TECHNOLOGY AND ENTERPRISE DEVELOPMENT

Also by Sanjaya Lall

ALTERNATIVE DEVELOPMENT STRATEGIES IN
  SUB-SAHARAN AFRICA
  (*editor with F. Stewart and S. Wangwe*)
CURRENT ISSUES IN DEVELOPMENT ECONOMICS
  (*editor with V. N. Balasubramanyam*)
DEVELOPING COUNTRIES IN THE INTERNATIONAL
  ECONOMY
MULTINATIONALS, TECHNOLOGY AND EXPORTS
THEORY AND REALITY IN DEVELOPMENT
  (*editor with F. Stewart*)
THE MULTINATIONAL CORPORATION

Also by Giorgio Barba Navaretti

TRADE POLICY, PRODUCTIVITY AND FOREIGN
INVESTMENT: The Textile and Clothing Industry in Europe
  (*with R. Faini and A Silberston*)

Also by Simón Teitel

INDUSTRIAL AND TECHNOLOGICAL DEVELOPMENT
TRADE, STABILITY, TECHNOLOGY AND EQUITY IN
  LATIN AMERICA (*with M. Syrquin*)
TOWARDS A NEW DEVELOPMENT STRATEGY FOR
  LATIN AMERICA

Also by Ganeshan Wignaraja

THE POSTWAR EVOLUTION OF DEVELOPMENT
  THINKING (*with C. Oman*)
PARTICIPATORY DEVELOPMENT: Learning from
  South Asia (*with P. Wignaraja, A. Hussain and H. Sethi*)

Technology and Enterprise Development

Ghana under Structural Adjustment

Sanjaya Lall
Lecturer in Development Economics
University of Oxford

Giorgio Barba Navaretti
Lecturer in Economics
University of Milan

Simón Teitel
Research Consultant
World Bank
Washington, DC

and

Ganeshan Wignaraja
Economist, Magdalen College
University of Oxford

St. Martin's Press

First published in Great Britain 1994 by
THE MACMILLAN PRESS LTD
Houndmills, Basingstoke, Hampshire RG21 2XS
and London
Companies and representatives
throughout the world

A catalogue record for this book is available
from the British Library.

ISBN 0–333–61884–X

Printed in Great Britain by
Ipswich Book Co Ltd
Ipswich, Suffolk

First published in the United States of America 1994 by
Scholarly and Reference Division,
ST. MARTIN'S PRESS, INC.,
175 Fifth Avenue,
New York, N.Y. 10010

ISBN 0–312–12149–0

Library of Congress Cataloging-in-Publication Data
Technology and enterprise development : Ghana under structural
adjustment / Sanjaya Lall . . . [et al.].
p.   cm.
Includes bibliographical references and index.
ISBN 0–312–12149–0
1. Technological innovations—Economic aspects—Ghana.
2. Structural adjustment (Economic policy)—Ghana.   I. Lall,
Sanjaya.
HC1060.Z9T48   1994
338'.064'09667—dc20   93–47038
                                             CIP

Contents

PART A   APPROACH AND BACKGROUND

List of Tables

viii

List of Figures

Preface

Technology is one of the primary determinants of the competitiveness of manufacturing firms. This is well understood in industrialised economies, where technological effort, generally in the form of developing new process or product know-how, is taken to be a vital basis of market success. In less industrialised countries, however, the significance of technological effort is generally less well appreciated. Since practically all the technologies in use are imported from the developed countries, and their application is known and understood, it is widely believed that developing country firms need to invest little on their own in technological effort. As passive recipients of technology, they only have to choose techniques that are appropriate to their factor endowments. It is assumed that thereafter they can use the technologies efficiently.

A body of recent research on technological capabilities in developing countries has shown that the process by which firms become technically proficient is far more complex and demanding. The selection, assimilation and effective deployment of technologies cannot be a passive process. The search for suitable technologies in imperfect markets for knowledge is difficult. The use of the technologies that are imported requires firms to seek new information, skills, material inputs and investment resources, the markets for which are prone to a range of imperfections in developing countries. Some firms are better equipped to undertake these efforts than others, and the degree of market failure varies by country and over time. Government policies and interventions may add to market failures or help remedy them. The nature of factor and product market imperfections and government interventions interact with the firm's own skills and entrepreneurship to determine how competitive it can become.

Research on technological capabilities has been confined to the relatively industrialised developing countries of Asia and Latin America. Practically no detailed research has been conducted on the process of technological development in the least industrialised countries of Sub-Saharan Africa. Yet the process of industrialisation there is just as complex and demanding as in other regions – perhaps even more so, because though the technologies used are simpler the market failures that confront firms can be greater. African countries have invested

xii

considerable resources in their industrial sectors, and have looked to manufacturing as the main vehicle of structural transformation and reduction of dependence on primary product exports. In general, these investments have produced far poorer results than in other developing regions.

Many African countries are now launching sweeping structural adjustment programmes. They are liberalising trade and exposing their industrial firms to the rigours of import competition. Are their firms technologically equipped to deal with such exposure? If not, can they incorporate and deploy new technologies at a rapid enough pace to expand industrial output and exports? If many protected activities are basically inefficient and die out, can new dynamic industrial firms emerge in the liberal setting to compete internationally? Are these countries, in sum, set to become 'newly industrialising economies' in the East Asian mould by structural adjustment and the removal of past interventions with market forces? These are questions of vital policy interest, to which existing knowledge on industry and technology in Africa offers scant answer.

This book is the first detailed attempt to assess technological capabilities in an African country. It is a study of a sample of manufacturing enterprises in Ghana, a country undergoing structural adjustment since the mid-1980s. It refines and applies the methodology used in past analyses of technological capabilities in developing countries. Its findings cast fresh light on the problems of industrial development in Africa and on the effects of rapid liberalisation programmes. The policy conclusions drawn are of relevance to other countries at early stages of industrial development.

This study was part of the World Bank's Regional Programme for Enterprise Development (RPED), which was intended to analyse the dynamics of enterprise growth in several countries in Sub-Saharan Africa. Ghana is the first country to be studied in this programme. Apart from this study of technology, there were several modules dealing with different aspects of enterprise development: finance, labour markets, business strategy and regulations. This study does not, therefore, attempt to address the issues covered by these other modules. Its focus is deliberately on technology, but there is no implication that technology is the only, or the main, determinant of enterprise development.

A large study like this one, which is part of an even larger project, accumulates many debts which are difficult to acknowledge properly. We are very grateful to the World Bank's RPED for asking us to conduct this research and allowing us to publish the findings. The interpretation and analysis is that of the authors alone and the Bank bears no responsibility for them. The constant support, advice and comments of Tyler Biggs, RPED's manager, were invaluable for the study. Melanie Mbuyi managed the difficult task of administering the project in the World Bank.

The study of Ghana was sponsored by the United Kingdom's Overseas Development Administration (ODA). In addition, a significant part of the financing of the technology module was provided by the Directorate General for Development Cooperation of the Italian Ministry of Foreign Affairs. We are very grateful to the ODA and the Italian Foreign Ministry for their backing.

Part of the study was based at the Oxford University Institute of Economics and Statistics, with administrative support from Gillian Coates. Part was based at the Centro Studi Luca d'Agliano in Turin, with statistical advice provided by Paolo Giudici and research assistance by Daniele Coen Pirani. Logistical support was also given by the Fondazione Eni Enrico Mattei in Milan.

The field work in Ghana was greatly facilitated by the help given by Seth Adoo and K. A. Nuhu of the Ministry of Industry, who advised us on which firms to see and arranged for our interviews. We shared some of the data collected for a larger panel study by a team from the Oxford Centre for the Study of African Economies and the University of Ghana (Legon), which conducted the panel survey and is in charge of its analysis for the RPED. To all the members of this team, and particularly Francis Teal and Tracy Jones, our thanks for their help and cooperation in the field and for making available the panel data in Oxford.

The enterprises in Ghana that gave generously of their time and information are too numerous to mention individually; and in any case the confidentiality we promised them precludes this. However, we are greatly in their debt.

Finally, to our families and friends who supported us in this work, and bore patiently with our absence and our distraction, warm thanks.

Sanjaya Lall
Giorgio Barba Navaretti
Simón Teitel
Ganeshan Wignaraja

Part A

Approach and Background

1 Introduction and Analytical Approach

SETTING THE SCENE

Sub-Saharan Africa's industrial development has been disappointing. This has been explained by two sets of factors. The first has traced it to external shocks such as declining terms of trade, droughts and civil unrest; the second to inappropriate policies, such as poor macro-economic management, inward-looking trade strategies, a predilection for public ownership, regulations on domestic competition, financial market segmentation and suppression, and restrictions on foreign investment. These two sets of explanations, with their associated recommendations, have tended to dominate discussions of African industrialisation . The remedies for the first set of deficiencies (primarily espoused by many African governments) have been to increase import capacity by giving more aid and to restore stable political conditions. For the second set (mainly from the multilateral aid agencies), they have been to achieve macroeconomic stability and more market-oriented policy regimes.[1]

There is little doubt that both external shocks and poor policies have adversely influenced the performance of African manufacturing. However, even taken together they do not fully explain the extent of industrial slack and uncompetitiveness in much of Africa.[2] In general, the achievements of manufacturing in the region are significantly below those of many other developing regions that have endured similar policies and shocks. In particular, Africa's virtual failure to enter the world market for manufactured products (apart from the sale of some processed primary products) indicates a widespread absence of competitiveness and dynamism. It is suggested here, therefore, that there are *other* constraints on industrial development in Africa. These are related to the lack of the skills and knowledge needed to set up and efficiently operate modern industry. It is argued that it is the lack of industrial capabilities that explain why so much of African manufacturing remains confined to the lowest end of the technology scale and why it responds poorly to the improved incentives that recent structural reforms have provided. To the extent that this is so, policy remedies have to address other issues than the ones noted above.

3

Not all analyses have neglected the role of industrial capabilities. For instance, in a perceptive review of the experience of African development, the World Bank's *Long Term Perspective Study* (1989) has this to say on industrialisation:

> Africa's post-independence industrialisation concentrated on creating physical capacity. Consistent with development theory at the time, it assumed that lack of capital constrained growth. Import substitution policies attracted foreign investment through protected markets. Agricultural taxation and foreign borrowing helped finance public investment in heavy industry, which served a narrow market at high cost. The capacity created was not well adapted to local demand and supply conditions, and much of it cannot be sustained.

> Modern manufacturing remains mostly small, stagnating at around 10 per cent of GDP and 9 per cent of employment between 1965 and 1987. *Most industries remain isolated from world markets and new technology, with high costs relative to best-practice operations elsewhere.* Protectionism has stimulated investment *but not innovation* to raise productivity or export growth to finance the import requirements. The future lies in shifting industrial structure towards high-growth, competitive enterprises that are linked to the domestic economy. . . .

> The most successful newly industrialising countries (NICs), while protecting domestic markets, have gradually opened them to competition, provided export incentives, and identified the educational and technical skills that build a flexible labour force. In Africa this implies a shift from central planning to a market-oriented approach, from regulation to competition, and from failed attempts to transplant technology to *systematic building up of capabilities.*

> *The core of this strategy is the step-by-step acquisition of skills necessary to operate and adapt new techniques.* Industrial strategy in Africa has tended to overstress the hardware (plant and machinery) and *neglect training labour and management to master new technologies.*[3]

The study goes on to discuss policy reforms that could help African countries to stimulate renewed and efficient industrial development, one that becomes an engine of structural transformation and export diversification instead of a costly burden on their fragile economies. On capability development the report argues:

Acceleration of industrial capacity growth will be wasted unless the capability to design, manage, and use it is also improved. Both the failures and successes of industrialisation are often traceable to a flaw or flair in entrepreneurship, management, or technology. . . . Improving technical and managerial capability is important to raise productivity and move from small- to medium- and large-scale modern enterprises. Although many countries have a surplus of well-educated labour, they do not always have the middle-level technical and supervisory skills needed . . . Better education and on-the-job training efforts are needed to raise the supply of good African professionals, managers and engineers.[4]

The Long Term Perspectives Study is, however, something of an exception to the way that most analysts approach the problems of African industrialisation. The role of capability factors in industrialisation continues to be relatively neglected, while adjustment programmes continue to be designed with almost exclusive focus on incentive factors.

The present study of enterprise development focuses on the development of technological capabilities in Ghana. It is particularly apt because Ghana has suffered one of the most punishing declines in manufacturing output experienced in Africa during the 1970s and early 1980s. Since the middle of the 1980s the Ghanaian Government has implemented a sweeping adjustment programme. This study seeks to identify the role of capability factors in the nature and quality of the response of manufacturing enterprises to the reformed incentive framework, and to explain why some firms are able to develop better capabilities than others.

WHAT ARE 'TECHNOLOGICAL CAPABILITIES'?

Technological capabilities (TCs) in industry are the information and skills – technical, managerial and institutional – that allow productive enterprises to utilise equipment and technology efficiently. Such capabilities are firm specific, a form of institutional knowledge that is made of the combined skills of its members accumulated over time. 'Technological development' may be defined as the process of building up such capabilities.

The development of TCs should not be thought of as the ability to undertake frontier innovation, though innovative capabilities are one form of TC. It comprises a much broader range of effort that every enterprise must itself undertake in order to absorb and build upon the knowledge that has to be utilised in production. The process is evolutionary, building upon past efforts and choices. It is not passive, but driven by conscious and purposive efforts undertaken by every enterprise.[5] It involves buying some skills and information from the market and providing others in-house, the choice depending on the technology, market conditions and firm strategies.

The successful transfer of a new technology to a developing country thus has to include a major element of capability building: simply providing equipment and operating instructions, patents, designs or blueprints does not ensure that the technology will be properly used. These 'embodied' elements of a technology have to accompanied by a number of 'tacit' elements, which have to be learned by the recipient. Only when such learning and adaptation have taken place can the technology be considered to be *'mastered'*,[6] that is, it is used at or near the ('best practice') level of technical efficiency at which it was designed.

Technological mastery is not an automatic or passive process. In order successfully to incorporate new technical information, certain prerequisites must be met by the importer of technology. In particular, adequate *'receivers' of technology* must be in place.[7] Qualified personnel and an appropriate organisation must be available before the transfer occurs, or must be developed rapidly by on-job training and other means.[8] Prior investments have therefore to be made in human capital and organisational capabilities to 'decode' new technical information, and to incorporate it into manufacturing processes. The skill requirements for technology absorption are not uniform across activities, but differ by the nature and tacitness of the technology, and by the level of mastery that is aimed at.[9]

Technological capability is not, however, simply the sum of the education and training of a firm's employees. It is based on the *learning undergone* by individuals in the enterprise and depends on the way in which the firm combines and motivates individuals *to function as an organisation.*[10] To some extent any enterprise that tries to use a new technology acquires some capabilities as an automatic result of the production process. Such *passive learning* goes some way to developing the necessary capabilities. In simple industries, say the assembly of imported kits or garment manufacture for the domestic market, this may be all that is needed. The skills needed are easily learned on the job, and there are few interlinkages with suppliers that involve technical problems and complex exchanges of information. Product designs are given by foreign suppliers of kits for assembly, or are easily adapted to local tastes in garments.

Such passive learning is, however, insufficient as the technology becomes more complicated or market demands more rigorous. Even in garment manufacture, for instance, a lot of effort is needed to raise quality and productivity, improve layout, introduce new supervision practices and so on, before an efficient producer for the local market becomes a competitive exporter (this is brought out clearly in this study). For more complex industries, to reach even static 'best practice' levels as established in advanced countries involves an enterprise in a longer and more demanding process.

But reaching a static level of competence is rarely enough to be competitive. It is generally necessary to adapt the technology in various ways, to smaller size of plant or production batch (termed 'downsizing'), different climate and raw materials, different product characteristics and different skill availabilities. Whatever the reason, the successful adaptation of a technology or machine requires engineering and technical skills and effort, the nature of these depending on the technology in question. Modifications of products, processes and equipment themselves create new knowledge, often leading to further improvements. This process of 'minor' innovation can accumulate over time to significant improvements in productivity, sometimes larger than major single jumps in technology.[11] The nature of this learning process means that different firms can have quite different rates of technological development, and end up with different levels of efficiency in using the same technologies.

Manufacturing enterprises do not develop capabilities in isolation. They generally operate in a *network of formal and informal relationships* with suppliers, customers, competitors, consultants, and technology, research and educational institutions. These networks take the form of complex contractual and non-contractual linkages.[12] These linkages help individual firms to deal with each other, specialise in their activities, gain access to expensive (lumpy) information and facilities. The need for such linkages differs by industry and enterprise. Some simple activities that rely mainly on primary inputs and use low skill techniques may not need many linkages to be efficient. Others need constant flows of information, skills and other inputs from outside to maintain their efficiency and to make rational decisions to invest in physical and human assets. As the role of complex activities grows with economic development, so does the need for inter-firm linkages.

The learning process for complex technologies can be *long* and *uncertain*. In a new environment, with new plant or process, different physical conditions, and fresh workers and managers, no technical process can be entirely predictable. Even the achievement of static efficiency (the solution, in other words, of the problems mentioned above) involves search, experimentation and interactions within firms as well as between them. When dynamic factors are introduced, the process of becoming and staying efficient is even more difficult. The real world is in a state of constant flux. Market conditions and tastes are changing, technologies improving, new competitors appearing, and relative costs of inputs, labour of various kinds and infrastructure shifting.[13] In addition, policy changes like import liberalisation can create urgent pressures to upgrade capabilities.

It may be useful to contrast this approach to capability development to the usual textbook analysis of how firms absorb and use technology: this is the analysis that underlies some of the policy recommendations of the get prices right variety.[14] In this world, firms in developing countries are assumed to operate with full knowledge of all possible technologies. Given the right (free market determined) prices for inputs and outputs, they pick the one that is appropriate to their national factor endowments. All firms in an industry facing the same prices choose the same technologies; otherwise they are allocatively inefficient. The international technology market is assumed to work efficiently, and all firms are taken to have full knowledge of the technologies available so that they can buy the right one 'off the shelf'. All firms can, moreover, immediately use imported technologies with the same degree of efficiency (and at best practice levels). There is thus no theoretical reason to expect the persistence of technical inefficiency. If such inefficiency exists, it is, *ex hypothesi*, due to managerial slack or incompetence, and to government interventions that allow inefficient firms to continue in production. In essence, *there is no process of acquiring TCs*.

Where extra costs of introducing new technologies in developing countries are admitted, a simplified view is taken of the learning process. The learning curve is believed to be fairly short and predictable: largely confined to 'running in' a new plant until it reaches rated capacity, and benefits of automatic learning-by-doing are realised. It is generally assumed that such costs are relatively trivial, predictable, and similar across industries. The learning process is, moreover, relatively passive rather than one that involves investment, risk and, in some activities, long maturation periods. Firms know what to do to reach best practice levels. There is consequently no need to devise measures to stimulate the capability to absorb new technologies, or to distinguish between industries in the financing of learning and start-up costs.

Firms are assumed to acquire and use technologies as individual units, essentially in isolation. There are no linkages between them, and no externalities resulting from individual efforts to generate skills and information. The development of specialisation among firms and industries thus relies on information exchanged in anonymous market transactions. There is no need to create or foster the information networks and institutions that have evolved in advanced industrial economies. Since there are no technological externalities, there is also no need to co-ordinate investment decisions (in physical assets or TC building) across activities that may have intense linkages.

It is assumed that firms have the foresight to finance 'running in' costs in capital markets. If capital markets are not fully efficient, the market failure has to be addressed at source. In the interim, infant industry protection (or subsidies) may be granted, only as a second best measure, at moderate levels and uniformly across activities to minimise the risk of resource misallocation. Since no technologies are more difficult, or involve more externalities, than others, there is no need for policy makers to be selective in their promotion of particular industries or technologies. There is also no need to devise different policies by the level of development of the countries in question, since markets are assumed to operate with equal degrees of efficiency.

In this essentially static framework, comparative advantage evolves according to the gradual accumulation of factor endowments, rather than by the deliberate efforts of industrial enterprises. As endowments grow, firms automatically move to the right factor combinations, costlessly absorbing the technologies concerned.

This approach gives rise to simple policy prescriptions. Interventions in efficient product and factor markets are undesirable, and immediate liberalisation of the trade and investment regime is desirable. In perfect markets, free trade and capital flows are the necessary and sufficient condition for achieving efficient resource allocation. In turn, efficient resource allocation leads to the optimal setting for growth and dynamic change. This is the implicit assumption of structural adjustment, and it follows logically from the premises about costless learning. On the empirical front, support for liberal policy prescriptions is derived from the rapid growth of the export-oriented economies of East Asia. This is attributed, in large part, to their general 'openness' to trade and technology transfer.

Once the simplifying assumptions about technological absorption and development are dropped and market failures in the learning process admitted, some of these sweeping prescriptions do not hold. The need for interventions to help the learning process, and for sustaining lengthy periods of learning or, in the case of existing firms that have to restructure and upgrade to face liberalisation, for relearning has to be taken into account. The need for adjustment remains, because there is no economic case for the kind of irrational interventions that most developing countries have imposed; but the duration, phasing and role of interventions in the process turn out to be very different from the standard structural adjustment package. The case of Ghana provides a useful illustration of this.

FUNCTIONAL CATEGORISATION OF TECHNOLOGICAL CAPABILITIES

Technological development is not a separate task in the care of a special department of an enterprise. The growth of TC can take place at almost any point in the manufacturing firm: shop-floor, quality control, process engineering, product design and testing, input procurement, formal R&D, and so on. It can take a variety of forms. To make the analysis of technological capabilities manageable, this section describes a simple functional categorisation of the technological tasks facing a manufacturing firm. This set of technological functions will be used in this study to analyse the capabilities and development of Ghanaian industrial firms.

The nature of TCs can be illustrated by a matrix (Table 1.1).[15] All manufacturing firms need to perform these tasks, but not necessarily all in-house. The tasks fall into three broad categories, which can be described briefly as follows.

First, *investment capabilities*. These are the skills and information needed to identify feasible investment projects, locate and purchase suitable (embodied and disembodied) technologies, design and engineer the plant, and manage the construction, commissioning and start-up. These functions are not always easy to perform. Industrial technology is not available in a codified form that can be easily bought 'off the shelf'. Many enterprises in developing countries find it difficult to decide on the best technology (or complex combinations of technologies) for their purposes. Technology markets may be fragmented, and it is often difficult for developing country firms to find the best suppliers and negotiate the most appropriate terms and prices.

Simply contracting out all investment functions to international engineering firms can get around some of these problems. However, it

Table 1.1 Illustrative matrix of technological capabilities

		Functional					
		Investment		*Production*			*Linkages*
		Pre investment	*Project execution*	*Process engineering*	*Product engineering*	*Industrial engineering*	*Linkages within economy*
DEGREE	BASIC SIMPLE, ROUTINE (Experience based)	Pre-feasibility and feasibility studies, site selection, scheduling of investment	Civil construction, ancillary services, equipment erection, commissioning	Debugging, balancing, quality control preventive maintenance, assimilation of process technology	Assimilation of product design, minor adaptation to market needs	Work flow, scheduling, time-motion studies. Inventory control	Local procurement of goods and services, information exchange with suppliers
OF COMPLE	INTERMED ADAPTIVE DUPLICATIVE (Search based)	Search for technology source. Negotiation of contracts. Bargaining suitable terms. Info. systems	Equipment procurement, detailed engineering, training and recruitment of skilled personnel	Equipment stretching, process adaptation and cost saving, licensing new technology	Product quality improvement, licensing and assimilating new imported product technology	Monitoring productivity, improved coordination	Technology transfer of local suppliers, coordinated design, Science & Technology links
XITY	ADVANCED INNOVATIVE RISKY (Research based)		Basic process design. Equipment design and supply	In-house process innovation, basic research	In-house product innovation, basic research		Turnkey capability, cooperative R&D, licensing own technology to others

may raise the capital costs of the project, and result in the technology being provided as a turnkey operation which the recipient does not participate in and finds difficult to master, and subsequently to adapt or upgrade. The experience of Japan and the Asian newly industrialising economies (NIEs) shows that growth in domestic ability to select technologies, negotiate favourable terms for its transfer and participate in the design and setting up of the plant can greatly reduce project costs and increase the subsequent capabilities for technology adaptation and improvement.[16]

More generally, the development of investment capabilities in an industry or country, rather than just in an enterprise, can be of great help in setting up plants economically and, later, expanding and improving upon them. This is one of the reasons, for instance, why Korea is renowned for having low project costs and rapid implementation of investments: its government made a deliberate effort to develop investment capabilities by helping firms to locate sources of technology and negotiate favourable terms, including the participation of local engineering firms in design and construction. By contrast, an important cause of high project costs in Africa has been the almost total absence of relevant local investment and engineering capabilities.

Second, *production capabilities*. These are the skills and knowledge needed for the operation and improvement of a plant. As the table shows, these can range from routine functions to intensive and innovative efforts to adapt and improve the technology. However, the classification of the degree of complexity, being purely relative, may be misleading. The acquisition of even 'basic' capabilities (like quality control, maintenance, scheduling, or reaching prescribed levels of machine efficiency) generally requires considerable time and effort in developing countries. Indeed, in recent years, the achievement of competitive levels of quality has become the subject of much technological and organisational effort even in developed countries.

The more advanced capabilities, for adaptation and innovation, generally require higher (or different) skills, and more time and investment. This is so even when new technologies are bought in rather than being created by the enterprise. The *absorption* of new technologies still calls for skill and know-how development, though clearly at a different, if not lower, level than those required for innovation. Most technologically mature enterprises tend to develop some element of in-house innovative capability. This is because fast-changing technologies can only be absorbed by formal or explicit R&D (i.e. research and experimental development separate from routine production).[17] Even for industries with slowly changing technologies, an independent design capability becomes desirable for firms that want to upgrade their products or move to different markets, and run into constraints in purchasing the latest vintage of technology from other firms.

Industrial engineering skills are required to improve the organisation of production. Industrial engineers seek continuously to improve productivity by changing the time and spatial sequence of manufacturing and auxiliary operations. The introduction of 'just in time' systems, for instance, calls for a different form of work organisation and procurement – industrial engineering is needed to design and implement such systems. Industrial engineers apply a variety of mathematical, statistical and organisational techniques, time and motion studies, layout and materials-handling analysis. Industrial engineering skills are universal in nature: they are valuable to all industries. Their absence may thus imply an important gap in the TC spectrum.

The technological effort needed varies by industry and the level of technology being used.[18] Metal working, electrical equipment, transport equipment and electronics (generally labelled 'engineering industries') have departments engaged in product design and the improvement of manufacturing methods. Chemical and other processing industries lay more emphasis on process optimisation . Such differences in technologies, with their underlying scientific and engineering knowledge, are important in determining the skill composition of the high-level technical workforce.

Third, *linkage capabilities*. These are the skills needed to establish and maintain production and technological links with other firms and institutions. Such relations are not the anonymous arm's length market transactions of textbook economics. In industrialised and developing countries alike, industrial linkages consist of a dense network of cooperative relationships that take much time and work to establish, and have a quasi permanent nature. They call for the transfer of technical information, skills and plans, all of which require capabilities to transmit and to receive.[19]

In developing countries, where supplier networks and institutions are generally at an infant stage, the effort needed is especially large. The principal firms, foreign or domestic, may have to 'bring up' suppliers rather than just establish linkages with existing enterprises. In many countries that are new to industrialisation, the absence of domestic procurement and subcontracting in manufacturing industry often reflects the lack of linkage capabilities and efforts by the major established manufacturers. On the other hand, where local absorptive capabilities are greater, some multinational enterprises and mature local firms are able to develop extensive local linkages. For instance, Ford helped create a network of local suppliers in Argentina after a concerted effort of 'vendor engineering' and the supply of technical assistance to Small and Medium Enterprises (SMEs). These efforts included visits by Ford engineers, contacts with suppliers abroad, help in getting technology licenses and so on. A similar process is observed in Malaysia, where Motorola has a large export-oriented semiconductor and wafer-making operation. Motorola actively helped local firms to design some capital equipment for its plant, and helped suppliers to set up and reach its exacting quality standards by technical training and other assistance.

As enterprises develop and mature, they tend to broaden and deepen their initial base of TCs. The *evolutionary nature* of the learning process generally means that firms develop along particular trajectories determined by their initial positions, entrepreneurial strategy and capabilities, and external stimuli.[20] These trajectories, once started, are difficult to change or reverse because firms accumulate knowledge along a certain path. They build up institutional routines and systems that allow them to absorb and process information and create in-house skills. Their internal organisations become more complex to allow specialisation by productive and technological functions.[21] They also learn better how to draw upon external sources of information, like consultants, suppliers and technology institutions, and feed these into the ongoing process of internal learning. However, some of the specific features of the determinants of technological learning in developing countries need discussion, and are taken up now.

DETERMINANTS OF TECHNOLOGY DEVELOPMENT

Introduction

What determines the ability and willingness of industrial enterprises in a developing country to invest in their own technological development and to seek information, skills and other resources from other enterprises and institutions? The determinants of industrial technology development (ITD) may be divided into three groups: the *incentive framework,* which determines the 'demand' side of technological capability building; the *'supply'* factors, constituted by skills, finance and information, and *institutions.* These factors may interact with each other in complex ways, but it is analytically useful to consider them separately for evaluating the determinants of TD in Ghana and the relevant policy implications. Finally, we consider the way in which the enterprise *organises* itself for technology development.

The Incentive Framework

The firm faces a set of market and non-market incentives that determine the 'demand' for technological effort. The most fundamental incentive for a firm to develop its technological capabilities arises initially from the *need to get into production*. This is true regardless of the nature of the trade and industrial regime, as long as the firm wants to succeed commercially and has the managerial autonomy to invest in ITD. However, the extent to which it invests in its capabilities to become domestically or internationally competitive, and the extent to which it sustains its efforts to adapt to changing conditions and diversify or deepen its base of capabilities, depends on incentives arising from the external environment and from government policies.

The *macroeconomic environment* and *growth prospects* for major markets, domestic or foreign, clearly exert a strong influence on decisions to invest in ITD. *Ceteris paribus*, a stable and high growth environment is more conducive to ITD investments than others. Since macro issues are beyond the scope of this study, they need not be discussed further here.

The *international or 'frontier' rate of technological progress* will also affect the pace and content of ITD. No modern manufacturing technology is static, and no country can afford to ignore world technological trends if it wishes to achieve international competitiveness in some manufacturing activities. The rate of technical change is very different across activities, and the incentives offered for ITD effort vary accordingly.[22] In all cases, even when the change originates elsewhere, *indigenous* technological effort is critical to coping with technical progress, since this is what determines how effectively local enterprises can deploy the new technologies in production.

The most important incentives to ITD arise from *competition*, both domestic and foreign. Competitive markets provide some of the most potent stimuli to investments in capability acquisition, and correct market signals can guide firms in investing to the right extent, and in the right forms, in ITD (market failures can, however, occur, and are mentioned below). Thus, artificial restraints to competition may hold back ITD investments, or may lead firms to develop the wrong kinds of capabilities. Many developing countries have imposed such restraints.

Domestic competition is often held back by barriers to entry by investment licensing, entry controls by size, ownership requirements, restraints on firm growth or diversification, and so on. Even if it were not, domestic competition by itself may not be able to stimulate fully competitive ITD if it took place in isolation from foreign competition. Highly protected industries in developing countries tend to be technologically backward even if there is domestic competition, because the average level of technical efficiency within domestic industry can be low and use of new technologies may lag behind world levels.

Exposure to *world competition* is thus a more powerful incentive to ITD in developing countries. However, because the process of capability development takes time and investment, there is a period during which the enterprise is less efficient than one that has already undergone the technological learning process. This period of *'infancy'* becomes important for policy for countries, like Ghana, that are new entrants to the industrialisation process. They face competition not only from the developed countries, which have much greater industrialisation experience and much better functioning factor markets and institutions, but also from other developing countries (like the NIEs) that are much further advanced in the process of technology acquisition and development. There is thus a case for interventions to promote the growth of infant industries: one of the most common means for doing this is to offer protection by intervening in trade.

The case for infant industry protection is based on the risk of market failure in investing in TC development.[23] Market failures may arise from gaps and deficiencies in the capital markets that finance investments in TCs, the lack of information on the benefits and process of capability investments and uncertainty and risk aversion. They may also arise from externalities such as the inability to reap the rewards of investments in skills or knowledge creation or technological linkages between enterprises,[24] which make it difficult for individual enterprises to anticipate each other's learning processes. These failures can lead firms to underinvest in their own technological development. Some of these market failures (as in capital markets) should be tackled directly, but this may take time, and protection may provide a solution in the interim. Others, like externalities and learning, may call for direct subsidisation or protection of the firms concerned.

While infant industry protection can provide the 'breathing space' in which new entrants can develop their capabilities, there are many potential dangers in such interventions and the *negative* aspects of protection have to be stressed. Protection can retard or distort the process of investing in ITD, especially if domestic competition is weak and the protection is granted in a widespread and indiscriminate manner. The general experience of import substituting regimes is that highly protected enterprises never mature to competitive levels because there is little incentive to invest in the capabilities needed.[25]

To ensure that infant industries invest in ITD, therefore, safeguards have to be instituted. The most effective safeguards are those that introduce market competition at the earliest possible time, such as time-bound programs of reduction in protection, immediate promotion of domestic competition, planned entry into export markets, or some combination of these. The ability to combine infant industry protection with a strong pressure to develop and deepen technological capabilities requires a clear strategic objective, administrative skills, flexibility, careful monitoring, and the correction or penalisation of poor performance. It requires, in other words, strong *government capabilities*.[26] These capabilities are often lacking in most developing countries, especially in Sub-Saharan Africa.

The experience of the larger East Asian NIEs suggests, however, that carefully designed interventions *can* produce high rates of industrial and technological development.[27] In the case of Korea, technologically the most dynamic of the NIEs, strong export orientation combined with highly selective infant industry protection, granted to a relatively few activities at a time, provided a powerful and effective spur to ITD.[28] Equally important, trade interventions were carefully monitored and supported by measures for building domestic technological capabilities. The deepening of such capabilities was promoted by a variety of measures: encouraging and subsidising private sector R&D, early entry into export markets, fostering the production of increasingly sophisticated capital goods (while continuing to import extensively other equipment, especially for export activities), investing in public sector R&D institutions that had strong links with domestic industry, and controlling the entry of foreign investors to minimise the dependence of local enterprises on 'ready made' technologies. Protection in this sort of trade regime is very different from that offered in typical import-substituting regimes, such as that prevailing in India until recently, or in Ghana until the launch of structural adjustment in 1986 (see Chapter 2).

Other incentives to ITD arise from *factor markets*. Changes in relative factor prices and availability can lead to considerable technological activity. It is important for policy purposes that these changes reflect true economic values to the enterprises concerned. Artificial input scarcities (as are often created in inward-oriented economies) can distort ITD by forcing firms to develop costly substitutes, often of low quality, that retard international competitiveness. Inflexibility and uncertainties in labour markets can also retard or distort the pattern of investment and capability building, as can imperfections in capital markets.

The 'Supply' Factors: Skills, Finance and Information

Given the 'demand' for ITD from the incentive framework, the supply response of the industrial sector depends on its access to some basic building blocks. While the final building of technological capabilities takes place inside manufacturing firms, these firms have to depend on external sources for resources that they cannot create easily. The three major building blocks to which firms need recourse are *skills* of the appropriate kinds, access to *technical information* to feed into in-house efforts, and *financing* for physical and other investment.

Each of these inputs has its own markets. Each market may suffer from failures. Many such market failures tend to be universal, borne out by the fact that all developed industrial countries have invested in setting up specific mechanisms and institutions to provide for education, training, technology finance, science infrastructure and research institutions.[29] However, it is generally accepted that factor market failures are greater and more widespread in developing countries, and that there is a correspondingly larger role for the government in remedying them. In addition, there is likely to be a greater risk of market segmentation in developing countries, giving some groups of firms better access to particular factors than others.

The significance of *skills* for the success of ITD is evident. Basic worker skills (literacy and numeracy) are necessary for almost all forms of industrial development. As industry moves into more complex products, specific types of higher technical (and other) skills become essential to efficient operation. Even 'simple' industries like garments or footwear need some high-level skills to operate at world standards of cost and quality. More complex industries have greater demands for advanced skills. Since many of these skills are specific to the technology being deployed, it is not only the total quantity (and quality) of technical skills produced that is relevant but also their composition.[30] The formation (or availability) of such skills may call for considerable government intervention in education markets. Industrial success in the NIEs has been closely linked to their investments in education, especially in engineering and technical education.[31]

Industrial enterprises created a significant amount of human capital with their own formal or informal training efforts. The provision of such training can suffer from market failure. The amount of employee training provided depends on firms' awareness of the benefits to be derived from investments in training, and the possibility of recouping the returns from those investments. If firms do not understand these gains, or if there is a significant risk that trained manpower will leave the firm, the private returns to training fall short of the social returns, and firms underinvest in training. This may be especially true of small firms that cannot pay high wages to retain trained manpower.

The ability of the capital market to *finance* investments in TC acquisition is another crucial element. At low levels of industrialisation, when firms are small and specialised in easy technologies, with low capital requirements and limited possibilities of improvements, the absence of a capital market with the capacity to finance risky innovation may not be critically important. Normal financing channels may cover production-related technological activities that are not separated into formal research and development. Even here, however, there is a risk that such financing will not meet training and other needs that are not strictly for working capital, and for which small firms may not be able to offer collateral. These constraints on technology development are likely to be far more serious in a period of structural adjustment,[32] when monetary and fiscal policies tend to be very tight, and smaller firms face particularly constricted access to formal sources of finance.

Enterprises have to draw heavily on *information* from other sources for gaining technological competence. These sources include the import of technologies from the advanced countries, advice and services from consultants, information from component and equipment suppliers, competitors, and a range of inputs from the industrial technology infrastructure (extension services, standards, metrology, basic research, contract R & D, and so on). Passive dependence on foreign technology may lead to good operational capabilities, but it is not necessarily the best way to *deepen* local TCs.[33] There may be no need to deepen local TCs in countries that can expect enough foreign direct investment to drive the industrial process, at least in certain high-technology areas. However, there will always remain large areas of industry where local enterprises have to develop, if only to serve local markets and as input suppliers to foreign firms. Thus the import of technology can never substitute completely for local capability development.

Local information support for technology development comes partly from other enterprises and partly from the science and technology (S&T)

infrastructure. The promotion of *inter-firm and inter-industry linkages* is a critical component of technological development. Specialisation and subcontracting tend to grow naturally over the course of industrial development. In most developing economies, however, this growth is slow and may need to be encouraged. In particular, in countries at early stages of industrialisation with weak capital goods and engineering industries, many of the linkages tend to remain with the developed countries, and firms that do deepen the production structure tend to be highly vertically integrated. This can impose high costs on local manufacturers and may hold back the diffusion of technologies within the country.

Linkages with the *S&T infrastructure* raise different sets of issues. The nature of such linkages varies with the stage of industrialisation. In early stages, simple testing, quality assurance, standards and extension and information services are the most important needs. Simply informing enterprises of the need to invest in TC development, and showing them how to go about it, may be a critical function of infrastructure institutions at this level. As firms get into more complex products and enter export markets, they have to be assisted with research into difficult manufacturing and design problems; standards become more demanding and the entire production process has to be set up to conform to exacting levels demanded by importing countries.[34] In even more advanced stages, basic research and coordination of information become predominant as firms grow and mature sufficiently to internalise many technological functions.[35]

In almost every country, an important problem with the S&T infrastructure has been its lack of effective linkages with the productive sector. Most developing countries have set up networks of technology institutions, but few have been able to harness them to raise productive efficiency in industrial enterprises. This does not mean that the institutions are unnecessary for ITD. They are vital to meeting certain needs, and their utility grows with the level of industrial complexity, but policies must be designed to link them intimately to the needs of manufacturing enterprises.

Institutions

In the broadest sense, institutions provide the 'rules of the game' within which enterprises operate and enter into contracts in the markets for factors and products (the intellectual property regime is an important element here). The lack of an appropriate contractual environment can hold back ITD because it can raise transactions costs and the risk of long-term investments (which necessarily require long-term commitments). However, this aspect of the institutional framework for ITD is not discussed here.

For present purposes, institutions in the narrower sense refer to the *organisations set up to support the functioning of the skill, capital and information markets* that are relevant to ITD. The main ones that are relevant in Ghana are education and training institutes, science and technology institutions, and others that support small-scale enterprises.

Organising for Technology Development

The absorption and adaptation of technology may occur in a deliberate and organised fashion or may be left to *ad hoc* entrepreneurial decision-making. Whether formally or informally, technology-related activities take place in most industrial firms, regardless of size and sophistication (though it is sometimes difficult to identify the agents of technical activity or to separate operational from technological tasks). Whether or not they take place in an organised form may affect their progress and efficacy. It is important, therefore, to understand how technological development is organised.

The functioning of modern industrial enterprises is generally facilitated by having differentiated and well-defined functions such as sales, production, R&D, finance, and so on, each with its own finer division of functions. The extent to which such divisions can be implemented is essentially a function of the size of the firm. Large firms can specialise in a different, wider range of technical functions than small firms, while micro- and small-enterprises cannot generally afford an internal organisational structure with well-defined division of labour for the major functions. Large firms can thus be technologically more competent *in certain activities or levels of technology where there is a certain size threshold for efficient technological activity* (for more complex organisational structures and a greater division of technical functions).

There may, in other words, be 'economies of size ' in technological activity which may or may not be related to economies of scale in production. Economies of size in technological activity are likely to be more prevalent in more complex activities, or in more advanced technologies within given activities. Thus, only firms over a certain size can be efficient in these activities because smaller firms cannot offer the necessary division of labour or range of specialist skills required. These economies may, of course, run out after a certain size, when the problems of internal coordination, information flow and decision making outweigh the benefits of greater specialisation and spread of advanced skills. However, for present purposes, this limit is not relevant since most developing country firms are well below sizes where diseconomies of information and coordination set in. In general, one would expect to find a positive relationship between size, capital intensity and skill endowments at the firm level.

This does not mean that *only* large firms can be technically efficient. Clearly this is not the case, since in every country, including the most developed, there are large numbers of dynamic and technologically progressive small firms. The point is rather that small firms are *efficient in certain activities or, within activities, in certain technologies*, that can be competitively operated with lower division of technical functions and with a smaller array of different skills. They have to specialise in simpler technologies where the range of technical functions can be covered by a few people, or they have to specialise in a particular subset of high-skill activities where they can buy in most of the functions they cannot afford in-house.

While such specialisation is common in developed countries, it is relatively uncommon in less industrialised developing countries. In developing countries, most small firms tend to exist in traditional, low technology, low skill activities that serve markets that do not compete directly with the modern manufacturing sector (in fact, what is called 'small' in developed countries is often regarded as large in developing ones). Sustained industrial development requires that these traditional firms be brought into the modern sector, either as complements or as competitors to larger-scale formal enterprises. This calls for new entrepreneurial skills and information to allow them to find and absorb modern technologies and to specialise in ways that allow them to stay competitive, and, over time, to grow to large size. It also often requires kinds of institutional development that very small firms cannot afford, so that they may die out before they can become capable enough to face competition.

The fact that many firms stay small in developing countries may also reflect a segmentation in factor markets whereby they find it more costly than large firms to obtain the inputs, credit, skills or information that they need.[36] However, it may reflect the lack of *internal* capabilities to compete and grow. The entrepreneurs may not have the skills, information or 'vision' that would allow them to seek the right inputs or adopt the right business strategies. This may account for the fact that many of the entrants into the modern small and medium sector of industry in developing countries tend to come from the modern sector itself rather than from the transformation of traditional enterprises.

Apart from the organisational needs of absorbing technologies, it is relevant to note that much of recent technological progress, especially in engineering industries, also has its counterpart in *organisational innovation*. Changes in organisational structure and work practices are becoming an integral part of international competitiveness in the more advanced countries (Hoffman, 1989). These innovations are required to keep up with the growing need for integrated and flexible systems in design, research, management and production. Thus, 'flexible automation technology and organisational innovations are coalescing into a new best-practice manufacturing system now diffusing throughout industry'.[37] While this may not appear relevant to the enterprises studied in this project, in the longer term it has serious implications for industry in all developing countries.

2. Background to Technology Development in Ghana

THE HISTORICAL SETTING

Ghana has a relatively brief history of modern manufacturing activity. The colonial legacy was one of economic activity based on primary product production and exports, and there was little manufacturing activity apart from traditional crafts and repair work associated with mining and plantation activities. As in many Sub-Saharan African countries, the post-independence government launched an industrialisation programme based on import substitution. In the absence of an African entrepreneurial class in manufacturing, a leading role was assigned to the public sector.[1] As the Government's recent Industrial Policy Statement says:

> With the attainment of political independence in 1957 and given the international situation at that time, Ghana was faced with two basic strategic options for economic development. The first was the gradualist approach, based on market forces and private enterprise; the second was a 'fast track' strategy founded on the notion that rapid economic development was feasible, provided the State assumed the entrepreneurial function. By adopting the accelerated strategy, the option propagated by leading development economists at that time, it was generally expected that development goals were best achieved through massive investments in industry.
>
> A number of factors governed the Government's decision to adopt the 'fast track' strategy. These included the rudimentary state of indigenous industry in the late fifties, the limited number of local entrepreneurs and the complete absence of a capital market. As a result, industrialisation efforts in the First Republic were based on a strategy of import substitution by the State. The Government embarked on an accelerated programme of establishing a large number of State-owned import substitution industries producing a wide range of previously imported consumer goods for the domestic market. By 1970, Ghana had one of the most diverse and dynamic manufactur-

24

ing sectors in sub-Saharan Africa, and the emerging industrial sector showed every sign of satisfactory performance and growth.[2]

After an early spurt of growth, the structural constraints under which Ghanaian industry laboured (discussed below) exercised a growing influence on the competitiveness and dynamism of its enterprises. As a consequence, growth rates slowed down and, with declining revenues from the primary exports that had financed industry, turned negative. It remained highly import dependent, largely uncompetitive in world markets and so unable to finance its own production or investment. Instead of becoming an engine of growth and structural change, manufacturing became a drag on Ghanaian economic development.

Following the approach of the last chapter, the reasons for the poor long-term performance of Ghanaian industry may be considered under the headings of the incentive framework, the supply of skills and technology, and the effectiveness of the institutional support system for industry. These are considered below, after briefly reviewing Ghana's industrial structure and recent manufacturing performance.

INDUSTRIAL STRUCTURE

The structure of Ghanaian industry reflects its early stage of development, its resource base and the specific interventions of the Government. Table 2.1 shows UNIDO data for the breakdown of manufacturing value added in 1980 and 1990, by industrial level activities grouped into heavy and light industry, for Ghana as well as Kenya and Cote d'Ivoire, and, for comparison with an NIE, Korea.

In 1990, total MVA (manufacturing value added) in Ghana came to around 60 per cent of Kenya's, 39 per cent of the Côte d'Ivoire's, and only 0.6 per cent of Korea's. Ghana had a somewhat larger weight of light industrial activity than its Africa counterparts, and this was rising over the 1980s, like Kenya but unlike the other two countries. This indicated a growth in Ghana of relatively 'easy' activities, and the contrast with Korea, where light industry fell from 41.5 to 29.6 per cent over the decade, is particularly striking. Within light industry, in contrast with the other two African countries, Ghana had a small food processing subsector, but larger beverage and tobacco industries and a much larger wood working industry.

In heavy industry, Ghana has (like Côte d'Ivoire) a large refining industry and, unlike the others, a large aluminium smelting facility

Table 2.1 MVA structure in selected countries by light and heavy industry, 1980 and 1990 (percentage)

Branch	Ghana		Kenya		Côte d'Ivoire		Korea	
	1980	1990	1980	1990	1980	1990	1980	1990
LIGHT INDUSTRY	57.8	59.9	52.7	55.2	58.5	50.5	41.5	29.6
311 Food products	8.2	9.2	23.4	27.2	23.8	18.8	7.8	6.0
313 Beverages	15.6	14.5	7.4	8.1	5.9	4.7	2.9	1.9
314 Tobacco products	13.1	14.0	2.5	2.7	5.2	4.4	5.9	3.4
321 Textiles	9.0	6.3	7.8	6.6	13.3	14.7	13.6	8.0
322 Wearing apparel	1.2	0.2	2.3	2.3	0.6	0.7	4.6	3.4
323 Leather and fur products	0.4	0.2	0.8	0.5	0.2	0.3	0.7	1.1
324 Footwear	0.4	0.2	1.2	1.1	0.6	0.9	0.6	0.6
331 Wood and wood products	6.6	13.3	2.6	2.0	5.3	3.7	1.2	0.8
332 Furniture and fixtures	0.8	0.7	1.2	0.9	1.6	1.0	0.5	0.9
342 Printing and publishing	2.0	1.0	2.9	3.0	1.8	0.9	2.3	2.4
361 Pottery, china and earthenware	0.4	0.0	0.1	0.1	0.2	0.3	0.5	0.3
362 Glass and glass products	0.0	0.3	0.4	0.6	0.0	0.0	1.0	0.9
HEAVY INDUSTRY	42.2	40.1	47.2	45.1	41.6	49.6	58.5	70.4
341 Paper and paper products	0.4	0.7	4.5	4.7	1.1	0.6	2.2	2.2
351 Industrial chemicals	0.8	0.3	3.3	2.0	1.7	1.3	5.1	3.7
352 Other chemical products	3.7	5.6	5.2	6.9	4.2	4.7	5.2	5.2
353 Petroleum refineries	15.2	14.0	2.0	1.6	14.2	17.3	3.9	2.4
354 Misc. petroleum and coal products	0.0	0.0	0.0	0.0	0.0	0.0	1.1	0.6
355 Rubber products	2.0	0.7	3.3	4.1	0.3	0.3	3.4	3.0
356 Plastic products	0.4	0.7	1.9	2.5	0.1	0.0	1.8	2.7
369 Other non-metal minerals	2.5	3.3	2.6	4.1	2.1	1.9	4.3	3.4
371 Iron and Steel	0.0	0.3	1.6	0.8	0.4	0.2	6.4	6.2

372 Non-ferrous metals	11.9	11.0	0.0	0.0	0.2	0.1	1.4	1.3
381 Metal products	2.9	2.1	7.3	6.6	5.5	4.3	3.3	5.3
382 Non-electrical machinery	0.0	0.0	0.8	0.7	0.2	0.2	3.4	6.8
383 Electrical machinery	0.8	0.7	5.3	4.3	1.6	1.2	8.1	15.6
384 Transport equipment	1.2	0.5	8.5	4.8	8.3	15.8	5.9	8.5
385 Professional and scientific equipment	0.4	0.2	0.1	0.2	0.0	0.0	1.1	1.3
390 Other manufacturing industries	0.0	0.0	0.8	2.0	1.6	1.7	1.9	2.1
TOTAL MVA (%)	100	100	100	100	100	100	100	100
TOTAL MVA (Current US$)	244	573	755	961	1273	1481	19 520	91 721

Source: UNIDO (1993) *Industry and Development Global Report* 1992/93, Vienna.

(both the result of specific government policies to enter heavy industry, in the latter case to exploit hydroelectric potential from the Volta river dam[3]). On the other hand, Ghana's equipment manufacturing industries are relatively underdeveloped, together accounting for 1.4 per cent of MVA in 1990 (down from 2.4 per cent in 1980). This compares with 10 per cent in Kenya (also down from 14.7 per cent in 1980), 17.2 per cent in Côte d'Ivoire (10.2 per cent in 1980), and a massive 32.2 per cent in Korea (up from 18.5 per cent in 1980).

The Ghanaian industrial structure is typical of low levels of industrialisation, showing a natural evolution from traditional to simple processing and assembly activities. The main departures from this are accounted for by foreign investments to process natural resources (in this case, aluminium from bauxite, based on cheap energy from the Volta river dam) or by specific heavy industries launched by the public sector. As with all such economies, the development of the engineering subsector, and the associated lack of metal working skills and facilities suited to modern industry, constitute an important source of weakness in its industrial structure.

The formal manufacturing sector in Ghana falls into three broad groups: a few large modern firms with the ability to produce to international standards; a larger population of small and medium sized firms using some modern technology but with low levels of efficiency; and numerous informal or micro enterprises with very simple or traditional technologies, serving limited local markets and lacking standardisation, quality control and modern management techniques.

The modern sector is concentrated in food processing and industries making industrial intermediates. It has relatively few indigenous private owners, being largely owned by foreign interests, the government or local non-Africans. It has strong technological connections with foreign companies, regardless of its ownership, but very little with the domestic economy. It has invested in training the local workforce to reasonable levels of efficiency, though it remains highly dependent on foreign sources for technology, high-level skills, equipment and components. Few of them (the aluminium company is an obvious exception) are likely to have reached levels of productive efficiency whereby they can withstand the full force of international competition, except when the 'natural' protection of transport costs is high.

The rest of modern or semi-modern enterprises operate at relatively small scales and use simple machinery. They are largely African owned, though there is a sprinkling of resident non-Africans. They generally appear to have low levels of worker and managerial skills, with little knowledge of the relevant material, product or processing technologies that they may need in order to be internationally competitive.[4] Their quality tends to be low, information about markets limited, and awareness of their own deficiencies poor. They draw on traditional methods of creating skills, obtaining information and organising production. There is practically no standardisation and little demand for modern technical services, design or consultancy (see below). There are few links with large scale enterprises.

The informal or artisanal sector, entirely African, is even further removed from modern technologies. It is geared to meeting very localised demands for simple, low cost products of low quality, using very little equipment and few skills that require formal training.

RECENT MANUFACTURING PERFORMANCE

Ghana's industrial growth record is disappointing. After an initial period of expansion of investment and output, the manufacturing sector suffered massive 'deindustrialisation' until the middle of the last decade.[5] By 1984, manufacturing output in Ghana was 39 per cent of the level achieved in 1977, and capacity utilisation in medium- and large-scale plants was down to a mere 18 per cent. From a peak contribution to GDP of 14 per cent in 1975, the share of manufacturing had dropped to 4 per cent in 1983.[6]

After the launch of the Economic Recovery Programme (ERP) in 1983, and particularly after the undertaking of structural reform policies in 1986, the performance of manufacturing industry improved sharply. In the first instance, this was due almost entirely to two factors: the availability of imported inputs and the rise in domestic demand from growing incomes, due to better cocoa prices and aid inflows. Thus, the real annual growth rate of MVA (manufacturing value added) was 12.9 per cent in 1984, 24.3 per cent in 1985, 11.0 per cent in 1986, and 10.0 per cent in 1987.

However, this pace of expansion could not be maintained. After easily usable capacity had been brought into production, the further growth of manufacturing activity called for more investments in refurbishing and modernising run-down facilities, the addition of new capacity, and, most important, increases in the efficiency of operations (a significant proportion had been run down to an extent that it could not be used as it stood). The need to improve technical efficiency became particularly pressing as the trade regime became more open and tariff barriers to import competition were reduced.

For a variety of reasons, discussed later, such investments were relatively slow to materialise. As a consequence, the rate of growth of MVA fell to 5.1 per cent in 1988, 3.1 per cent in 1989 and 2.5 per cent in 1990. There are few signs of a revival thereafter. By the start of the 1990s, therefore, manufacturing had not regained its peak 1970s share of GDP of 14 per cent. In the adjustment period itself, this share had fallen from 11.5 per cent in 1985 to 9.2 per cent in 1990. Total manufacturing production was 63 per cent of its 1977 level in 1990.

These broad trends conceal important variations in the performance of individual activities. For instance, two subsectors, cement and non-ferrous basic metals (aluminium), had reached their earlier peaks (Table 2.2). Beverages, petroleum refining and wood products also fared relatively well (reaching 70 per cent or more of their 1977 volume). These were industries that had a strong local resource base (like wood or beverages), other cheap inputs (aluminium), 'natural' protection from high transport costs (cement), or else had attracted government investments in upgrading and equipment (petroleum refining). Industries that did rather badly (below 50 per cent of the 1977 volume) were textiles, garments, leather, iron and steel products, electrical equipment, and transport equipment (though index numbers for this last activity are not given, there is anecdotal evidence that import liberalisation has hit it badly). The others turned in an indifferent performance.

MANUFACTURED EXPORTS

The state of development of Ghanaian industry is also indicated by its manufactured export performance. Data extracted from the Ghana Export Promotion Council's figures for non-traditional exports in 1986 and 1991 show that the absolute values involved are extremely small. At ruling exchange rates, total Ghanaian manufactured exports in 1986 come to $3.5 million. The adjustment programme offered much better returns to exporting, and the volume of manufactured exports did lead to an increase, to $14.7 million by 1991.[7] At first sight, this suggests that there was a dynamic growth of competitive manufacturing activity and a shift of resources from inefficient to efficient industries.

This reading would be premature. The disaggregated data show that the growth came mainly from resource-based industries that were already established in export markets. Moreover, the rates of expansion should be treated cautiously because of the very small base from which they start. The leading performers were wood and aluminium products, both

Table 2.2 Index numbers of manufacturing production (1977=100)

Sector	Weight	1984	1986	1988	1989	1990
Food Processing	15	29	41	54	48	58
Beverages	8.1	60	75	89	98	94
Tobacco	7.8	63	58	58	51	57
Textiles, clothing, leather	13.7	16	23	29	24	38
Wood	7.2	60	80	98	80	74
Paper, printing	1.9	72	71	53	48	54
Petroleum refining	19	63	77	68	87	71
Other chemicals	6.6	40	38	68	62	58
Cement	3	42	47	73	100	117
Iron & steel products	3.3	26	39	18	12	5
Basic non-ferrous metals	9.6	n.a.	73	97	101	104
Non-ferrous metal products	0.5	10	55	46	48	55
Electrical equipment	1.5	19	51	47	14	26
Transport equipment	3	–	–	–	–	–
All Manufacturing	100	39	54	62	63	64

Source: *Quarterly Digest of Statistics* (Statistical Service, Republic of Ghana, December 1991).

with long experience of international markets. The values of the main non-traditional manufactured exports in 1991 were: aluminium $5.5 m., wood products $6.2 m. (of which furniture accounted for $3.6 m. and other wood products for $2.6 m.), canned foods $0.3 m., tobacco $0.4 m., soaps $0.6 m., machetes and iron rods $0.8 m., and others 1.3 m. There were, in addition, handicraft exports of just under $1 m. (see Figure 2.1).

There was, however, little sign of the emergence of new exports that went beyond the processing of local resources. In particular, in contrast to the early expansion of exports in East Asia, the availability of cheap labour (as shown later, wages are now relatively low in Ghana) has so far failed to emerge as a source of comparative advantage. There is also little sign that local enterprises are entering new areas even within the category of resource-based exports, where the natural cost advantage may be expected to stimulate local entrepreneurs. Aluminium exports are accounted for by two long-established foreign firms, while one Scandinavian firm alone accounts for around 95 per cent of furniture exports. In general, Ghana's manufactured export growth to date has been below the modest targets set by the Export Promotion Council.

This is an important reflection on the analytical basis of structural adjustment. Adjustment is premised on the expectation that 'getting

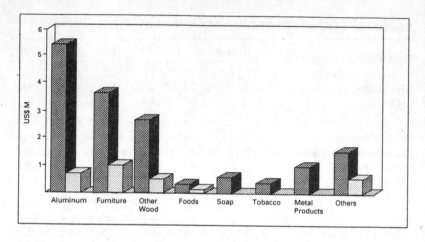

Figure 2.1 Manufactured exports, US $ m. (1986 and 1991)

Source: Ghana Export Promotion Council.

prices right', rapidly and across the board, is both necessary and sufficient for achieving sustained industrial and export development. The response capacity is assumed to be present and all relevant markets to work efficiently. This view derives from a simple neoclassical interpretation of the technological learning process. In particular, as noted in the last chapter, it ignores the cost, difficulties and market failures involved in enterprises becoming efficient. In a country at Ghana's stage of development, all these problems loom much larger, even for the restructuring of relatively simple labour-intensive operations.

An understanding of the technological capability building process would have led to the expectation that local enterprises in Ghana would find it very difficult to develop the technological and other capabilities that are needed for world class competitiveness. Unlike liberalisation in countries with more advanced industrial capabilities and better functioning markets, it would have been expected that in Ghana a considerable period of 'learning' and 'relearning' would be involved. In addition, the learning process within firms would need considerable assistance from external institutions before prices did their work.

This theme will be developed through the study. The rest of this chapter describes the incentive framework and the broader setting for capability development in Ghana. The following part takes up the more detailed examination of the technological capabilities of industrial firms.

REASONS FOR POOR PERFORMANCE

Incentive Framework

The *incentive framework* under which enterprises operated during the past regime is critical to an understanding of their technological development today. The present shape of Ghanaian industry has been determined more by the policies pursued over the two decades before the launch of ERP and structural adjustment than by the policies thereafter. The incentive framework can be considered under two closely related headings: trade policies and industrial policies.

Trade Policies. Restrictive import licensing was introduced in Ghana at the end of 1961 to deal with a deteriorating balance-of-payments caused by rising import demand and stagnant export revenues. Import controls quickly became entrenched in Ghana's trade regime and determined domestic prices and the ability to obtain intermediate inputs. While the industrial sector generally benefited from the high levels of protection offered, it suffered from periodic cuts in production when the reserve situation called for a tightening of imports. These scarcities increased over time and, by the early 1980s, had brought the highly import-dependent sector to gross underutilisation of capacity. The atmosphere of uncertainty, falling demand and general economic malaise compounded the existing disincentives to investments in technological activity.

As in other countries pursuing unselective industrialisation policies behind high barriers of protection, Ghanaian industry failed to develop adequate industrial capabilities and infrastructure.[8] In addition, its poor initial base of industrial skills and its macroeconomic and primary sector policy mistakes exacerbated the problems created by the trade regime, leaving Ghana with a much lower capability to respond to changes in the incentive framework than other import-substituting economies that had a much larger initial base of skills, like India or Mexico.

In common with highly inward-oriented regimes, the effective rates of protection offered in Ghana were high, and also highly variable across activities. Calculations by the World Bank show that by 1972, nearly half of Ghanaian industry had effective rates of protection (ERPs) of over 100 per cent, and 43 per cent of 400 per cent or more, including several with negative value added at world prices.[9] However, the calculation of domestic resource cost ratios for a sample of firms suggested that a significant number of them were *potentially* competitive if they could operate at full capacity and achieve the requisite standards of quality and design. These were industries that used local resources intensively, did not have large minimum scales of production, and had technologies that were easy to master (or else could use traditional technologies competitively). Activities like food, beverages and tobacco emerged as the best placed to compete in world markets.[10]

The liberalisation that started with the structural adjustment programme of 1986 transformed the trade regime. Quantitative restrictions on imports were removed entirely, and tariffs were lowered and rationalised. Official restrictions on access to imported inputs, equipment and technology were removed. By 1992, most tariffs were concentrated around 25 to 40 per cent, with an average effective rate of protection of around 25 per cent. They were due to be lowered further during 1992.

The trade regime in Ghana is now *relatively open*, and exposes much of the Ghanaian manufacturing sector to strong world competition. Once the reforms underway are fully implemented, there will remain little or no overall incentive bias towards the home market. However, a few activities may be given a degree of protection from local taxes, while some others may suffer from negative effective protection if their output is sold at world prices while their non-traded inputs (particularly energy) are more expensive than to overseas competitors.

Industrial Policies. The main area of industrial policy of relevance to technology development concerns the ownership policies pursued in the past and the development of private enterprises in the future. The post-independence leadership in Ghana strongly promoted public ownership of industry, both to speed up the industrialisation process and to establish socialism. However, the government's strategy was to have a blend of a strong state presence alongside an active private sector, rather than to expropriate the latter completely.

The attitude toward the private sector varied over time. The military regime of 1972–9 extended the scope of the state in production, marketing, distribution, pricing and resource allocation, but was unable to suppress a private economy that took advantage of the growing distortions introduced by the controls. The subsequent regimes tried to control corruption and profiteering with tighter controls on the private sector. Ultimately, the new policies, launched after the ERP, introduced comprehensive reforms and much greater freedom for the private sector.

According to the latest figures available on the ownership breakdown of Ghanaian industry, for 1986, the small and micro enterprise sector (concentrated in traditional activities with low productivity technologies and low quality products) is entirely in the local private sector (Table 2.3). The medium- and large-scale sector, in more modern and capital intensive activities, was originally dominated by wholly foreign-owned

Table 2.3   Ownership of Ghanaian enterprises, 1986 (percentage shares)

Ownership	Wholly foreign	Foreign/local joint ventures[1]	State/local private joint ventures	Wholly state
% share of total	9	39	22	30

[1] This includes joint ventures with both public and private sector firms.

enterprises (in 1962 they accounted for 68 per cent of value added by large and medium enterprises, with another 12 per cent from joint ventures). Over time, the role of the public sector grew, reaching a peak of 30 per cent of value added in 1986. The public sector also had a number of joint investments with foreign and local enterprises, accounting for 14.4 per cent of value added in 1986. The number of joint ventures between Ghanaian and foreign enterprises increased ten fold over 1962–82, because of the requirement that foreign firms take local partners. The number of wholly private enterprises also rose in this period, despite the discrimination against them.

The post-ERP regime improved significantly the environment for private business in Ghana. Among the reforms under way in the early 1990s is the liberalisation of entry to all private investors, local or foreign.[11] While the 1985 Investment Code is still in force in the early 1990s, its application is more relaxed and a new Code is under preparation. The approval process has been considerably speeded up. The government plans to improve the efficiency of state-owned enterprises and to divest them gradually. All enterprises that remain in state ownership will be encouraged to operate on commercial principles and will be granted greater autonomy.

There are, however, few indications of a significant growth in the interest of foreign investors in Ghanaian manufacturing industry. Table 2.4 gives details of foreign direct investment (FDI) approvals in manufacturing over 1986–90. The data show that there was a burst of approvals in 1987 over 1986, doubling the figure from $5.7 to $11.7 million. In 1989 there was another increase to a peak of $19 million, followed by a decline to $14.3 million. The cumulative figure for approvals was $62.9 million over the five years, an average of $12.6 million per year. However, approval data are not usually a good indicator of actual arrivals of FDI into a country: in most developing countries the ratio between approvals and arrivals is generally 60:40. Actual FDI arrivals are likely to have been in the range of $5–6 million per annum, a very low figure indeed.

Table 2.4   Branch distribution of foreign investment approvals in Ghana,
1986–1990[a]

Industry group	Annual FDI Approvals (US $ millions)					Cumulative FDI approvals	
	1986	1987	1988	1989	1990	US $ (1986–1990)	% share
Food, beverages and tobacco	1.4	1.7	2.1	4.0	2.3	11.5	18.3
Textiles and garments	0.0	0.3	0.2	0.0	0.1	0.6	1.0
Leather products	0.0	0.0	0.0	0.1	0.0	0.1	0.2
Wood and wood products	2.5	5.1	2.9	7.0	0.6	18.1	28.8
Paper and paper products	0.0	1.4	0.0	1.4	1.2	4.0	6.4
Chemicals	0.3	0.6	0.9	1.3	4.9	8.0	12.7
Rubber and plastic products	0.4	0.0	2.4	4.6	1.4	8.8	14.0
Non-metallic minerals	0.2	0.1	0.1	0.0	1.8	2.2	3.5
Basic metals	0.0	0.0	0.0	0.0	1.3	1.3	2.1
Fabricated metal products	0.9	2.5	2.6	0.5	0.4	6.9	11.0
Electrical products	0.0	0.0	1.0	0.1	0.3	1.4	2.2
Total manufacturing	5.7	11.7	12.2	19.0	14.3	62.9	100

[a] Approvals. Data on actuals not available.

Source: Ghana Investment Centre, Accra.

The bulk of FDI approvals, 47 per cent of the total value over the
period, has gone into two activities: food processing and wood products. These are relatively simple resource-based industries, with reasonable
export prospects because of their local material inputs. However, these
investments may not signify much upgrading of industrial capabilities
in Ghana, because they have few linkages with the rest of manufacturing. Intermediates like chemicals and rubber have got about 27 per
cent of total approvals, while capital goods (even if fabricated metals
are included in this category) have received very little.

This pattern is not surprising. In the absence of protection from imports,
the main draw for manufacturing FDI into high value-added activities
in a developing country is a good base of local skills and technical
expertise, together with a network of efficient subcontractors and suppliers. This Ghana cannot offer at this stage (see below).[12] FDI inflows have therefore to rely on cheap raw materials and natural protection
given by transport costs. What is less expected is the inability to attract more foreign interest in labour-intensive activities. Ghanaian labour
is now relatively cheap, and the country enjoys, with most of Sub-

Saharan Africa, special access to the EC market. Its failure to draw the relocation of garments and other assembly activities from the developed and newly industrialising economies points to low labour productivity and/or infrastructural deficiencies. Some of these problems are found in the present case studies.

Skills and Technological Activity

Ghana has a well-deserved reputation for possessing a large base of skilled labour by Sub-Saharan African (SSA) standards. In the mid 1960s, it had a primary school enrolment ratio of 69 per cent and a secondary enrolment ratio of 13 per cent. By 1989, these ratios had increased to 74 and 39 per cent respectively In primary enrolments, Ghana was among the top 5 SSA countries in 1965 and the top dozen in 1985; in secondary enrolments, it ranked among the top three in both periods (only Zimbabwe and Mauritius did better). Its tertiary enrolment ratio, at 2 per cent, though not high, was average by SSA standards.[13] In addition, Ghana has a stock of educated people living abroad that may constitute a valuable potential base of industrial skills.

Table 2.5 shows enrolment rates at the three levels in Ghana and five other African countries as well as Korea. It suggests that Zimbabwe has the best general skill base in Africa, but that the African countries all lag seriously behind the NIEs of East Asia. It is useful to supplement these data with figures on tertiary level enrolments in technical subjects that are likely to be of direct relevance to capability building in manufacturing. Table 2.6 shows enrolments at three levels of aggregation in science-related subjects. The category of 'natural science, mathematics, computing and engineering' is perhaps the closest to industrial needs. Here, the proportion of enrolments to population comes to 0.01 per cent in Ghana, the same in Zimbabwe and slightly less than that in the other four African countries. This can be compared to 0.76 per cent in Korea.

Vocational training enrolments in Ghana are shown relative to these other countries in Table 2.7. Here Ghana fares better than Kenya and Nigeria, but worse than the other African countries (Cameroon has a particularly good performance). Ghana's figure, relative to population, is *just over* 5 per cent of the figure for Korea.

While these figures cannot be taken as they stand as measures of the human capital base for industrialisation, they are highly suggestive. By comparison with the newly industrialising countries of East Asia or Latin America, the base of manufacturing skills in Ghana seems

Table 2.5 Educational attainments in selected African countries

Country	Numbers enrolled in school as percentage of age group						Tertiary level No. of students per 100 000 inhabitants (year)	Adult illiteracy rate 1990
	Primary[a]		Secondary		Tertiary			
	1965	1989	1965	1989	1965	1989		
Ghana	69	75	13	39	1	2	132 (1985)	40
Kenya	54	94	4	23	0	2	121 (1987)	31
Zimbabwe	110	125	6	52	0	6	383 (1988)	33
Côte d'Ivoire	60	n.a.	6	n.a.	0	n.a.	200 (1985)	46
Nigeria	32	70	6	19	0	3	239 (1985)	49
Cameroon	94	101	5	26	0	3	227 (1987)	46
S. Korea	101	108	35	86	6	38	3688 (1988)	5

[a] For some countries with universal primary education, the gross enrollment ratios may exceed 100 per cent because some pupils are younger or older than the country's standard primary school age.

Sources: World Bank (1992), *World Development Report 1992*, Washington; UNESCO (1990), *Statistical Yearbook 1990*, Paris.

Table 2.6 Tertiary level students in technical fields (in numbers and as a percentage of total population) in selected African countries

Country	Year	General science[a]		Natural science, mathematics, computing and engineering		Engineering only	
Ghana	1987	3 516	0.02	1 886	0.01	722	0.005
Kenya	1987	12 588	0.05	5 470	0.02	3 438	0.01
Zimbabwe	1987	1 723	0.02	888	0.01	389	0.005
Côte d'Ivoire	1987	6 344	0.05	2 574	0.02	365	0.003
Nigeria	1987	45 018	0.04	23 524	0.02	8 068	0.008
Cameroon	1980	3 127	0.03	1 983	0.02	373	0.005
S. Korea	1988	609 650	1.45	320 666	0.76	227 640	0.543

[a] Includes natural science; mathematics and computer science; medicine; engineering; architecture; trade and crafts; transport and communications; agriculture, forestry and fishing.

Source: UNESCO (1990), *Statistical Yearbook 1990*, Paris.

Table 2.7　Pupils enrolled in vocational education in selected African countries

Country	[1] 1975	[2] Latest year a	[3] 2 as % pop.
Ghana	18 919	14 915	0.10
Kenya	5 468	8 880	0.04
Zimbabwe	1 312	11 104	0.12
Côte d'Ivoire	15 758	25 328	0.24
Nigeria	27 843	87 846	0.09
Cameroon	36 262	93 651	0.88
S. Korea	436 538	723 193	1.72

a Latest refers to 1988 or 1989.

Source: UNESCO (1990), *Statistical Yearbook 1990*, Paris.

very small. Korea and the other NIEs had relatively high levels of human capital, and especially technical human capital, at the *start* of their industrialisation drive in the 1960s. This was essential to their ability to achieve international competitiveness in a rapidly diversifying range of manufacturing activities. Ghana lacks a similar base even today, though it has been attempting to industrialise for almost as long as Korea.

Ghana's present endowment of skills appears to be sufficient, if sufficient specialised industrial training can be provided, to allow it to progress with some large-scale industrial development, and to undertake the upgrading of its traditional small and medium manufacturing activities. However, it may not be sufficient to permit a sustained expansion into a more sophisticated range of industrial activities. The base of technical skills may even be insufficient to take it into the relatively advanced technologies that may be needed to be internationally competitive in some of the activities that already exist in the country. The recent trends in engineering education, in particular, are not encouraging.[14] In the University of Science and Technology in Kumasi, the only university that gives engineering degrees in Ghana, the number of engineering graduates has gone up from 125 in 1984 to 193 in 1991 (see Table 2.8). However, the percentage of graduates in manufacturing-related subjects (chemical, electrical, electronic and mechanical engineering) has fallen from 48.8 per cent to 38.9 per cent. Similarly, the proportions of engineering diploma holders (52 in number in 1984

Table 2.8   University engineering graduations in Ghana, number and by specialization 1970–1991

	1970	1980	1984	1990	1991
No. of B.Sc. engineering degrees[a]	58	95	125	160	193
No. of B.Sc. engineering degrees per 100 000 inhabitants	0.7	0.8	1.0	1.1	1.2
Engineering degrees by specialization (%)					
Agriculture	0.0	2.1	6.4	15.6	12.4
Chemical	0.0	7.4	12.8	7.5	7.8
Civil	29.3	36.8	24.0	25.0	19.7
Electrical/electronic	32.8	18.9	18.4	9.4	11.4
Geodetic	1.7	8.4	4.8	6.3	13.0
Mechanical	36.2	12.6	17.6	20.0	19.7
Mining	0.0	13.7	16.0	16.3	16.1
Total	100	100	100	100	100
No. of engineering diplomas	47	77	52	45	23
No. of engineering diplomas per 100 000 inhabitants	0.6	0.7	0.4	0.3	0.2
Engineering diplomas by specialization (%)					
Civil	0.0	0.0	40.4	53.3	13.0
Environmental health tech	0.0	0.0	0.0	8.9	30.4
Electrical	44.7	29.9	9.6	15.6	8.7
Geodetic	14.9	26.0	9.6	20.0	30.4
Mechanical	40.4	44.2	40.4	2.2	17.4
Total	100	100	100	100	100

[a] Four year degree programme.

Source: University of Science and Technology, Kumasi, Ghana.

and only 23 in 1991) in manufacturing-related disciplines fell from 50 per cent to 26.1 per cent.

These impressions of skill deficiencies in manufacturing are supported by a recent report prepared for the Government on science and technology.[15] This report surveys each of the major manufacturing industries in the country, and comments at length on available technological capabilities. In almost every case, it notes the shortage of skilled and technical manpower, especially at the middle levels, as a major cause of technological backwardness. It also comments repeatedly on the widespread absence of formal technological activity by enterprises and the neglect of training of employees. As a result, practically each subsector of Ghanaian industry appears to operate with obsolete, often inappropriate, technologies that are poorly mastered and rarely improved.

What is perhaps more surprising is that the skills available in the country are not utilised by enterprises. There is unemployment among technically qualified graduates. Despite the low levels of skill with which their firms operate, many Ghanaian managers thus seem to be *unaware* of the needs of their firms for skill upgrading and for technological effort. This is also found in the case studies, and exceptions are noted and explored below.

Coming now to *formal technological effort* in Ghanaian manufacturing, practically all industrial R&D in Ghana is conducted by public institutions rather than by enterprises. The available data on national R&D in Ghana are shown in Table 2.9. The data may not be very reliable, but they suggest that R&D effort has declined sharply in the 1980s, presumably as a result of the adjustment programme. This is common to many countries undergoing rapid structural adjustment.

The level of R&D as a percentage of GNP in Ghana is low in comparison with newly industrialising countries or Malaysia (which are around 1–2 per cent of GNP), but is about the norm for several African countries like Nigeria, Côte d'Ivoire, Mauritius or Kenya, as well as less industrialised countries like Sri Lanka, Thailand and Indonesia.[16] For our purposes these figures are difficult to interpret , since the bulk of R&D in most of these countries is related to agriculture, and it is not possible to compare how much technological effort is devoted to manufacturing.

For Ghana, however, we are able to identify the institutions responsible for industry-related R&D. There are three bodies in the Council for Scientific and Industrial Research (CSIR) network that are involved in such work: the Industrial Research Institute (IRI), the Scientific Instrumentation Centre (SIC), and the Food Research Institute (FRI).[17] The functions of these institutions are to develop and disseminate technologies for use in manufacturing industry, and to conduct contract technological work for industrial enterprises.

In addition, two institutions are responsible for the identification, development and diffusion of intermediate technologies for small and micro enterprises: Development and Application of Intermediate Technologies (DAPIT), and Ghana Regional Appropriate Technology Industrial Service (GRATIS), but these do not do their own research. Their main function is to encourage the commercial application of known technologies by small- and medium-sized enterprises (SMEs); any fur-

Table 2.9   R&D expenditures in Ghana, 1975–1987

Year	Cedis Million (current)	As % of GNP
1975	30.2	0.6
1979	212.5	0.8
1983	100.2	0.1
1987	2262.2	0.3

Source: Moore (1989), Table 5.

ther development or adaptation is commissioned to one of the CSIR institutes noted above.

The National Board of Small Scale Industries (NBSSI) also helps SMEs with the provision of training (technical as well as entrepreneurial), finance, advice and extension. The Technology Transfer Centre (TTC), set up by the University of Science and Technology (UST) in Kumasi, provides training and promotional services to SMEs and commercialises technologies developed by the University (including the manufacture of certain tools and equipment). The UST is the only other focus for industry-related R&D in Ghana apart from the CSIR institutes.[18] The Ghana Standards Board provides some basic support in the field of standards and quality assurance, and is about to launch metrological services.

In 1989, the three CSIR institutes directly concerned with industry (IRI, SIC and FRI) together employed 282 people (90, 57 and 135 respectively). The total number of 'scientific' staff (degree holders in technical fields engaged in research) was 45 and technical support staff (diploma holders) 123. The total funding of the three institutes in 1989 was Cedis 238.8 million (around $31 m. at the prevailing rate of exchange), which came to *0.02 per cent of GDP.*[19]

This suggests that R&D effort in Ghana relevant to manufacturing industry is minuscule, well below the critical mass needed to make a significant contribution to the absorption, adaptation or creation of technology.[20] Even if the technological efforts of the UST and the institutions supporting SMEs are added in, the total is likely to remain very small. Apart from the quantity of technological work, moreover, there are serious problems concerning its quality and relevance. Many reports, official and other, give the impression that the work carried out by the CSIR institutes is largely unrelated to the problems facing Ghanaian manufacturing enterprises, and very little of the R&D results in commercial application.[21] The quality of the work is variable, often rather low. The laboratories are poorly equipped and staffed. The management of research projects tends to be unwieldy and is not oriented to achieving practical results in defined periods.[22] Too much emphasis seems to be laid on developing indigenous technologies rather than on assimilating and diffusing technologies available in developed or more industrialised developing countries. Some useful services are provided by the CSIR to industry, but, judging from the data on the sources of funding, these are a tiny fraction of the work undertaken.

Because of the importance of product quality to the development of efficient manufacturing, it is worth reporting on the system for *standards, metrology and calibration* in Ghana. In 1987, the International Standards Organisation published the International Standard for Quality Management Systems, ISO 9000 series.[23] This series seeks to bring about a harmonisation of quality standards on an international scale, and no enterprise with export ambitions can ignore it. The European Community will require all enterprises exporting to it to have a recognised quality management system in place. Thus, the assurance of quality by installing a proper system is now an essential prerequisite for achieving international competitiveness in manufacturing industry. Such a system calls, not just for enterprise level efforts and skills to reach a certifiable level of quality management, but also for a supporting infrastructure of technical consultancy services, standards, metrology and calibration.

The Ghana Standards Board (GSB) has the responsibility for drafting and implementing national standards in the country. So far its efforts have been devoted largely to foods and drugs, though the Board also has responsibility for engineering products. The engineering sector in Ghana lacks a comprehensive range of product standards, and tends to use a variety of foreign standards which may not match each other, and some of which may not represent a good choice of technology. Along with the absence of quality control systems, there is a widespread *lack of appreciation of standards in Ghanaian industry*. This reflects the previous protected regime under which it operated, as well as the lack of qualified personnel able to understand and implement the technical aspects of standardisation. The GSB lacks the resources (financial and human) to prepare engineering standards, to encourage industry to use them, and to enforce standards in a meaningful way. Its attitude to promoting standards has been very passive.

GSB operates a mandatory system of product certification under which all manufacturers are required by law to have their products certified as being of acceptable quality. This requirement is largely theoretical, since the severe shortage of resources means that there is no way the GSB can check satisfactorily the quality of a range of manufactures. The absence of a range of approved and published engineering standards means that there is a danger of substandard specifications being used to define product performance, with consequent effects on sales and exports. Thus, *GSB certification has correspondingly little value in countries that adhere to international standards.* These issues are evidently very important for the technological development of Ghanaian manufacturing, and will be touched on again.

3 Methodology and Sample Characteristics

INTRODUCTION

The study of technological capabilities in Ghana is based on the findings of two surveys of manufacturing firms. The main part of the study, forming Part C of this book, derives from a case study sample of 32 firms that were interviewed in depth. There was also a larger panel survey with quantitative information, the findings of which are analysed in the next chapter. This chapter describes the methodology and background to the firms in the surveys. Both surveys were undertaken in August and September 1992.

The study covered four industries: *textiles and garments, food processing, wood working* and *metal working*. The purpose of the case study and panel data surveys was to analyse: (1) the process of acquiring technological capabilities in firms; (2) the technological strengths and weaknesses of different types of firms; and (3) the influences on technological capability acquisition in firms. This chapter describes the survey methodology and highlights some of the important characteristics of the sample firms: size, age in production, ownership and market performance. It ends with a brief discussion of adjustment effects on the panel and case study firms.

METHODOLOGY

This study uses a survey methodology as its source of primary data. The survey had two main components: a *panel questionnaire* applied to 200 manufacturing firms and a *case-study questionnaire* applied to 35 firms. The case study survey included 27 firms which were also part of the panel survey. Of the original number of firms in the panel survey, 12 questionnaires could not be completed in time for this book and 24 were omitted because of missing or incomplete information, thus reducing the size of the panel sample to 164 firms. Out of the 35 firms in the case study survey, 3 were eliminated because of incomplete or questionable data. This analysis of technological capabilities in the 32 case study firms draws primarily on the results of the case study questionnaires but also makes some use of the panel questionnaires.

The division of labour contemplated in the two surveys was as follows. The panel questionnaires, administered to a large number of firms, were expected to provide quantitative information on capital stock, recent new investments, human capital and some specific technology indicators (such as licenses and technical assistance, expatriates employed, R&D expenditures, productivity improvement personnel and sources of technological information). The case-study questionnaires, administered to a small number of firms, sought information on the acquisition of technology, the nature of in-house technological activities, training programmes, local production linkages, the relationship with technical institutions, the impact of adjustment and future firm strategies. These questionnaires also elicited quantitative information on the ownership structure, the skill levels of technical manpower, the educational background of entrepreneurs and production managers, local market position, export behaviour, and several performance indicators.

The selection of firms for the technology case studies was not random. It was attempted to survey a mix of firms from different size classes (small, medium and large), ownership forms (foreign, local non-African, local African and state) and market performance categories (growing, reviving, stagnant and dead). Although some smaller firms were included, the attempt to choose firms which were technologically interesting led to a focus on more medium- and large-sized firms. A number of particular firms were also selected on prior knowledge of exceptional technological activity.

Table 3.1 provides information on the product mix and the location of the sample firms. Of the 32 case study firms, there are 8 in textiles and garments, 7 in food processing, 8 in wood working and 9 in metal working. The firms are identified only by number to preserve confidentiality. The prefixes TG, FP, WW and MW refer respectively to textiles and garments, food processing, wood working and metal working.

The firms in these sectors differ substantially in terms of product-mix and thus technology of production. *Textiles and garments* are quite different activities. Textiles is now generally a capital intensive activity with a substantial degree of mechanisation, while garments is much more labour intensive and uses simple, manually operated, machinery such as sewing and cutting machines. *Food processing* ranges from biscuit manufacturing and flour milling to subsidiaries of multinational corporations making sophisticated processed foods. *Wood working*, which

Table 3.1 Background: location, size, age in production, ownership structure and principal products

Firm	Location[a]	Employment 1991 (nos)	Sales 1991 (US$ '000)	Age in production in 1992 (years)	Ownership structure[b]	Principal products
Textiles and garments						
TG1	A	90	194.7	18	100% LNA	Uniforms (95%), printing T-shirts (5%)
TG2	A	73	163.1	8	100% LNA	Synthetic leather (90%) and derivatives (Tarpaulin)
TG3	K	42	66.6	18	100% LA	Uniforms
TG4	A	30	93.7	16	100% LNA	Nets (50%), polyester fabrics (50%)
TG5	A	24	49.9	22	55% LNA, 45% LA	Knitwear (mainly T-shirts)
TG6	A	15	20.1	24	100% LA	Uniforms
TG7	K	13	n.r	17	100% LA	Traditional garments
TG8[c]	A	0	0.0	(1968–87) 19	100% LA	Used to make shirts, trousers and knitwear
Food processing						
FP1	A	650	82918.7	31	55% State, 45% Foreign	Evaporated milk, cocoa beverage, infant cereals
FP2	A	246	2990.5	23	100% Foreign	Cocoa beverages, drinking chocolate, toffees
FP3	A	228	644.3	31	100% State	Fruit juice and other processed foods
FP4	A	216	830.4	36	100% LNA	Biscuits
FP5	A	200	8155.9	3	100% LA	Flour
FP6	A	172	7612.2	32	60% Foreign, 40% LA	Dairy products
FP7	A	80	543.7	8	100% LA	Fruit juices and drinks

Wood working

WW1	A	267	1359.3	14	60% LA, 40% Foreign	Wood furniture
WW2	A	225	489.4	65	100% LA	Lumber (80%) and wood furniture (20%)
WW3	A	147	407.8	10	100% LA	Wood furniture
WW4	A	135	40.8	41	100% LA	Wood furniture
WW5	K	65	81.6	16	50% LNA, 50% LA	Wood furniture
WW6	K	41	21.7	14	100% LA	Wood furniture
WW7	K	16	8.4	6	100% LA	Wood furniture
WW8	A	10	4.9	7	100% LA	Cane furniture

Metal working

MW1	T	430	5200.6	27	40% State, 60% Foreign	Structural steel rods
MW2	A	150	2718.6	5	100% LA	Pots and pans
MW3	A	71	1141.8	21	100% LA	Aluminium doors, windows, ceilings, partitioning
MW4	A	30	40.8	35	40% Foreign, 60% LA	Aluminium doors, windows, ceilings, partitioning
MW5	A	28	34.0	35	100% LA	Machines for agriculture and food processing
MW6	K	28	32.6	17	100% LA	Water tanks, metal gates, metal doors
MW7	K	19	51.7	20	100% LA	Machines for food processing and wood working
MW8	K	16	23.3	7	40% State, 60% LA	Spare parts for auto industry
MW9	K	13	n.r	29	50% LNA, 50% LA	Fabricated mining equipment

[a] A = Accra, T = Tema (near Accra), K = Kumasi.
[b] LA = Local African, LNA = Local non-African.
[c] Dead firm had 160 employees at its peak in 1986. n.r = not reliable.

includes furniture and cabinet-making, covers a broad range of activities and technologies from the use of manual tools to well-equipped modern furniture-making factories. Finally, in *metal working* there are small-scale producers of pots and pans, at one end, to relatively large mills pressing steel and aluminium products, at the other. Included in this group are also producers of various types of machines and other equipment.

The case study firms were located in Accra (including Tema) and Kumasi, 23 in the former and 9 in the latter. The firms surveyed in Accra cover all four industries. Those in Kumasi consist of 2 textile and garment firms, 3 wood working firms and 4 metal working firms.

SAMPLE CHARACTERISTICS: THE TECHNOLOGY CASE STUDIES

Firm Size

Table 3.1 contains two measures of firm size (total employment, and sales in current US$) for the case study firms. Following the approach of the Ghanaian Census, firms are grouped according to employment into: large (over 100 employees), medium (30–99 employees) and small (29 or less employees).[1] Of the 32 sample firms, 12 are large (38 per cent), 9 medium (28 per cent) and 11 small (34 per cent). Most of the 8 largest firms (in terms of turnover) are of foreign origin. Half of them are in food processing and a third in metal working. As noted, small firms account for only 34 per cent of the case study firms, in contrast to the panel survey (see below), which is more representative of the industrial structure and has a larger proportion of small firms.

Age in Production

Table 3.1 also shows the age of the case study firms, in terms of years in production by the beginning of 1992. There is considerable variation in the age of the firms – ranging from 3 years for the youngest to 65 years for the oldest. 25 of the 32 case study firms (78 per cent) commenced production prior to the 1983 Economic Recovery Programme. Nearly all the foreign and local non-African firms in the case study survey belong to the pre-1983 group. Interestingly, most of the new firms (i.e. post-1983) are of local African origin. Some features of the pre- and post-ERP firms are considered below.

Ownership

The ownership of the firms is shown by foreign, state and local private ownership. A further distinction is made within local private ownership between local African (LA) ownership and local non-African (LNA) ownership (these are non-Africans resident in Ghana, of Syrian or Lebanese origin). Six of the firms (19 per cent) have some proportion of foreign equity; seven (22 per cent) have some proportion of local non-African equity, including 4 wholly non African-owned firms and 3 with about equal shares of local non African equity and African equity. Of the remainder (59 per cent), 17 are wholly local African owned, one has majority local African equity and minority state equity and one is wholly state owned.

Market Performance

Table 3.2 sets out some performance indicators for the case study sample in aggregate and by industry. Three measures of performance are provided: (i) sales growth rate between 1988 and 1991, (ii) employment growth rate between 1988 and 1991, (iii) the capacity utilisation rate in 1991. The sales growth rate for the case study sample in aggregate could only be estimated for 22 case study firms. Data on employment growth rate were slightly better, for 24 firms, while average capacity utilisation rate could be estimated for 28 firms.

Sales Growth. In aggregate, the case study firms registered a high average annual sales growth rate, measured in current SDRs, of 33.5 per cent in 1988–91. However, only 13 firms out of 22 (under 60 per cent) had positive rates: the high aggregate growth rate reflects the influence of a couple of large rapidly growing firms. If the two best performing firms (FP6 and MW2) are excluded, the overall growth rate falls to 10.6 per cent. This growth rate nevertheless remains impressive when compared to the −2.0 per cent rate recorded for the larger panel survey (see below).

The growth rates for the firms differ by industry and size of firm. They are positive in metal working (44.2 per cent), food processing (40.4 per cent) and wood working (24.1 per cent), but negative in textiles and garments (−17.3 per cent). Again, if the two best performing firms are excluded, the growth rate in metal working falls to 31.1 per cent and in food processing to 9.7 per cent.

By size, large firms (over 100 employees) fare best, with a sales growth rate of 40.4 per cent (excluding the two best performing firms,

Table 3.2 Market performance: a comparison of the case study firms and the panel data firms by industry (percentages)

	Textiles and garments	Food processing	Wood working	Metal working	All firms	All firms excluding top 2 firms[b]
Case study firms						
Av. annual employment growth rate in 1988–91 (%)	−3.9	3.4	1.4[a]	0.8	0.9	0.1
Av. annual sales growth rate in 1988–91 (current SDRs) (%)	−17.3	40.4	24.1	46.1	33.5	10.6
% growing firms (i.e. those with positive emp. growth)					63.0	
% growing firms (i.e. those with positive sales growth)					59.0	
Sales growth rate in small firms in 1988–91 (current SDRs)					27.6	
Sales growth rate in medium firms in 1988–91 (current SDRs)					9.5	
Sales growth rate in large firms in 1988–91 (current SDRs)					40.4	13.2
Unweighted average capacity utilization rate (%)	23.0	67.0	57.0	47.0	47.0	
Panel data firms						
Av. annual employment growth rate in 1988–91 (%)	−15.0	−6.0	6.0	4.0	−2.0	
Av. annual sales growth rate in 1988–91 (current SDRs) (%)	−16.0	−5.0	−4.0	−7.0	−6.0	
% growing firms (i.e. those with positive emp. growth)	46.7	45.8	73.9	82.1	64.4	
% growing firms (i.e. those with positive sales growth)	28.6	26.3	41.7	53.8	36.4	
Sales growth rate in micro firms in 1988–91 (current SDRs)					−43.0	
Sales growth rate in small firms in 1988–91 (current SDRs)					6.0	
Sales growth rate in medium firms in 1988–91 (current SDRs)					−2.0	
Sales growth rate in large firms in 1988–91 (current SDRs)					−9.0	

The growth rates were calculated using the compound method.
[a] Excludes an outlier (WW2).
[b] Excludes FP6 and MW2.

however, this falls to 13.2 per cent). Small firms record sales growth of 27.6 per cent and medium-sized firms of 9.5 per cent.

Employment Growth. The rate of employment expansion in this period is far lower. In aggregate the case study firms record an average annual employment growth rate of 0.9 per cent in 1988–91, which falls to 0.1 per cent if the two best performing firms are omitted. About 63 per cent of the case study firms (15 out of 24) had positive employment growth rates. As with sales, the employment growth rate for the case study sample is higher than the −6.0 per cent recorded for the panel sample (see below). The different growth rates of sales and employment indicates that firms have been shedding labour in recent years, reflecting the stringency imposed by the stabilisation programme and increased competitive pressures. This increased labour productivity is, however, highly concentrated in a few firms.

Employment growth rates vary by industry and by size of firm. Employment growth rates are negative in textiles and garments (−3.9 per cent) and positive in the three other industries (3.4 per cent in food processing, 1.4 per cent in wood working and 0.8 per cent in metal working). Excluding the two best performing firms (FP6 and MW2 again) reduces the employment growth rate to −3.3 per cent in metal working but that in food processing remains unchanged. Large firms had positive employment growth rates (2.6 per cent) while small and medium firms recorded negative growth rates (−3.7 and −1.8 per cent, respectively).

Capacity Utilisation. The unweighted average capacity utilisation rate for the case study sample in 1991 was 47 per cent. Textiles and garments have the lowest rate (23 per cent), followed by metal working (47 per cent), wood working (57 per cent) and food processing (67 per cent).

Exports by the sample firms are negligible. Only 3 of the case study sample firms exported in 1991. FP3 exported 26 per cent of sales, WW1 30 per cent and MW2 3 per cent. The poor export showing of the sample firms is symptomatic of the general lack of competitiveness of Ghanian manufacturing.

Table 3.3 sets out some performance indicators for the individual case study firms. Four measures of performance are shown: (i) sales growth rate, (ii) employment growth rate, (iii) capacity utilisation rate, and (iv) exports to sales ratio.

Sales growth is probably the single most useful quantitative indicator of performance of individual firms. Unfortunately, its utility in this sample is limited by incomplete information and the short period for which most of the data are available (in most cases 1988–91). Even

Table 3.3 Performance indicators for individual case study firms

Firm	Sales growth rate (current SDRs)		Employment growth rate		Capacity utilisation rate (%)		Exports 1991 (% of sales)	Overall classification
	Period	Av. annual growth rate (g) %	Period	Av. annual growth rate (g) %	Earlier	1991		
Textiles and garments								
TG1	1985–91	−16.9[e]	1988–91	7.7		65	Nil	Growing
TG2	1988–91	0.5	1988–91	15.0	75 (1985)	15	Nil	Stagnant
TG3	1988–91	185.1[c]	1988–91	61.3[c]		20	Nil	Stagnant
TG4	1988–91	−33.0	1988–91	−33.3	80 (1986)	20	Nil	Stagnant
TG5	1988–91	−20.2	1988–91	−24.2		10	Nil	Reviving
TG6		n.a.		n.a.	50 (1980)	9[a]	Nil	Stagnant
TG7	1988–91	145.3[c]	1988–91	17.6[c]	80 (1980)	22	Nil	Stagnant
TG8[b]		0.0		0.0		0	Nil	Dead
Food processing								
FP1	1988–91	n.a.		n.a.	15 (early 1980s)	50	Nil	Growing
FP2	1988–91	−1.7		n.a.		n.a.	0.5[f]	Stagnant
FP3	1988–91	1.5	1988–91	−5.7	80 (early 1980s)	50	26	Stagnant
FP4	1988–91	61.2	1988–91	18.4		100	Nil	Reviving
FP5		n.a.		n.a.		62	Nil	Growing
FP6	1988–91	115.5	1988–91	3.6		100	Nil	Growing
FP7	1988–91	30.3		n.a.	20 (1987)	40	Nil	Growing
Wood working								
WW1	1988–91	81.9	1988–91	2.7		95	30	Growing
WW2		n.a.	1988–91	−10.5		n.a.	Nil	Stagnant
WW3	1988–91	12.3	1988–91	7.0		75	Nil	Growing
WW4	1988–91	−6.9	1988–91	−5.7	50 (early 1980s)	17	Nil	Stagnant
WW5	1988–91	−0.4		n.a.		n.a.	Nil	Stagnant

WW6	1989–91	−38.3	1988–91	1.7		50	Nil	Stagnant
WW7	1988–91	−31.1	1988–91	38.7		50	Nil	Stagnant
WW8	1988–91	−32.8	1988–91	26.0		n.a.	Nil	Stagnant
Metal working								
MW1		n.a.	1988–91	n.a.	10 (late 1980s)	35[a]	Nil	Reviving
MW2	1987–91	35.8	1988–91	7.7	75 (1989)	75	3	Growing
MW3	1988–91	31.7	1987–91	13.9	20 (1986)	60	Nil	Growing
MW4		n.a.	1988–91	−12.6	65 (1986)	40	Nil	Stagnant
MW5		n.a.	1988–91	0.0	100 (1986)	25	Nil	Stagnant
MW6		n.a.	1988–91	23.1		50	Nil	Growing
MW7	1988–91	27.1	1988–91	−1.7		100	Nil	Growing
MW8	1988–91	15.9[d]	1988–91	13.3[d]		5	Nil	Stagnant
MW9		n.a	1988–91	−9.8		20	Nil	Stagnant

[a] 1992.

[b] Dead firm which had 160 workers at its peak in 1986.

[c] Sales and employment growth rates appear very high between 1988–1991 but this is because it shut down for two years in mid-1980s. Capacity utilisation remains v. low.

[d] Sales growth was achieved by activating the machine shop rather than the foundry which is the main manufacturing facility.

[e] Sales appear to have grown between 1988–91 but data are not available.

[f] 1989–1990.

[g] Compound growth method. n.a = not available.

longer-term growth rates would, however, have been difficult to interpret in terms of gauging which firms are more competitive. The effects of import compression of the pre-1983 period, that led to drastic reductions in operations, and the subsequent Economic Recovery Programme, with its attempt to stabilise the economy, imposed severe stresses that make it difficult to separate 'good' firms from others. Data on employment growth suffer from similar constraints.

In the absence of a single measure of performance, a *synthetic indicator* was constructed for individual firms, combining the data on sales growth, employment growth and capacity utilisation rates with interview impressions. Table 3.3 ends with a classification of individual firms by this indicator into four groups: growing (sales have risen over the past 3–4 years); reviving (sales declined initially but have picked up in the past year or two); stagnant (constant or declining sales); and dead (ceased operations). Of the 32 firms, 11 are classified as growing, 3 as reviving, 17 as stagnant and 1 as dead. Thus, only 44 per cent of the sample firms can be categorised, as growing or reviving. The majority of the growing or reviving firms are in food processing and metal working.[2]

SAMPLE CHARACTERISTICS: THE PANEL[3]

Firm Size

Let us now come to the larger sample of firms covered by the panel data. Table 3.4 shows the employment size distribution of the panel and case study firms. Of the 168 panel firms, 12 per cent are large, 19 per cent are medium and 69 per cent are small or micro, with the largest share of small and micro enterprises in textiles and garments and food processing. The panel distribution reflects the structure of Ghanaian industrial enterprises in general, with its predominance of relatively small firms in simple activities. As noted earlier, this differs from the size distribution in the case studies, where only 34 per cent of the firms are small and 66 per cent are medium and large, reflecting the purposive nature of the case study sample, focusing on the technologically more active firms.

Age in Production

A comparison of the age in production of the panel and case study firms shows that the former has a somewhat lower proportion of

Table 3.4 Summary characteristics of the 32 case study firm and the 164 panel data firms by industry (percentage of firms in each category)

	Textiles and garments	Food processing	Wood working	Metal working	All firms
A. CASE STUDY FIRMS					
1. Firm size categories:					
Small firms (<29 employees)	50.0	0.0	25.0	55.6	34.4
Medium firms (30–99 employees)	50.0	14.3	25.0	22.2	28.1
Large firms (>100 employees)	0.0	85.7	50.0	22.2	37.5
2. Ownership categories:					
Firms with foreign equity	0.0	42.9	12.5	22.2	18.8
Firms with local non-African equity	50.0	14.3	12.5	11.1	21.9
Firms with local African equity	50.0	28.6	75.0	55.6	53.1
Firms with state equity	0.0	14.3	0.0	11.1	6.3
3. Age in production categories:					
Firms which began production before 1983	87.5	71.4	75.0	77.8	78.1
Firms which began production after 1983	12.5	28.6	25.0	22.2	21.9
B. PANEL DATA FIRMS					
1. Firm size categories:					
Micro firms (0–9 employees)	41.2	46.2	31.8	30.8	37.2
Small firms (10–29 employees)	29.4	28.2	38.6	30.8	32.1
Medium firms (30–99 employees)	17.6	15.4	18.2	25.7	19.3
Large firms (>100 employees)	11.8	10.3	11.4	12.8	11.5
2. Age in production categories:					
Firms which began production before 1983	54.1	70.0	48.6	64.3	59.6
Firms which began production after 1983	45.9	30.0	51.4	35.7	40.4

pre-1983 firms, with the largest share older, panel, firms in textiles and garments.

Ownership

80 per cent of the firms in the panel are under local private ownership, reflecting again the dominance of small enterprises (of local African origin) in the general population of Ghanaian firms. No information is, however, available on the breakdown of local private ownership of panel firms into local African and local non-African origin. The ownership distribution of the case study sample is similar to that of the panel sample.

Market Performance

Table 3.2 above set out some performance indicators for the panel sample in aggregate and by industry. Two measures of performance were provided, both for 1988–91, sales growth and employment growth.

Sales growth. In aggregate, the panel firms register negative growth rates of sales (−6.0 per cent) in 1988–91. The rates are negative in all four industries: −16.0 per cent in textiles and garments, −7.0 per cent in metal working, −5 per cent in food processing, and −4.0 per cent in wood working.[4] Only 36.4 per cent of the firms in the panel sample had positive rates.[5] Metal working had the highest proportion of growing to declining firms (53.8 per cent), followed by wood working (41.7 per cent), textiles and garments (28.6 per cent) and food processing (26.3 per cent).

Small firms (10 to 29 employees), with 6.0 per cent sales growth, are the best performers in the panel. In sharp contrast, micro enterprises (less than 9 employees) record annual declines (of −43.0 per cent). Medium (30–99 employees) and large firms (above 100 employees) also show negative rates of −2.0 and −9.0 per cent, respectively. Thus the adjustment and stabilisation has hit the micro enterprises the hardest, but larger firms have also suffered; it is small firms that have benefited from the rising demand and availability of imports (see below).

Older panel firms, which began production before 1983, declined less (at −2.0 per cent per annum) than firms which began production after 1983 (at −19.0 per cent).[6]

Employment growth. In aggregate, the panel firms register negative growth rates of employment (−2.0 per cent) during 1988–1991. This varies by industry and firm size. Textile and garments and food processing record employment declines (−15.0 per cent and −6.0 per cent per annum, respectively), while wood and metal working show increases (6.0 per cent and 4.0 per cent). By size, small (10–29 employees) and micro enterprises (less than 9 employees) are the best performers, each with 3.0 per cent employment growth. Medium (30–99 employees) and large firms (above 100 employees) show negative employment growth rates.

It is interesting to compare the panel findings with that of the survey by Steel and Webster (1992), conducted in late 1989 to assess the impact of the structural adjustment on small enterprises in Ghana. The survey covered 82 firms, of which 33 were micro enterprises (1 to 3 employees), 42 small enterprises (4–29 employees) and 7 medium and large enterprises (30 plus employees). The period covered was before the import liberalisation really started to 'bite', 1990 and later. Nevertheless, the period 1983 to 1989 is interesting to analyse. In that time sharp rises in import prices (arising from massive devaluation) and the stabilisation measures (that reduced credit and significantly raised interest rates), combined with the lifting of quantitative restrictions on imports and easier domestic entry, led to much greater competition for established firms and to easier access to foreign inputs.

Steel and Webster's survey found that many new small enterprises emerged in this period. However, the total numbers involved were small, and the 'quality' of the response to the liberalisation was weak: only 39 per cent of the sample managed to increase production in 1983–9. Of the remainder, 43 per cent suffered declines and 18 per cent stagnated. One important finding was that declining firms were concentrated in the set of enterprises started *before* the ERP (1983). Micro enterprises (with less than 4 employees) fared particularly badly regardless of their age. Newer firms had the largest proportion of those with rising production, with the best performers among those with employment of 4 to 29 workers.

Three sets of comparisons can be made between the two sets of surveys: (i) the percentage of growing firms; (ii) the performance of firms of different size classes; and (iii) the performance of firms started before and after the launch of the ERP. It should be noted that the panel sample is more representative of the population of Ghanaian firms, because it has a larger coverage and its sampling procedure was carefully designed.

(i) The present panel survey confirms Steel and Webster's finding that supply response to import liberalisation continues to be weak in Ghana. In the panel 36.4 per cent of the firms have positive sales growth compared to Steel and Webster's 39 per cent. Thus, the later period, when the liberalisation had gathered momentum, did *not* witness a strengthening of enterprise growth.

(ii) The panel survey confirms Steel and Webster's findings on the relative performance of firms of different size classes. Thus, small firms performed best, amongst all size classes, while micro firms performed worst (the size measures used by Steel and Webster differ from the one used here, but this does not differ in general conclusion). It is not immediately obvious why this pattern should exist, but one explanation may be that medium and large firms are more concentrated in tradable products that face direct import competition and are losing markets to foreign products (this is the finding of the case studies later in this study). In the 'non-tradable' section of the market served by small and micro enterprises, the former are gaining at the expense of the latter, presumably because micro enterprises lack the minimum skills and equipment to cope with competition and are particularly hard hit by stabilisation measures. We do not examine this issue, since there are no micro enterprises in the case study.

(iii) The panel's results on the performance of firms of different age groups differ from that of Steel and Webster. The latter found that, declining firms were concentrated in the set of enterprises started *before* 1983, and suggested that new enterprise formation was healthier in response to a more competitive environment. The panel data show, however, that firms founded before the ERP declined considerably less (at −2 per cent) than those founded after 1983 (−19.0 per cent). There thus seems to be no clear evidence that the general pattern of enterprise formation had improved over time.

Interestingly, small firms both in Steel and Webster's as well as the panel survey felt that their major competition came from other small firms rather than from imports. In a period of sweeping import liberalisation this suggests that small enterprises were serving local niche markets that were naturally protected from foreign products,[7] or that import competition had not yet started to reach these markets. The technology case study also finds this for many of the firms in wood and metal working (see below).

This concludes the description of the background to the sample firms. The next chapter analyses in greater detail the technological characteristics of the large panel sample.

4 Technological Characteristics of Panel Sample

INTRODUCTION

The development of TCs is based on the interaction of physical capital (equipment) and human capital (skill recruitment and training, combined with technological effort), driven by entrepreneurial responses to product and factor market conditions. Only some of these variables can be captured in an analysis of the quantitative data obtained in the panel sample. This chapter analyses information for the 164 panel firms on capital-labour ratios, the stock of human capital and investment patterns between 1983 and 1991. This analysis gives a number of insights into technology development in Ghanaian manufacturing, a valuable supplement to the detailed firm-level examination of the case studies of the 32 firms reviewed in the next part of the book.

This chapter will assess the following issues. First, if there are firms with different levels of technological capabilities (as measured by stocks of equipment and human capital) within the same industry. Second, whether differences in TC levels are continuous or discrete. If there are discrete differences, this implies that there are factors that hamper the smooth transition of firms across different levels of technology and cause them to 'cluster' in particular segments of the spectrum. Clustering may be an important phenomenon to analyse for policy purposes. Third, what the determinants of any observed technological clusters are: size, factor or product market segmentation, or those related to the process of technological learning. The former are emphasised by neoclassical approaches to adjustment, while the latter are stressed by the TC approach.

THEORETICAL FRAMEWORK

It may be useful to reiterate the key theoretical assumptions, derived from the approach laid out in Chapter 1, on which this empirical analysis is based. From the perspective of the manufacturing firms, the inputs that go into the development of TCs can be classified into external and internal. External inputs are the machines, skilled personnel, licences and manuals, trainers, and technical information that can be acquired in the market. Internal or in-house inputs have to be developed through search, training, experimentation and research. The processes of acquiring the two types of inputs are interactive: internal effort is affected by the external inputs and the ability to search for, acquire and utilise external inputs is affected by the nature and the extent of internal efforts. This has three implications.

First, *TCs are costly to acquire*. The decision to develop TCs is like any other investment decision: it implies a sunk cost and it brings uncertain long-term benefits. And, like any other rational investment decision, it will be based on the present value of future expected benefits. Given the perceptions, abilities and risk profile of the entrepreneur, this will depend on demand and competition in the product market (the incentive framework) and on the characteristics of the markets for the relevant inputs.

Second, *TCs are to a large extent firm specific*, for four reasons. First, because, given the very large number of TC inputs, possible input combinations are infinite and these may differ from firm to firm. Second, there is a possibility of market failures in any individual input market, which may also vary by firm. Third, to the extent that TCs are developed inside the firm, they are determined by the nature of the individual learning process of each firm, uncertainty, and by the costs and market failures that arise for transactions internalised by the firm. Finally, the efficiency of investments in TC is frequently affected by scale economies, thus relating capability acquisition to the size of the firm.

Finally, *TCs are technology specific*. In other words, the know-how developed relative to a given technology does not completely spill over to other technologies.[1] For example, 'the basic concept of weaving is involved in virtually all textile production, but much of the technical knowledge associated with modern automated factory production is inapplicable to hand-loom technology' (Stiglitz 1987).

These hypotheses provide a useful base for exploring the empirical issues raised above. The premise that TCs are costly and firm specific implies that the optimal level of TCs differs for each firm, and may explain why there are firms with different levels of technological capability within the same industry. The technology-specific nature of TCs can explain technological clusters, discrete levels of technology within the same industry. Firms may develop the capabilities required to use efficiently a given technology, but lack the ability to create the TCs necessary to move to the next level of technology.

Firm and technology specificity imply that the relevant set of production technologies is no longer clearly defined and cannot be represented by the standard isoquant. At any time there are only a limited number of techniques that a firm can easily control and efficiently use. Standard neoclassical theory usually explains differences in technology in terms of firm size and factor market segmentation. Such explanations are complementary to, and not necessarily in conflict with, the TC approach. For instance, when there are increasing returns to scale in investing in TCs, size is one of the factors that can determine firm capabilities. If factor markets are 'segmented' (that is, different firms face different prices, availability or quality of factors), upgrading to superior technological clusters can be constrained by factor market segmentation as well as by the fact that TCs are technology specific.

There are important policy implications arising from this analysis. In developing countries, it is generally considered desirable to reduce technical inefficiency and bring the less efficient firms nearer to the efficiency frontier; in other words, to reduce technological segmentation. If factor market imperfection were the only constraint, policy interventions aimed at liberalising markets and eliminating market imperfections would suffice to let dynamic firms move to better technologies. However, if upgrading is held back by the lack of TCs, interventions aimed directly at improving TCs would be necessary. Liberalisation by itself would not suffice.

The next section examines the broad relationship between technology and firm size and carries out a complete mapping out using a statistical clustering technique. It is followed by an assesment of whether factor markets segmentation provides a full explanation of the formation of the clusters. The subsequent section looks at the relationship between technology and growth performance. The main conclusions are drawn in the final section.

MAPPING OUT TECHNOLOGICAL INPUTS

Data on Skills, Technology and Size

The data available on the panel sample are not ideal for analysing technological capabilities. In particular, the only quantitative indicator of the kind of technology employed is the value of physical equipment.

The measurement of capital is always fraught with problems, and these problems are compounded in developing countries where the smaller enterprises keep little or no accounts and often buy second-hand machines. Even if accurate capital data were available, and could be adjusted for inflation and depreciation, it is not necessary that capital intensity (value of equipment per employee) would be a true indicator of the nature of the technology. However, we have to manage with the data that are available, and every effort has been made to adjust the firm responses for distortions and inflation. It is assumed that capital-intensity *within a given industry* measures the 'level' (that is, the complexity and sophistication) of the technology. It is not in fact an implausible assumption that more advanced technologies are more capital intensive. Using it allows us to analyse the available information in interesting ways.

Such a measure of technological levels within industries may be hypothesised to have certain characteristics that can be tested with the data:

- Large firm size is expected to be positively associated with technological levels, since within every activity large-scale operation is normally more capital intensive.
- Physical and human capital are expected to be positively correlated, since more complex technologies involve greater skill inputs to operate efficiently.
- Within similar size classes of firms, however, there are expected to be technological and skill differences because of the firm-specific nature of capability acquisition.
- Across size classes there are expected to be technological and skill differences caused, not just by scale factors, but also by segmentations in factor markets which affect different firms differently.

These hypotheses are *not* directed at the firm level capability building or at technical efficiency. The capital intensity of an enterprise has no necessary connection with how capable it is at using its technology, and there is no presumption that large firms are more capable than small ones. As noted in Chapter 1, large firms tend to specialise in different market and technological segments from small ones in the same industry, and it is only in very special circumstances that size *per se* is an indicator of greater technical efficiency.

Coming now to the data, the distribution of the sample firms by size (note that this distribution is shown by four rather than three groups) is given in Table 4.1. The majority of firms (112 of the total 164)

Table 4.1 Distribution of sample by size and industry

Size (no. of employees)	Textiles & garments number of firms	frequencies %	Food processing number of firms	frequencies %	Wood working number of firms	frequencies %	Metal working number of firms	frequencies %	Total number of firms	frequencies %
equal or more than 100	4.00	10.50	4.00	9.80	5.00	10.90	5.00	12.80	18.00	11.00
from 30 to 99	7.00	18.40	7.00	17.10	10.00	21.70	10.00	25.60	34.00	20.70
from 10 to 29	10.00	26.30	11.00	26.80	17.00	37.00	12.00	30.80	50.00	30.50
from 0 to 9	17.00	44.70	19.00	46.30	14.00	30.40	12.00	30.80	62.00	37.80
TOTAL	38.00	100.00	41.00	100.00	46.00	100.00	39.00	100.00	164.00	100.00

employ 29 or fewer workers each, and at the other end there are only 18 firms with over 100 employees. As noted in the last chapter, this is typical of Ghanaian industry at large, with its preponderance of micro and small firms.

Table 4.2 shows data for the sample firms on the value of fixed capital, investments in equipment (in 1983–91) and the skill levels of the entrepreneur and employees. Table 4.3 gives the correlation coefficients for these variables. The evidence suggests that both human and physical capital intensity increase with firm size. Capital per employee is 8–9 times higher for large firms than for firms with less than 10 employees. Cumulative investments per employee are also much larger for firms with more than 100 employees.

Table 4.4 presents evidence on some influences on the investment decision of the sample firms. As far as the initial investment (nearly all of which involves imported equipment) is concerned, there is a marked difference by size of firm on access to foreign sources of information. Large firms have a much higher propensity to get information from overseas, with the implied ability to make a better selection of machinery. The purpose of investment does not show clear differences by size, and it is interesting to note that only the middle range of firms seems to regard the introduction of new products as an important objective. The impact of new investments seems to be that more larger firms enjoy lower costs of production than do smaller ones, while the latter seem to have the same costs, suggesting that they are adding to capacity but not introducing new technology. Few firms seem to carry out technical adaptations; what there is seems to be concentrated in the small and medium firms. However, all these answers here are difficult to interpret, and the distributions should be treated with care.

Table 4.5 shows differences in sources of financing by firm size, export performance, main sources of competition and the labour market used for recruitment. There is a clear difference across firm size in access to bank finance, with smaller firms having very limited access. Exports are practically confined to the larger firms, while the pattern of competition does not show a systematic pattern. The use of apprentices is negatively correlated with firm size, and small firms rely on informal recruitment while larger firms use formal methods of advertising for and selecting workers.

This evidence suggests that there is segmentation in the markets facing firms of different sizes. However, this is only preliminary: as they stand, the data cannot explain the phenomenon properly in statistical

Table 4.2 Human capital and technology by size groups: the whole sample[d]

	Total capital[b] (mean)	Total investments[ce] (mean)	Total sales (mean)	Education of: entrepreneur[a] (median)	Education of: management[a] (median)	Capital per employee (mean)	Investments per employee (mean)	Sales per employee (mean)
SIZE								
from 0 to 9	4 998	1 047	3 349	3	4	1 195	258	953
from 10 to 29	73 141	4 113	54 513	3	6	4 827	224	3 266
from 30 to 49	290 895	16 215	166 645	4	7	7 920	469	4 375
from 50 to 99	573 634	45 915	377 891	6	7	8 644	870	5 453
equal or more than 100	1 995 487	323 150	2 827 393	8	7	8 008	833	7 523
INDUSTRY								
Textile & garments	211 238	1 515	766 658	4	6	1 720	129	1 740
Food processing	475 763	14 037	160 400	4	7	5 314	381	3 177
Metal working	372 454	23 946*	481 200	4	7	7 338	229	5 967
Wood working	203 260	87 050	184 011	3	7	3 682	757	1 995
TOTAL	318 081	43 195	380 610	3	7	4 603	392	3 238

[a] 1=none; 2=primary school; 3=middle school; 4=secondary school; 5=vocational; 6=polytechnic; 7=professional; 8=university.

[b] replacement value of plant and equipment at the end of 1991.

[c] sum of the three most recent investments in plant and equipment since 1983 in current US dollars.

[d] all values are expressed in US dollars (1991 exchange rate).

[e] this result is obtained excluding the sample's biggest firm; if it is included in the computation of total investments, it becomes 41 326.

Table 4.3   Correlation matrix: technology and size[a]

	KL	CAP	SLAB	SAL	TINV	INKA	EMP	EDMAN	EDPRO	EDENT
KL[b]	1	0.62**	0.47**	0.46**	0.22*	−0.13	0.29**	0.28**	0.36**	0.4**
CAP	0.62**	1	0.62**	0.84**	0.42**	−0.05	0.77**	0.2**	0.6**	0.48**
SLAB	0.47**	0.62**	1	0.61**	0.35**	0.17	0.32**	0.05	0.4**	0.3**
SAL	0.46**	0.84**	0.61**	1	0.46**	0.11	0.77**	0.15	0.63**	0.42**
TINV	0.22*	0.42**	0.35**	0.46**	1	0.55**	0.39**	−0.03	0.22*	0.12
INKA	−0.13	−0.05	0.17	0.11	0.55**	1	0.05	−0.03	0	−0.11
EMP	0.29**	0.77**	0.32**	0.77**	0.39**	0.05	1	0.13	0.50**	0.38**
EDMAN	0.28**	0.2**	0.05	0.15	−0.03	−0.03	0.13	1	0.25**	0.23**
EDPRO	0.36**	0.6**	0.4**	0.63**	0.22*	0	0.50**	0.25**	1	0.39**
EDENT	0.4**	0.48**	0.3**	0.42**	0.12	−0.11	0.38**	0.23**	0.39**	1

[a] ** = significant at 0.001 level; * = significant at 0.01 level.
[b] See table 4.6 for the variables' description.

Table 4.4 Description of firms, investment decisions: the whole sample

	Size					
	0 to 9	10 to 29	30 to 49	50 to 99	⩾100	TOTAL
INVESTMENT'S DESCRIPTION						
Average cost in US dollars						
(1991 exchange rate)	2 663	4 650	20 364	68 136	494 543	77 992
% of new equipments	83.30	75.00	75.00	70.00	78.60	76.80
First source of info on equipment (%):						
Local source[a]	45.00	36.70	40.00	18.20	21.40	34.10
Foreign involving search						
and foreign without search[b]	0.00	16.70	20.00	45.50	57.10	22.80
Other	55.00	46.70	40.00	36.40	21.40	43.20
Purpose of investment (%):						
Same product-improve process	37.50	18.80	33.00	27.30	21.40	28.10
Same product-add to capacity	37.50	46.90	33.00	54.50	64.70	44.80
Introduce new products	8.30	0.00	33.00	0.00	7.10	7.30
Different variety of						
similar product	0.00	3.10	0.00	0.00	0.00	1.00
Other	16.70	31.30	0.00	18.20	7.10	18.70
Impact on cost of production (%):						
Higher than before	5.90	10.30	16.70	22.20	10.00	11.00
Same as before	64.70	62.10	66.70	44.40	20.00	53.40
Lower than before	35.30	27.60	16.70	33.30	70.00	35.60
Impact on product quality (%):						
Higher than before	60.00	33.00	83.30	66.70	45.50	59.00
Same as before	40.00	67.00	16.70	33.30	54.50	41.00
Lower than before	0.00	0.00	0.00	0.00	0.00	0.00
% of firms which carried out						
technical adaptation	4.30	20.00	18.20	9.10	0.00	12.00

[a] local sources=trade fairs, business association, other local firms, technology institutions, other.
[b] foreign source involving search=indepent foreign supplier of plant and equipment, foreign technical consultants, publications, foreign trips. Foreign sources without search=foreign joint venture partner, parent company, foreign buyers.

terms. First, it is not clear whether the correlations are on a continuum, or if there are discrete jumps. It is quite possible that, if TCs are technology-specific, firms do not face a continuum of alternative input combinations. They face instead limited sets of technological options and choose their technology according to their own absorptive level, depending on their starting technological capacities. Second, it is also important to understand whether differences in technology may also emerge independently of size. There may, in other words, be important

Table 4.5   Labour, finance and product markets segmentation: the whole sample[a]

	Size					
	0 to 9	*10 to 29*	*30 to 49*	*50 to 99*	*100+*	*TOTAL*
Sources of financing (in %):						
Profits	63.00	66.70	57.10	58.30	72.20	63.80
Personal savings	27.70	28.60	28.60	0.00	0.00	23.20
Borrowed from friends or relatives	12.80	9.50	0.00	0.00	5.90	9.50
Borrowed from bank	4.30	4.80	14.30	36.40	25.00	10.40
Borrowed from supplier	2.20	0.00	7.10	9.10	11.80	3.70
Borrowed from money lender	0.00	0.00	0.00	0.00	0.00	0.00
Average % of production exported[b]:	0.62	1	n.a.	35	39	17
Main source of competition:						
None	5.3	10	6.3	0	5.6	7.4
Domestic firms	89.5	72	68.8	85.7	77.8	79.8
Foreign competitors in exports markets	0	4	6.3	14.3	5.6	3.7
Imports	5.3	14	18.8	0	11.1	9.2
% of apprentices on total employment	70	36	30	11	6	43
source of workers recruitment:						
Formal[c]	6	33.3	41.6	50	62.5	27.6
Informal[d]	94.6	66.7	58.3	50	37.5	72.4

[a] each cell gives the percentage of firms which answered positively to that question.
[b] only 25 observations available for obtaining these results.
[c] formal advertising, labour office, trade or technical schools, other.
[d] relative or friend of owner or of current employee, suggestion from supplier or business associate, word of mouth.

differences in technology within size groups that this type of evidence does not capture. At the same time, firms may face identical factor markets but have different technological responses because of their differing TC development. The broad indication that small firms tend to operate in different market segments than large ones may hide these facts.

The following section addresses the question of whether firms are grouped according to similar technological characteristics, using more appropriate statistical techniques. These techniques use cluster analysis and principal components. Both are described below.

Principal Components and Clusters

The clustering technique is probably the most useful statistical tool to analyse whether or not differences in groups of firm characteristics (capital intensity, skills, labour productivity and new investments) are characterised by discrete jumps across the size spectrum of sample firms. The technique groups firms according to the degree of vicinity of a selected set of variables. If such clusters emerge, with significant differences between the groups in the technological variables taken together, the hypothesis that there are discrete changes in technology is supported.

In order to form the clusters we used four sets of variables, listed in Table 4.6, measuring size (number of employees, sales and total capital), technology (indicated by capital intensity and sales per employee), human capital (education levels of entrepreneurs, managers and production workers) and investments (cumulated investments and an index of renewal of the capital stock). To derive a more general description of the relationship between the variables than could be obtained from a correlation matrix, and to obtain a clear visual representation of the grouping of firms, we used principal component analysis to reduce the number of the variables without loosing much of the original explanatory power.

A principal component summarises sets of closely related variables. Principal component analysis allows us to transform the original ten variables into ten new variables, each having a much higher explanatory power than the original. Each principal component is a synthetic variable, embodying all the original variables, with the advantage that by using just principal components (three in our analysis) we can explain a large share of the sample variance.[2] The obvious question is what does each principal component represent. The ideal situation is when a component can be identified as summarising sets of closely related variables. This is the case when the component is strongly correlated to a set of variables which express similar economic content. For example, if principal component 1 is only correlated to size variables, component 1 can be interpreted as a size indicator. The correlation between principal components and the original sample variables is shown in Table 4.7.[3] The technical appendix provides a formal explanation of how principal components and the clusters were constructed.

We constructed principal components for each of the four industries separately, since each had different technologies. Three components

Table 4.6   Variables used for the derivation of the clusters

---

1. Size Variables

Sales (SAL)	Logarithm of Sales in 1992 (in 1992 US$)
Employment (EMP)	Logarithm of Employment in 1992 (including apprentices)
Capital stock (CAP)	Logarithm of replacement value of capital in 1992 (in 1992 US$)

2. Technology indicators

Capital labour ratio (KL)	Replacement value of capital in 1992 on total employment in 1992
Productivity of labour (SLAB)	Sales in 1992 on total employment in 1992

3. Human capital indicators

Experience and education of the entrepreneur (EDENT)	Managers' average wages for equivalent education multiplied by an experience weight *
Education of the managers (EDMAN)	Managers, average wages in the firm
Education of the workers in production (EDPRO)	Workers in production average wage in the firm

4. Investment variables

Total Investments (TINV)	Cumulated investments between 1983 and 1992 in current US$
Replacement of the capital stock (INKA)	Cumulated investments between 1983 and 1992 in current US$ on replacement value of capital in 1992.

---

* The education variables are discrete. In order to use them for clustering we needed to transform them into continuous variables, therefore we used wages as a proxy for education (the preliminary report 'Economic Reform and the Manufacturing Sector in Ghana' shows that the two are highly correlated). For the entrepreneurs there are obviously no wages. So we used manager wages for an equivalent level of education. The experience weight is given by the ratio between the number of years worked in the same industry and 30 years, which is the maximum experience available in the sample.

were selected for each industry, allowing us to explain more than 60 per cent of the sample variability in each case (Table 4.7). Clusters were formed on the basis of the principal components, so that the clusters group firms which are homogeneous in terms of the principal components. At this stage we only look at what we have defined as 'structural'

Table 4.7 Rotated factor matrix by industry[a]

Variables	Metal working			Variables	Wood working			Variables	Food Processing			Variables	Textiles & garments		
	Factor 1	Factor 2	Factor 3		Factor 1	Factor 2	Factor 3		Factor 1	Factor 2	Factor 3		Factor 1	Factor 2	Factor 3
TINV[b]	0.44	0.22	0.72	TINV	0.1	0.84	0.1	TINV	0.27	0.85	0.007	TINV	0.18	0.89	-0.04
CAP	0.74	0.55	-0.001	CAP	0.69	0.25	0.56	CAP	0.88	0.19	0.33	CAP	0.96	0	0.02
SAL	0.81	0.43	0.14	SAL	0.6	0.48	0.32	SAL	0.8	0.44	0.22	SAL	0.89	0.18	0.16
EMP	0.86	0.11	0.05	EMP	0.32	0.32	0.75	EMP	0.89	0.14	0.1	EMP	0.75	0.28	-0.08
INKA	-0.24	-0.17	0.86	INKA	-0.04	0.91	0.001	INKA	-0.22	0.8	-0.12	INKA	-0.02	0.83	-0.13
SLAB	0.36	0.73	0.07	SLAB	0.47	0.64	0.001	SLAB	0.27	0.74	0.16	SLAB	0.6	0.55	0.17
KL	0.1	0.93	-0.09	KL	0.9	-0.07	0.03	KL	0.55	0.04	0.73	KL	0.77	-0.35	-0.15
EDMAN	0.81	0.15	0.1	EDMAN	0.72	0.24	0.43	EDMAN	0.031	-0.12	0.91	EDMAN	0.8	0.21	0.03
EDPRO	0.81	0.14	-0.03	EDPRO	0.27	0.08	0.74	EDPRO	0.36	0.18	0.78	EDPRO	0.85	0.08	0.03
EDENT	0.68	0.26	-0.16	EDENT	-0.06	-0.27	0.61	EDENT	0.79	0.13	0.19	EDENT	0.01	-0.11	0.96
EXPLAINED VARIABILITY	51.70%	13.60%	10.20%		46.60%	17.70%	9.50%		47.80%	20.30%	11.20%		48.90%	18.80%	10.10%

[a] This matrix provides the correlations between variables and components.

[b] See Table 4.6 for the variables' description.

clusters, those based only on the size and capital intensity components. Later, we examine 'dynamic' clusters, those which also take into account the investment components.

Figures 4.1 to 4.4 give a graphic representation of the 'structural' clusters for each of the four industries. The axes represent the two principal components used to form the clusters. Next to each figure, the correlation ratio of each component to the original variables (the rotated factor matrix) is shown.[4] These ratios help explain the economic meaning of the components. We have arranged the figures so that the vertical axis corresponds to the principal component mostly correlated with size variables and the horizontal axis with the principal component mostly correlated with capital intensity. Each dot represents one firm in the sample. The boxes or circles around groups of firms represent the clusters. The 'structural' cluster analysis has six major results:

1. All the four industries are characterised by clear-cut clusters of firms with similar values of the physical and human capital indicators. This suggests that there are multiple equilibria in investments in TCs, with different groups of firms responding in different ways.
2. The type of technology, as measured by these variables, is generally different in each of the clusters (see below). Thus, firms do not seem to operate over a continuum of alternative technological options: changes in the type of technology are generally few and discrete in each industry.
3. The structure and the nature of the clusters is different for each of the industries and depends on the features of the technology in the industry itself.
4. For each of the four industries, the inferior technological cluster (with lower capital and skill intensity) is always composed of micro enterprises.
5. There is, as expected, a positive and consistent relationship between size and human and physical capital intensity.
6. However, size does not always differ across technological clusters: because of firm level differences in the TC building process, there are clusters which are explained by differences in technology but not size.

Let us examine these results at greater length. Figures 4.1 to 4.4 show that three clusters emerge for metal working, wood working and food processing, and two for textiles and clothing. Tables 4.8 to 4.11

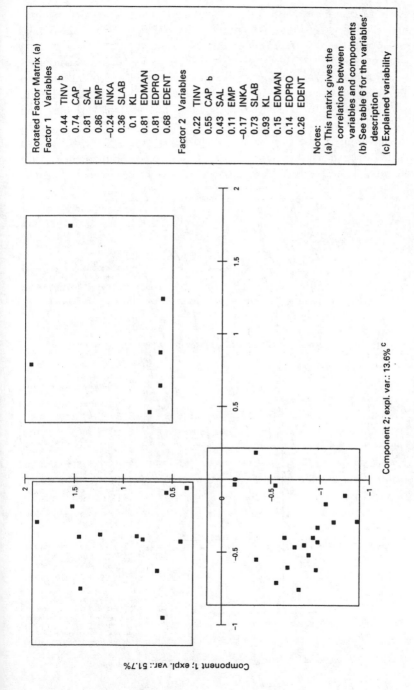

Figure 4.1 Structural cluster in metal working

Component 2; expl. var.: 13.6%^c

Component 1; expl. var.: 51.7%

Rotated Factor Matrix (a)	
Factor 1	Variables
0.44	TINV [b]
0.74	CAP
0.81	SAL
0.86	EMP
−0.24	INKA
0.36	SLAB
0.1	KL
0.81	EDMAN
0.81	EDPRO
0.68	EDENT
Factor 2	Variables
0.22	TINV
0.55	CAP [b]
0.43	SAL
0.11	EMP
−0.17	INKA
0.73	SLAB
0.93	KL
0.15	EDMAN
0.14	EDPRO
0.26	EDENT

Notes:
(a) This matrix gives the correlations between variables and components
(b) See table 6 for the variables' description
(c) Explained variability

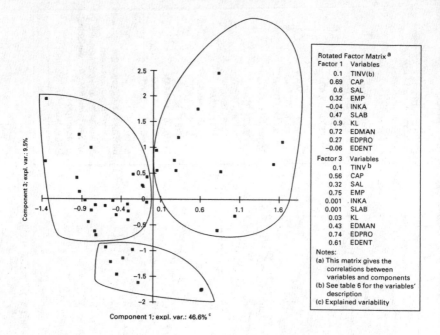

Figure 4.2   Structural cluster in wood working

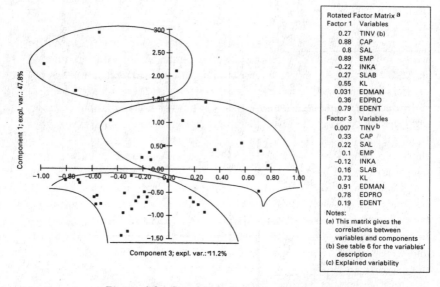

Figure 4.3   Structural cluster in food processing

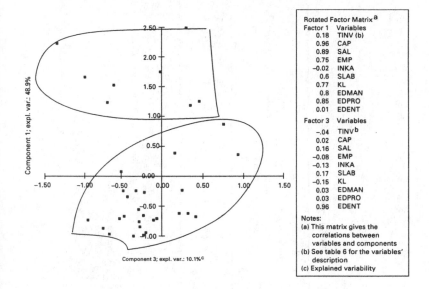

Rotated Factor Matrix [a]	
Factor 1	Variables
0.18	TINV (b)
0.96	CAP
0.89	SAL
0.75	EMP
-0.02	INKA
0.6	SLAB
0.77	KL
0.8	EDMAN
0.85	EDPRO
0.01	EDENT
Factor 3	Variables
-.04	TINV [b]
0.02	CAP
0.16	SAL
-0.08	EMP
-0.13	INKA
0.17	SLAB
-0.15	KL
0.03	EDMAN
0.03	EDPRO
0.96	EDENT

Notes:
(a) This matrix gives the correlations between variables and components
(b) See table 6 for the variables' description
(c) Explained variability

Figure 4.4   Structural cluster in textiles and garments

give the average values for some key variables characterising the firms in the clusters. The clusters are called A, B and C in each industry (A and B in textiles and clothing), where cluster A represents the most advanced technologies and C the least. In other words, average capital intensity and human capital increase when we move from C to A.[5] In every industry, cluster C comprises micro enterprises with uneducated personnel mostly using hand tools. The characteristics of the higher clusters depend on the different industries, which are discussed in turn.

In the case of *metal working*, firms in cluster B use manual or powered machine tools. The capital–labour ratio is about four times higher than for cluster C, and human capital increases significantly for all the three categories considered (entrepreneurs, managers and production workers). In cluster A, we have either firms using more sophisticated machine tools, sometimes with numerical control (for example for the production of high-quality window and door frames) or firms which use large-scale technologies, like rolling mills. It is interesting to note that firms in cluster A are on average younger (6 years old) and were founded after the ERP in 1983. This tendency for more capital intensive technologies to be launched after ERP may run counter to the intuitive belief that liberalisation pushes industry to use technologies

Table 4.8 Major clusters' characteristics: Metal working

Cluster	Number of firms[a]	Average number of employees in 1991	Average firm age in 1991	Average education of production workers[b] (median)	Average education of management[b] (median)	Average education of entrepreneur[b] (median)	Average capital per employee (in 1991 US$)	Share of foreign ownership %[c]	Share of public ownership %[c]
A	6	118	6	5	7	8	17 728	16.7	16.7
B	12	60	15	4	7	6	4 465	33.3	8.3
C	19	10	10	1	n.a.	3	1 338	10	0

[a] this column gives the number of firms which form the cluster.

[b] 1=none; 2=primary; 3=middle school; 4=secondary; 5=vocational; 6=polytechnic; 7=professional; 8=university.

[c] this column gives the percentage of firms in the cluster which are entirely owned by private foreign owners or are joint ventures between private Ghanaians and foreign owners.

[d] this column gives the percentage of firms in the cluster which are entirely owned by the State or with public participation.

Table 4.9 Major clusters' characteristics: wood working

Cluster	Number of firms[a]	Average number of employees in 1991	Average firm age in 1991	Average education of production workers[b] (median)	Average education of management[b] (median)	Average education of entrepreneur[b] (median)	Average capital per employee (in 1991 US$)	Share of foreign ownership %[c]	Share of public ownership %[d]
A	11	93	15	4	6	6	7818	20	20
B	24	21	9	2	6	3	2439	4	0
C	8	3	7	3	3	3	1068	0	0

[a] this column gives the number of firms which form the cluster.

[b] 1=none; 2=primary; 3=middle school; 4=secondary; 5=vocational; 6=polytechnic; 7=professional; 8=university.

[c] this column gives the percentage of firms in the cluster which are entirely owned by private foreign owners or are joint ventures between private Ghanaians and foreign owners.

[d] this column gives the percentage of firms in the cluster which are entirely owned by the State or with public participation.

Table 4.10 Major clusters' characteristics: food processing

Cluster	Number of firms[a]	Average number of employees in 1991	Average firm age in 1991	Average education of production workers[b] (median)	Average education of management[b] (median)	Average education of entrepreneur[b] (median)	Average capital per employee (in 1991 US$)	Share of foreign ownership %[c]	Share of public ownership %[c]
A	4	424	33	3	5	8	10089	0	75
B	13	37	10	3	7	6	7111	25	25
C	23	7	11	3	n.a.	3	1278	8	0

[a] this column gives the number of firms which form the cluster.

[b] 1=none; 2=primary; 3=middle school; 4=secondary; 5=vocational; 6=polytechnic; 7=professional; 8=university.

[c] this column gives the percentage of firms in the cluster which are entirely owned by private foreign owners or are joint ventures between private Ghanaians and foreign owners.

[d] this column gives the percentage of firms in the cluster which are entirely owned by the State or with public participation.

Table 4.11 Major clusters' characteristics: textiles and garments

Cluster	Number of firms[a]	Average number of employees in 1991	Average firm age in 1991	Average education of production workers[b] (median)	Average education of management[b] (median)	Average education of entrepreneur[b] (median)	Average capital per employee (in 1991 US$)	Share of foreign ownership %[c]	Share of public ownership %[c]
A	8	112	14	4	6	4	5769	37	25
B	28	9	9	3	2	3	460	0	4

[a] this column gives the number of firms which form the cluster.

[b] 1=none; 2=primary; 3=middle school; 4=secondary; 5=vocational; 6=polytechnic; 7=professional; 8=university.

[c] this column gives the percentage of firms in the cluster which are entirely owned by private foreign owners or are joint ventures between private Ghanaians and foreign owners.

[d] this column gives the percentage of firms in the cluster which are entirely owned by the State or with public participation.

that are more 'appropriate' to the labour-abundant factor endowments of a country like Ghana. It may be that distortions remain in factor markets that favour capital-intensive technologies. It may, on the other hand, be the case that the dichotomy based on a simple two-factor model is misleading, and that firms are in fact choosing the most efficient technologies with the precision and scale needed.

In *wood working*, differences between clusters C and B are less dramatic than in metal working. Average capital intensity in wood working cluster B is roughly double that in C, and the type of equipment firms use is still extremely simple. Managers have a higher level of education, but average schooling does not change for the entrepreneur and the production workers (for the latter it even declines). Firms in cluster B have permanent locations, in contrast to firms in C which generally have temporary ones. The technology gap is larger between clusters B and A. In A, capital-intensity is three times higher and the average entrepreneur has polytechnic education (compared to middle school in cluster B). Firms in cluster A tend to be modern furniture manufacturers with expensive equipment like kiln dryers and electric machine tools. Only three of the 11 wood cutting firms in the sample are in cluster A. Therefore, the jump in capital intensity between A and B does not reflect a shift towards more capital-intensive products.

In *food processing*, cluster C has the usual group of micro enterprises, mostly bakeries. Between clusters C and B there is a considerable technological jump. Cluster B has small-medium firms with highly skilled personnel (particularly managers) and capital-intensity five times higher than in cluster C. Finally, cluster A has the largest group of firms in the whole sample. However, in contrast to the rest of the industry, these firms have poor human capital (the average education of the managers is low) and capital intensity does not increase proportionally with size.[6] Firms in cluster A are relatively old, with old equipment which has not been renewed. Firms in cluster B are much younger and use relatively advanced processing technology.

Finally, in *textiles and clothing,* four of the firms in the sample are in textiles and 32 in clothing. Only two significant clusters emerge. Cluster B is made of informal tailoring shops, while cluster A has larger firms with more complex organisations and higher capital intensity. The average education of the entrepreneur is higher in cluster A, but it is much lower than in the top clusters of the other industries. Three of the four textile firms are in cluster A. This is expected because textile plants are always more capital-intensive than clothing manufacturers. However, the other five firms in the A cluster are garment firms, suggesting that the increase in capital intensity between the two clusters is not due only to changes in the product.

There are inter-industry differences which are also worth noting. These are particularly marked between the two relatively capital-intensive industries (metal working and food processing) and the labour-intensive ones (particularly wood working, because the results for textile are not particularly revealing). First, the change in the production technology between clusters C and B seems much larger for the capital-intensive industries. This result suggests that in the simpler labour-intensive industries, the discrete jump in the technology is smaller and there exist opportunities for some technological upgrading at the lower end of the technological spectrum. This possibility appears to be more limited for firms in capital-intensive industries: upgrading from the micro cluster implies a more radical change in technology. Second, metal working and food processing firms in the top cluster (A) are more physical and human capital intensive than their counterparts in wood working and textiles and clothing.

Finally, the relationship between technology and size. Although firms in the top cluster are on average larger than others, size and technology are not consistently correlated. Some of the clusters differ in terms of technology and human capital, but not in terms of size (A and B in metal working and food processing).[7] Technology seems to be more independent of size in more capital-intensive industries and for the higher technological clusters. In both metal working and food processing, size has a strong explanatory power independent of capital intensity, and capital-intensity has an explanatory power which is independent of size. In contrast, size and capital-intensity are highly correlated in industries with simple technologies (textiles and garments and wood working). In other words, firm size seems to be important when changes between relatively simple technologies are taken into account. However, for changes to higher technological levels in metal working and food processing, size (and thus economies of scale) do not seem to matter substantially for the technologies chosen.

Human capital emerges as a key factor both for technological levels and firm growth. Firms with superior technologies have better-educated entrepreneurs, managers and production workers. On average, technological upgrading requires an overall change of the skill structure in the firm.[8]

TECHNOLOGICAL CLUSTERS AND MARKET SEGMENTATION

This section considers the role of market imperfections in explaining the formation of clusters. Three different markets are taken into account. First, the market for capital equipment. The source of information on the capital equipment purchased is considered – whether the source is local or foreign, the assumption being that, with imperfect information, larger firms have better access to the foreign sources with information on more advanced technologies. Second, the labour market. The recruitment of workers from vocational training schools and through other formalised channels is compared to informal, 'word of mouth' methods of recruitment. The qualification of new recruits is also considered. Finally, the financial market. The source of financing of the capital equipment is analysed, to see whether firms finance their purchase of capital equipment through banks and other formal financial institutions or through informal channels and their own savings.

The analysis is conducted in two stages. First, the percentage of firms which used one of the two segments of these markets is measured for each cluster (Tables 4.12 to 4.15). Second, measures of association (Cramer's V) between the clusters and the different market segments are computed (Tables 4.16 to 4.19). A measure of association between discrete variables is equivalent to a measure of correlation between continuous variables.[9]

Let us consider the results by industry. In *metal working*, firms in cluster C are clearly in different market segments from those in clusters A and B. Table 4.16 shows a positive measure of association, significant at more than 99 per cent for all the segments. The analysis is carried out by first comparing cluster B with C, and then by joining clusters A and B and comparing them with C. The association between the clusters and the source of information of capital is the strongest, and that with the financial markets the weakest. There is no significant market segmentation between clusters A and B, although some of the firms in B use local sources of information on capital (none in A) and a smaller percentage of them use formal sources of financing. This suggests that in this industry it is the first stage of upgrading that confronts significant market segmentation.

Wood working provides a different picture. Segmentation is significant between clusters A and B (Tables 4.13 and 4.17) rather than between C and B. This suggests that the first stage of upgrading and growth does not require a shift to higher market segments, while segmentation becomes significant for larger size classes. Production techniques are

Table 4.12 Technological clusters and market segmentation: metal working (frequencies)

Cluster	Source of info on k purchase: last invest.			Source of info on k purchase: initial invest.			Source of workers' recruitment		Source of k purchase financing	Percentage of apprentices in the firm
	Foreign[a]	Local[b]	Other	Foreign	Local	Other	Formal[c]	Informal[d]	Bank	
A	50%	0%	50%	50%	0%	50%	67%	33%	17%	13%
B	40%	30%	30%	20%	40%	40%	75%	25%	20%	15%
C	0%	46%	54%	0%	42%	58%	21%	79%	0%	65%

[a] Independent foreign supplier of plant; foreign joint venture partner; foreign buyers; foreign technical consultants; publications; foreign trips.
[b] Trade fairs; business associations; other local firms; technology institutions.
[c] Formal advertising labour office; trade or technical schools.
[d] Relative or friend of owner/of current employee; suggestion; from supplier or business associate; word of mouth.

Table 4.13 Technological clusters and market segmentation: wood working (frequencies)

Cluster	Source of info on k purchase: last invest.			Source of info on k purchase: initial invest.			Source of workers' recruitment		Source of k purchase financing	Percentage of apprentices in the firm
	Foreign[a]	Local[b]	Other	Foreign	Local	Other	Formal[c]	Informal[d]	Bank	
A	50%	37%	13%	45%	27%	28%	67%	33%	20%	17%
B	9%	33%	58%	11%	23%	66%	30%	70%	0%	56%
C	0%	50%	50%	0%	50%	50%	0%	100%	0%	59%

[a] Independent foreign supplier of plant; foreign joint venture partner; foreign buyers; foreign technical consultants; publications; foreign trips.
[b] Trade fairs; business associations; other local firms; technology institutions.
[c] Formal advertising labour office; trade or technical schools.
[d] Relative or friend of owner/of current employee; suggestion; from supplier or business associate; word of mouth.

Table 4.14 Technological clusters and market segmentation: food processing (frequencies)

Cluster	Source of info on k purchase: last invest.			Source of info on k purchase: initial invest.			Source of workers' recruitment		Source of k purchase financing	Percentage of apprentices in the firm
	Foreign[a]	Local[b]	Other	Foreign	Local	Other	Formal[c]	Informal[d]	Bank	
A	67%	33%	0%	75%	0%	25%	75%	25%	25%	0%
B	14%	29%	57%	60%	30%	10%	67%	33%	25%	0%
C	17%	50%	33%	0%	20%	80%	8%	92%	6%	14%

[a] Independent foreign supplier of plant; foreign joint venture partner; foreign buyers; foreign technical consultants; publications; foreign trips.
[b] Trade fairs; business associations; other local firms; technology institutions.
[c] Formal advertising labour office; trade or technical schools.
[d] Relative or friend of owner/of current employee; suggestion; from supplier or business associate; word of mouth.

Table 4.15 Technological clusters and market segmentation: textiles and garments (frequencies)

Cluster	Source of info on k purchase: last invest.			Source of info on k purchase: initial invest.			Source of workers' recruitment		Source of k purchase financing	Percentage of apprentices in the firm
	Foreign[a]	Local[b]	Other	Foreign	Local	Other	Formal[c]	Informal[d]	Bank	
A	20%	0%	80%	67%	0%	33%	50%	50%	14%	5%
B	8%	50%	42%	8%	46%	46%	42%	58%	8%	55%

[a] Independent foreign supplier of plant; foreign joint venture partner; foreign buyers; foreign technical consultants; publications; foreign trips.
[b] Trade fairs; business associations; other local firms; technology institutions.
[c] Formal advertising labour office; trade or technical schools.
[d] Relative or friend of owner/of current employee; suggestion; from supplier or business associate; word of mouth.

Table 4.16 Technological clusters C & B and market segmentation; a measure of independence: metal working

Variables	DF[a]	Cramer's V[b]	Significance[c]
Structural clusters & source of lab. recruitment[d]	1	0.52	0.004
Structural clusters & source of financing[e]	1	0.48	0.007
Structural clusters & source of info on k (first inv.)[f]	1	0.61	0.0006
Structural clusters & source of info on k (last inv.)[f]	1	0.68	0.0001

Technological clusters C & (A, B) and market segmentation; a measure of independence: metal working

Variables	DF[a]	Cramer's V[b]	Significance[c]
Structural clusters & source of lab. recruitment[d]	1	0.52	0.001
Structural clusters & source of financing[e]	1	0.4	0.01
Structural clusters & source of info on k (first inv.)[f]	1	0.58	0.0004
Structural clusters & source of info on k (last inv.)[f]	1	0.66	0.00005

[a] Degrees of freedom.
[b] Cramer's V is defined as the square root of Pearson's chi-square previously divided by the sample's size times the minimum between the number of rows and columns (minus 1) of the contingency table.
[c] Observed significance level; if it is less than 0.05, the hypothesis that the two variables are independent is rejected.
[d] Binary variable which assumes value 1 if the firm recruits workers by: formal advertising, labour office, trade or technical schools; and value 0 if it recruits workers by: suggestion from supplier or business associate, suggestion from relative of owner or of current employee, word of mouth.
[e] Binary variable which assumes value 1 if a bank is among the firm's main sources of financing and 0 if not.
[f] Binary variable which assumes value 1 if the main source of information on the purchase of capital equipment has been a foreign one, i.e.: an independent foreign supplier of plant, foreign joint venture partner, foreign buyer, foreign technical consultant, publication, foreign trip; and value 0 if the main source of information has been a trade fair, business association, other local firm, technology institution.

Table 4.17 Technological clusters (C, B) & A and market segmentation; a measure of independence: wood working

Variables	DF[a]	Cramer's V[b]	Significance[c]
Structural clusters & source of lab. recruitment[d]	1	0.6	0.001
Structural clusters & source of financing[e]	1	0.28	0.07
Structural clusters & source of info on k (first inv.)[f]	1	0.5	0.001
Structural clusters & source of info on k (last inv.)[f]	1	0.48	0.002

Technological clusters B & A and market segmentation; a measure of independence: wood working

Variables	DF[a]	Cramer's V[b]	Significance[c]
Structural clusters & source of lab. recruitment[d]	1	0.72	0.001
Structural clusters & source of financing[e]	1	0.32	0.16
Structural clusters & source of info on k (first inv.)[f]	1	0.57	0.01
Structural clusters & source of info on k (last inv.)[f]	1	0.49	0.03

[a] Degrees of freedom.

[b] Cramer's V is defined as the square root of Pearson's chi-square previously divided by the sample's size times the minimum between the number of rows and columns (minus 1) of the contingency table.

[c] Observed significance level; if it is less than 0.05, the hypothesis that the two variables are independent is rejected.

[d] Binary variable which assumes value 1 if the firm recruits workers by: formal advertising, labour office, trade or technical schools; and value 0 if it recruits workers by: suggestion from supplier or business associate, suggestion from relative of owner or of current employee, word of mouth.

[e] Binary variable which assumes value 1 if a bank is among the firm's main sources of financing and 0 if not.

[f] Binary variable which assumes value 1 if the main source of information on the purchase of capital equipment has been a foreign one, i.e.: an independent foreign supplier of plant, foreign joint venture partner, foreign buyer, foreign technical consultant, publication, foreign trip; and value 0 if the main source of information has been a trade fair, business association, other local firm, technology institution.

Table 4.18   Technological clusters C & B and market segmentation; a measure of independence: food processing

Variables	DF[a]	Cramer's V[b]	Significance[c]
Structural clusters & source of lab. recruitment[d]	1	0.55	0.001
Structural clusters & source of financing[e]	1	0.31	0.06
Structural clusters & source of info on k (first inv.)[f]	1	0.76	0.00001
Structural clusters & source of info on k (last inv.)[f]	1	0.21	0.2

Technological clusters C & (A, B) and market segmentation; a measure of independence: food processing

Variables	DF[a]	Cramer's V[b]	Significance[c]
Structural clusters & source of lab. recruitment[d]	1	0.59	0.0002
Structural clusters & source of financing[e]	1	0.31	0.05
Structural clusters & source of info on k (first inv.)[f]	1	0.8	0
Structural clusters & source of info on k (last inv.)[f]	1	0.37	0.02

[a] Degrees of freedom.
[b] Cramer's V is defined as the square root of Pearson's chi-square previously divided by the sample's size times the minimum between the number of rows and columns (minus 1) of the contingency table.
[c] Observed significance level; if it is less than 0.05, the hypothesis that the two variables are independent is rejected.
[d] Binary variable which assumes value 1 if the firm recruits workers by: formal advertising, labour office, trade or technical schools; and value 0 if it recruits workers by: suggestion from supplier or business associate, suggestion from relative of owner or of current employee, word of mouth.
[e] Binary variable which assumes value 1 if a bank is among the firm's main sources of financing and 0 if not.
[f] Binary variable which assumes value 1 if the main source of information on the purchase of capital equipment has been a foreign one, i.e.: an independent foreign supplier of plant, foreign joint venture partner, foreign buyer, foreign technical consultant, publication, foreign trip; and value 0 if the main source of information has been a trade fair, business association, other local firm, technology institution.

Table 4.19   Technological clusters A & B and market segmentation; a
measure of independence: textiles and garments

Variables	DF[a]	Cramer's V[b]	Significance[c]
Structural clusters & source of lab. recruitment[d]	1	0.56	0.001
Structural clusters & source of financing[e]	1	0.08	0.63
Structural clusters & source of info on k (first inv.)[f]	1	0.48	0.004
Structural clusters & source of info on k (last inv.)[f]	1	0.56	0.001

[a] Degrees of freedom.
[b] Cramer's V is defined as the square root of Pearson's chi-square previously
   divided by the sample's size times the minimum between the number of
   rows and columns (minus 1) of the contingency table.
[c] Observed significance level; if it is less than 0.05, the hypothesis that the
   two variables are independent is rejected.
[d] Binary variable which assumes value 1 if the firm recruits workers by:
   formal advertising, labour office, trade or technical schools; and value 0 if
   it recruits workers by: suggestion from supplier or business associate, suggestion from relative of owner or of current employee, word of mouth.
[e] Binary variable which assumes value 1 if a bank is among the firm's main
   sources of financing and 0 if not.
[f] Binary variable which assumes value 1 if the main source of information
   on the purchase of capital equipment has been a foreign one, i.e.: an independent foreign supplier of plant, foreign joint venture partner, foreign buyer,
   foreign technical consultant, publication, foreign trip; and value 0 if the
   main source of information has been a trade fair, business association, other
   local firm, technology institution.

more labour intensive in the wood-working industry, and diseconomies
emerge at higher size level, than in metal working. The relative simplicity of the techniques is supported by the finding that a large percentage of wood-working firms in cluster A use local sources of
information, in contrast to firms in cluster A in the metal working,
which all use foreign sources of information. The source of labour
recruitment is the most significant segmentation for the wood-working
industry. This result probably derives from the fact that the industry is
very labour intensive. Finance is only significant if we join B and C
and compare it against A.

   Food processing shows results similar to that of metal working, once
more reflecting the relative complexity of the technology (Tables 4.14
and 4.18). Market segmentation characterises the shifts from clusters

C to B, while there is no significant segmentation between the two higher clusters. The source of information on capital equipment is the most significant segmentation. Finance is only significant at 95 per cent when we join A and B and compare them to C.

Finally, in *textiles and garments*, there are only two clusters and there is clear evidence of market segmentation across them.

These results suggest that some of the technological clustering *is* explained by market segmentation. Taking all the activities together, it seems that market segmentation is a significant constraint at an intermediate level of the technology spectrum. This appears in the move to more complex technologies and when the change in technology is associated with a significant increase in firm size. On the other hand, market segmentation does not affect small changes between simple technologies (clusters C and B in wood working). At the higher end of the technology spectrum, on the other hand, market segmentation is not binding, and does not appear to be a significant explanation of differences in the levels of technology employed. These differences have to be explained by other factors.

Market segmentation is thus significant in the move from micro-small size to small-medium size, and it affects intermediate changes in technologies, but not the very basic ones nor the ones at the top of the technology spectrum. The former do not require substantial changes in capital equipment and upgrading in skills. By contrast, firms in the top technological clusters face very similar factor markets: a shift to a higher technology does not require entry into different factor market segments. Finally, the way in which market segmentation affects technological upgrading, and growth and upgrading, changes from industry to industry.

Once firm size and market segmentation have been taken into account, other determinants of technological clusters must be considered. Clusters B and A in the two capital-intensive industries (particularly metal working), suggest that TCs are technology specific and that technological upgrading can be independent of size. Firms in cluster B can move to A only by heavily investing in TCs. It appears, however, that their particular circumstances (note that movements from B to A are not constrained by market segmentation) make such investment too expensive, and the firms stay at a lower technology equilibrium.

A similar tendency (to a lower level equilibrium) is apparent for clusters C and B in wood working (we analyse in the next section whether such shifts actually take place). Firms in cluster C might be unwilling to improve their technology because their TCs are low and lead to low expected returns from technical effort. However, the shifts between the two clusters do not require large investments in human capital and technology. Differences between the two clusters are mostly captured by average size. As we will see in the next section, (unobserved) technical effort is probably the major ingredient of any upgrading from C to B. Technical effort can allow these firms to improve either efficiency or product quality and grow, but it is not sufficient to take them to the top technological cluster (A). For this jump to take place, more sophisticated capital equipment and skills and entry into superior market segments are necessary.

GROWTH AND INVESTMENTS

Until now, we have considered a static mapping out of technology, human capital and size. But what about technological development? Do the characteristics of the clusters change with time? Do firms in higher clusters upgrade from lower ones or do they start already in their present state?

Let us start with upgrading across clusters. To understand the dynamic technological process it would have been ideal to have the same set of data for an earlier period, and to analyse how clusters change and whether firms move across clusters. Unfortunately, we only have historical data for employment, and we are confined to computing average employment growth rates within each cluster. Tables 4.20 to 4.23 also show the number of employees at foundation and today for all the firms in the sample within each cluster. Differences in performance within clusters could probably be explained by different investments in TCs that the previous analysis does not capture.

For all the four industries, firms in the lower clusters C are on average younger and faster growers. This is probably due to the very high mortality rate in this segment, easier entry requirements, and the tiny base from which growth calculations are made. The only industry where there is upgrading from the micro cluster is wood working. Firms in cluster B are fast growers (23 per cent per year) and many of them graduated from being micro enterprises. Firms in the top cluster generally started as small or medium, showing little upgrading from lower clusters. Their average rate of growth is much lower.

Some upgrading from a micro size can also be observed in cluster B of the metal working industry. This is still not a very dynamic cluster, certainly much less so than cluster A, which has an average growth

Table 4.20 Cluster's long-run growth rates: metal working

Cluster A			Cluster B			Cluster C		
Total no. of firms	Average no. of employees when founded	Average no. of employees 1991	Total no. of firms	Average no. of employees when founded	Average no. of employees 1991	Total no. of firms	Average no. of employees when founded	Average no. of employees 1991
6	44	118	12	27	60	19	2	10
Case nos	No. of employees when founded	No. of employees 1991	Case nos	No. of employees when founded	No. of employees 1991	Case nos	No. of employees when founded	No. of employees 1991
20	5	150	3	40	24	11	1	16
26	n.a.	30	21	6	28	37	7	5
31	16	130	76	3	19	38	n.a.	8
127	23	40	119	n.a.	504	44	10	20
150	130	150	126	2	90	49	0	12
177	n.a.	32	129	n.a.	33	50	0	2
			134	3	100	53	3	11
			136	n.a.	51	54	0	4
			141	18	75	55	1	1
			147	130	70	70	1	28
			156	13	71	94	1	5
			178	30	58	108	0	11
						117	0	1
						139	1	3
						162	n.a.	1
						171	0	21
						172	0	6
						184	0	8
						189	0	9
Average firm age in 1991	Growth rate of cluster A[a]	Average firm age in 1991		Growth rate of cluster B	Average firm age in 1991			Growth rate of cluster C
6	18% [4 obs.][b]	15		5% [9 obs.]	10			20% [17 obs.]

[a] Annual compound growth rate for all the firms in the cluster over the average age of the firms in the cluster.
[b] Number of data available for computing the growth rate.

rate of 18 per cent and very young firms (average age 6 years). Most of the firms in A started as small- or medium-sized enterprises and grew larger. In the food processing industry, on the other hand, there does not seem to be much movement across the clusters. Micro firms stay small, very large ones started as such and are declining dramatically under liberalisation. Firms in cluster B are relatively dynamic, some of them growing and some declining. Little movement across

Table 4.21   Cluster's long-run growth rates: wood working

Cluster A			Cluster B			Cluster C		
Total no. of firms	Average no. of employees when founded	Average no. of employees 1991	Total no. of firms	Average no. of employees when founded	Average no. of employees 1991	Total no. of firms	Average no. of employees when founded	Average no. of employees 1991
11	44	93	24	3	21	8	0	3
Case nos	No. of employees when founded	No. of employees 1991	Case nos	No. of employees when founded	No. of employees 1991	Case nos	No. of employees when founded	No. of employees 1991
7	232	119	2	7	45	43	1	3
8	14	95	9	n.a.	17	56	0	1
72	76	25	10	2	10	61	0	8
77	n.a.	143	12	0	10	81	n.a.	1
85	5	42	22	1	13	85	n.a.	1
106	2	6	27	1	11	96	0	0
118	10	40	32	7	14	115	1	5
128	8	50	48	0	6	123	0	3
160	n.a.	20	51	0	41	188	0	0
			52	0	16			
			90	2	18			
			93	n.a.	7			
			97	5	7			
			103	17	17			
			109	0	50			
			110	2	17			
			114	10	368			
			124	5	14			
			164	6	7			
			166	1	50			
			173	2	40			
			174	4	15			
			186	2	14			
			194	n.a.	21			
Average firm age in 1991	Growth rate of cluster A[a]	Average firm age in 1991		Growth rate of cluster B	Average firm age in 1991			Growth rate of cluster C
15	5% [8 obs.][b]	9		23% [20 obs.]	7			30% [7 obs.]

[a] Annual compound growth rate for all the firms in the cluster over the average age of the firms in the cluster.
[b] Number of data available for computing the growth rate.

Table 4.22 Cluster's long-run growth rates: food processing

Cluster A			Cluster B			Cluster C		
Total no. of firms	Average no. of employees when founded	Average no. of employees 1991	Total no. of firms	Average no. of employees when founded	Average no. of employees 1991	Total no. of firms	Average no. of employees when founded	Average no. of employees 1991
4	850	424	13	22	37	23	3	7
Case nos	No. of employees when founded	No. of employees 1991	Case nos	No. of employees when founded	No. of employees 1991	Case nos	No. of employees when founded	No. of employees 1991
25	n.a.	216	6	50	33	19	1	35
107	152	159	35	9	24	39	0	1
113	2000	885	36	8	25	40	10	10
200	400	228	41	10	30	47	2	4
			75	n.a.	20	82	5	3
			101	30	24	87	4	4
			112	32	97	95	n.a.	4
			116	n.a.	25	99	12	10
			138	4	11	100	0	4
			142	45	68	104	n.a.	25
			152	13	45	111	2	0
			175	22	17	155	7	9
						169	n.a.	4
						170	3	1
						182	7	7
						183	3	4
						187	0	4
						190	n.a.	4
						191	5	8
						192	1	1
						193	0	7
						195	3	6
						196	n.a.	3
						198	2	11
Average firm age in 1991	Growth rate of cluster A[a]	Average firm age in 1991		Growth rate of cluster B	Average firm age in 1991			Growth rate of cluster C
33	−2% [3 obs.][b]	10		5% [10 obs.]	11			6% [19 obs.]

[a] Annual compound growth rate for all the firms in the cluster over the average age of the firms in the cluster.
[b] Number of data available for computing the growth rate.

Table 4.23   Cluster's long-run growth rates: textiles and garments

Cluster A			Cluster B		
Total no. of firms	Average no. of employees when founded	Average no. of employees 1991	Total no. of firms	Average no. of employees when founded	Average no. of employees 1991
8	84	112	27	2	9
Case nos	No. of employees when founded	No. of employees 1991	Case nos	No. of employees when founded	No. of employees 1991
13	15	48	29	0	0
14	n.a.	14	45	2	13
17	28	37	46	0	1
18	50	267	58	3	2
42	80	42	59	0	1
130	259	259	60	0	4
143	n.a.	1276	63	n.a.	1
157	75	24	64	15	0
			65	0	27
			66	0	1
			67	0	7
			68	2	5
			69	4	11
			71	0	4
			84	0	2
			91	6	15
			92	0	30
			98	0	17
			102	0	1
			105	0	10
			121	n.a.	118
			133	n.a.	6
			137	n.a.	54
			140	1	4
			163	1	35
			165	0	10
			167	0	5
			168	0	4
Average firm age in 1991		Growth rate of cluster A[a]	Average firm age in 1991		Growth rate of cluster B
14		2% [6 obs.][b]	9		15% [25 obs.]

[a] Annual compound growth rate for all the firms in the cluster over the average age of the firms in the cluster.
[b] Number of data available for computing the growth rate.

clusters is also shown in textiles and garments.

In general, there seems to be relatively little movement across clusters, as far as data on employment growth show. In particular, except for wood working, there is no upgrading at all from the micro cluster.

It is also interesting to look at the relationship between growth and investments. The first important result is that firms in the top technology clusters are not necessarily those which invest more (Figures 4.5 to 4.8). Taking the ratio between total investments and the stock of capital (an indicator of how much the physical capital stock has been renewed in the last ten years) as a measure of investments (along with total investments), large investors are found at both ends of the technology spectrum. Thus, micro firms also invest, though in proportion to their capital stock. For the more dynamic wood and metal-working industries, as shown in Figures 4.9 and 4.10, almost all the firms which have invested are growing. In this respect, renewal of capital equipment appears to be necessary for growth in dynamic industries.

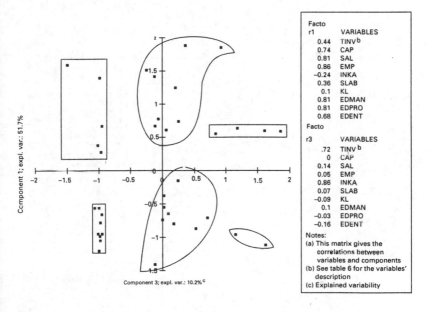

Facto r1	VARIABLES
0.44	TINV [b]
0.74	CAP
0.81	SAL
0.86	EMP
−0.24	INKA
0.36	SLAB
0.1	KL
0.81	EDMAN
0.81	EDPRO
0.68	EDENT

Facto r3	VARIABLES
.72	TINV [b]
0	CAP
0.14	SAL
0.05	EMP
0.86	INKA
0.07	SLAB
−0.09	KL
0.1	EDMAN
−0.03	EDPRO
−0.16	EDENT

Notes:
(a) This matrix gives the correlations between variables and components
(b) See table 6 for the variables' description
(c) Explained variability

Figure 4.5   Rotated factor matrix a: metal working

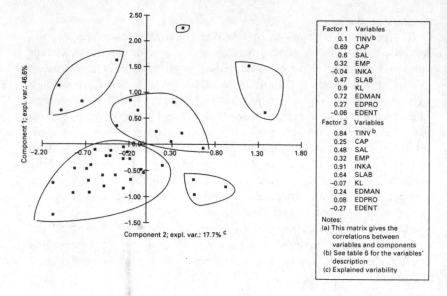

Figure 4.6   Rotated factor matrix a: wood working

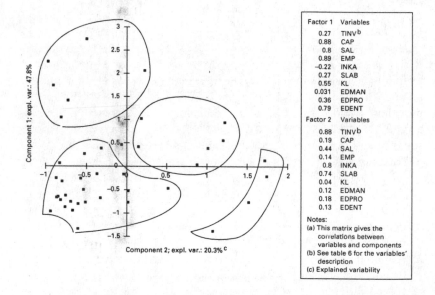

Figure 4.7   Rotated factor matrix a: food processing

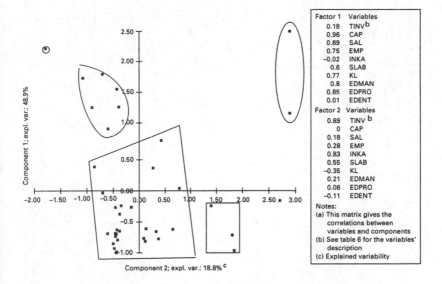

Figure 4.8 Rotated factor matrix a: textiles and garments

CONCLUSIONS

In conclusion, cluster analysis has turned out to be extremely useful in 'mapping out' the technological features of the firms in the panel sample. It has been useful in highlighting some of the major constraints to technological upgrading. However, the analysis is based on a limited number of imperfect quantitative indicators, which clearly fall short of providing a complete picture of the technological development process in a firm. The detailed case studies in the rest of the volume try to capture some of the qualitative factors that the large data set could not.[10]

To summarise the main findings of this analysis:

1. All the industries in the sample are characterised by clear clusters of firms defined by size, physical capital and human capital. This confirms the hypothesis that there are multiple equilibria in investments in technology.
2. Although firms in the top clusters are on average larger, size and technology are not consistently correlated. Some of the clusters observed differ in terms of technology and human capital, but not in terms of size.

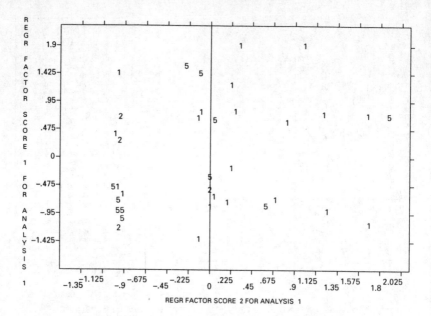

Figure 4.9   Metal working: plot of component 1 with component 3
controlled for growth rates

Legend: 1 = Positive employment's or/and sales' growth rates
        2 = Negative growth rates in employment and sales
        5 = Missing data

3. Segmentation in factor markets affects technological upgrading at intermediate technological levels. It does not, however, bind upgrading at the lowest and highest ends of the technology spectrum.
4. Part of the reason for clustering in terms of physical and human capital lies in the fact that TCs are firm and technology specific. In other words, the level of capabilities is determined by the firm's own decision to invest in their acquisition, and in certain cases capabilities in the firm are too low to make the shift to a more advanced technology worthwhile.
5. There is very little evidence of upgrading across technological clusters, particularly when large changes in technology are necessary and market segmentation exists.

These results have interesting policy implications. In line with the structural adjustment approach, market segmentation exists and con-

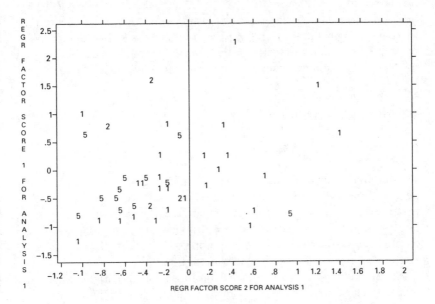

Figure 4.10   Wood working: plot of component 1 with component 2
for growth rates

Legend: 1 = Positive employment's and/or sales' growth rates
         2 = Negative employment's and/or sales' growth rates
         5 = Missing data

strains growth and upgrading in some of the technological clusters. Policy intervention aimed at improving factor markets and reducing segmentation might be helpful for enterprise development. However, it would not be sufficient, if only particular factor markets are addressed and TC needs are not taken into account. Take, for instance, a cluster which is constrained by segmentation in the financial market: small firms have no access to formal credit. The government may set up a fund for lending to small enterprises. Assuming that such a fund can be operated efficiently (a major assumption, given the transactions costs and risks inherent in lending to small and micro enterprises), is this sufficient to ensure that the firms concerned invest and upgrade their technology? Not necessarily. To use new technologies, many firms would need to develop new sets of technological capabilities. For some, the process may be too costly and risky, or it may be constrained by other factor-market imperfections, e.g. a shortage of skilled technicians.

Furthermore, policies aimed at removing market imperfections would have no effect on upgrading across clusters when this is not constrained by market segmentation. The need to promote the technological learning period by infant industry promotion may also be a necessary part of the policy support needed to dynamise manufacturing enterprises.

TECHNICAL APPENDIX[11]

Handling Missing Data

The original sample consisted of 188 firms and 234 variables. As many observations were missing for some of the variables, the problem was first tackled by selecting 50 crucial variables, each of them having at least 90 observations. 24 firms were dropped from the sample because of measurement errors in many important variables. The subsequent analysis has therefore been made on 164 firms.

All the methods considered for handling missing data belong to the 'explicit imputation methods' family, which tries to find a replacement value as similar as possible to the value of the missing item. Similarity is defined according to values of a set of assignment variables, statistically related to the variables with missing data and available for both respondents and nonrespondents. In particular, two methods were considered.

(i) *Mean-value imputation.* If observation y_i of variable Y is missing, this method simply substitutes y_i with the mean of character Y in the population. A more sophisticated version of this method controls for a certain number of assignment variables i.e. if variables $X_1, X_2, ..., X_n$ are thought to be relevant in grouping observations, y_i is not substituted by the overall mean of the population, but by the mean of Y controlled for the relevant level of $X_1, X_2, ..., X_n$. The same procedure applies if Y is a qualitative variable: in this case the imputed value will be character Y's median instead of its mean. The advantage of this method is ease and rapidity. It bears one important disadvantage: it distorts the sample distribution of Y, since item nonrespondents can only take on values of the imputation cell means, greatly reducing the sample variance.

(ii) *Regression imputation.* y_i is computed by building up the following regression, and by using observation for which the data set is complete:

$$Y = b_0 + b_1 X_1 + ... + b_n X_n + e,$$

where $b_i i = 1,2,...,n$ are estimated parameters; if for element i of the population $X_{1i}, X_{2i},...,X_{ni}$ are available without missing values, it is possible to predict y_i on the basis of the estimated coefficients. If Y is a qualitative variable, the regression model can be substituted with a logit model. The advantage of this method – given a good fit and a correctly specified model – is the maintenance of the statistical association of the Y and the assigned variables.

We opted for the first method mentioned, controlling for an industry and a size qualitative variable (on 5 levels). Thus, if a sales datum concerning firm i – belonging to the food processing industry and employing 60 employees – was missing, the mean of variable 'total sales' calculated among food processing firms with more than 50 and less than 100 employees (this was the appropriate size level) was used to substitute for it.

There are three reasons for the choice of this method. First, there is a lack of strong predictors for the variables with missing data. Second, there was widespread lack of data among variables, making the availability of the data set for element i – necessary for computing $y(i)$ – impossible. Third, the higher time and cost of using the regression-based model.

Descriptive Statistics

The construction of descriptive tables used the canonical instrument, i.e. the analysis of marginal association between variables. In this phase only pre-imputed data were used, since mean-value imputed ones would only reinforce the results already obtained.

At this stage, a correlation matrix among quantitative variables, and a measure of association among couples of qualitative variables, were produced; the latter is a Pearson's χ^2 based measure – Cramer's V – defined as $[\chi^2/n*\min(\#\text{rows} - 1; \#\text{columns} - 1)]^{1/2}$, where n is the sample size and #rows the number of rows of the contingency table. It varies from 0, which means absence of association, to 1, which means perfect association, independently from its direction (positive or negative).

In the tables, Cramer's V is accompanied by the χ^2 test of independence, a test based upon the χ^2 statistics, whose null hypothesis is known as 'marginal independence of the two variables considered in the contingency table'. An observed significance level smaller than the fixed significance one (usually 0,05 or 0,01) will imply rejection of the null hypothesis, i.e. the two variables are in some way correlated to each other.

Principal Components

Ten theoretically important (imputed) quantitative variables were selected, yielding a data matrix of the order (164,10). Since we wished to get a clear visual representation of the information contained in this matrix, and since the correlation matrix showed quite high correlation among variables belonging to certain homogeneous economic subgroups, it was thought feasible to reduce the number of variables without losing much of the statistical information contained in the original 164*10 modalities.

Principal components analysis has been used as a method to implement this reduction. Let $X(164,10)$ be the original data matrix, the first principal components of $X(164,10)$ is, by definition:

$$P(1) = \Sigma_i a_{i1} * X_i = X(164,10)a_1$$

where a_1' is a row-vector with elements $(a_{11}, a_{21},...,a_{k1})$, and X_i a column-vector of $X(164,10)$; a_1 is determined by the following maximization process:

$$\max (S_1^2) \text{ s.t. } a_1'a_1 = 1$$

where S_1^2 is the sample variance of $P(1)$. The result is that the first principal component $P(1)$ is a linear combination of the k original variables $(X_1, X_2,..., X_k)$ with coefficients equal to the elements of the eigen vector associated to the greatest eigen value of the variance-covariance matrix of $X(164,10)$.

The second principal component $P(2) = X(164,10)a_2$ is computed similarly,

$$\text{maximizing } (S_2^2) \text{ s.t. } a_2'a_2 = 1 \text{ and } a_1'a_2 = 0$$

where the second constraint means that component $P(1)$ and $P(2)$ are not correlated. The same procedure applies to the other principal components. (Note that the number of components of a matrix is equal to its rank i.e. to the number of its noncorrelated columns.)

There are two major properties of principal components: (i) they are orthogonal, with no 'overlapping' information among them: each explains a specific amount of the sample variability. (ii) Since the result of the optimization shown above is:

$$\max (S_i^2) = l(i) = \mathrm{Var}(P(i))$$

where $l(i)$ is the i-th eigenvalue in decreasing order,

$l(i)/\Sigma_i\ l(i)\ 100$

will be ith's principal component contribution to the explanation of original data's total variability. We have thus obtained 10 (=rank of $X(164,10)$) new (noncorrelated) variables of decreasing importance and maximum variance.

We chose the first three principal components, retaining a percentage of total original data's variability equal to $l(1) + l(2) + l(3) / \Sigma_i$ $l(i)$ 100 (in our case never less than 60 per cent).

Unfortunately, components are not always correlated in an interpretable pattern. Thus, a rotation phase of components analysis attempts to transform − by rotating components' axes − the initial factor structure matrix into one that is easier to interpret. Varimax, the algorithm we used, attempts to minimize the number of variables which are correlated with one component, preserving distances between them.

Cluster Analysis

Clustering algorithms were run at an industry level because no clusters could be detected at the whole sample level (as was expected from biplots). The first decision referred to the variables to be utilized in forming clusters: the 10 original variables or the three chosen principal components? We opted for the second because of consistency with the analysis so far accomplished and because experience suggests that differences in results are negligible. Moreover, the smaller the number of included variables the easier are the clusters to interpret.

The second choice concerns the algorithm to be used. Empirical studies show that different algorithms give the same clusters, if groups possess a spheric shape. Particularly, splitting methods, which form groups by dividing the original statistical population, are not likely to determine non-spheric clusters, while aggregating algorithms, which aggregate objects around predetermined centres, can only create non-spheric clusters. It turned out from biplots that some clusters do not have a spheric shape. For this reason an aggregating method was chosen. Aggregating methods operate in the following way:

- initially n clusters $(c_1,c_2,...,c_n)$ – each made up of one element of the population – are considered;
- a new partition is then built up by minimizing $d(c_i,c_j)$ relative to i and j, (where d is a distance function), and aggregating the nearest groups c_i and c_j in a new one, thus obtaining n-1 clusters;
- new distances among groups are calculated and a new partition of the n-1 clusters is built up using the same procedure;
- the procedure is iterated until all the n original objects are assembled in one unique cluster.

It is therefore clear that what makes the difference between alternative clustering methods is the way in which the distance between clusters is defined, or, more precisely, the way in which the new centroid of a merged cluster is calculated: this will vary with the desired clusters' characteristics. The median method – the algorithm we used – determines:

$$d(c_ic_j,c_k) = 0,5d(c_i,c_k) + 0,5d(c_j,c_k) - 0,25d(c_i,c_j),$$

where $d(c_ic_j,c_k)$ is the distance between cluster c_k and the cluster obtained by merging clusters c_ic_j's.

There are two main characteristics of this method. First, the two combined clusters are equally weighted in the centroid computation, regardless of the number of cases in each; thus this method is robust. Second it should not suffer from 'chain effects', i.e. progressive agglomerations of objects which are not homogeneous with regard to one principal component.

An important problem was then deciding how many clusters to choose, since hierarchical methods (like the median one) provide many alternatives (from n to 0 groups). This was done by cutting the dendrogram (the 'tree' which describes the grouping dynamics) above the low aggregations (which bring together the elements that are very close to each other), and under the high aggregations (which lump together all the groups in the population).

Part B

Process and Determinants of Technological Development

5 Technological Capabilities: A Summary Evaluation

INTRODUCTION

This part of the study deals with a firm-level qualitative analysis of the technological capabilities in the smaller sample of Ghanaian firms. In this chapter we present a 'mapping out' of firm-level capabilities. This was carried out for each of the four industry groups separately, based on the data collected in the interviews (the detailed assessment of TCs, on which this chapter is based, is reported in appendices A–D). For each of the capabilities, the discussion is divided to the extent possible according to industry. The chapter ends with a list of technologically 'competent' firms, whose characteristics reveal some of the main influences on technology development. The next three chapters discuss these influences under separate headings.

The first chapter presented a breakdown on TCs by three major functions: investment, production and linkages. Each of these functions is performed, implicitly or explicitly, by every manufacturing firm, with a combination of its own efforts and those of others. Each requires its own special kinds of skills and information, and so can be more or less well done depending on the firm's ability to mobilise internal and external resources and its willingness to invest those resources. Let us see how the Ghanaian sample fares in each category.

INVESTMENT CAPABILITIES

Introduction

All manufacturing activity starts with the investment needed to set up the productive facility. The process of defining the equipment and technology needed, finding and buying them at the right price and on the right conditions, installing and absorbing the tacit elements of the technology, and getting into production – these are usually fairly complex tasks for most manufacturing activities. They require the development of skills and the collection of information in fragmented markets for technology. However, not all investments require the same intensity of search and effort. The appropriate investment capabilities vary by industry, the level of technology used, the scale of the operation and the nature of the market (local or foreign, niche or exposed to international competition). Not all enterprises need possess equal levels of skills and information to set up facilities efficiently, and there are a number of specialised agents (like engineering contractors, capital goods manufacturers or foreign investors) who can undertake some or most of the investment activity. For a developing country firm entering into production itself, however, a certain minimum level of capabilities is needed to set up the basic parameters of the project and to evaluate and monitor external sources of assistance.

The significance of investment capabilities to the success of the enterprise increases with the capital-intensity of the facility and the complexity of the process. In any given technology, both tend to rise with the size of the operation.[1] Thus, activities with mature technologies, simple processes, and small-scale facilities generally have relatively low skill and information needs for investment. Those with new technologies and large-scale, complex processes have high transaction costs in locating, designing, engineering and setting up an efficient facility.

General Findings

The Ghanaian sample firms span a range of investment needs, but within each industry they tend to be concentrated in the simpler end of the technological spectrum. Practically all the equipment is imported, since the local capital goods industry is relatively undeveloped. Table 5.1 presents information on the age of equipment, origin of equipment, whether the initial equipment was new or used, and the most important source of information for the initial investment by the 32 sample firms. It also shows the available data on the number and value of "major" new investments since the ERP started. The impressions conveyed by this table may be summarised as follows:

• There is a high propensity to start with used equipment: of the 32 firms, 15 launched themselves exclusively with used equipment while another 2 had a mixture of new and used equipment. Each of the four industries does this, but the metal working subsector seems to have a slightly higher propensity. This is not undesirable *per se*, if the choice of equipment is appropriate to the technical needs of the

Table 5.1 Investment in plant and equipment

| Firm | Initial investment in plant and equipment | | | | Major subsequent investments | |
| | Average age of equipment (years) | New/used equipment | Sources of information for initial investment in equipment: | | Total value of major additions since 1983 US$ '000 (number) | Sources of information: General |
			Specific	General		
Textiles and garments						
TG1	14–17 years old	New	Local dealer	L	1 729 (2)	FWS
TG2	Over 16 years old[a]	Used	Trade fairs	FWS	n.a.	n.a.
TG3	About 17 years old	New	Foreign cloth supplier	FNS	n.a.	n.a.
TG4	Over 30 years old	Used	Own search abroad	FWS	n.a. (1)	FWS
TG5	Over 15 years old	New	Foreign agent	FWS	0	
TG6	About 25 years old	New	Foreign equip. mfrer	FWS	0	
TG7	n.a.	Used	None, (subcontracted)	L	0.3 (1)	L
TG8	16–24 years old	Used	None, (subcontracted)	L	0	
Food processing						
FP1	Mix of 30 year old and new	New	Foreign parent	FNS	n.a.	n.a.
FP2	Mostly 40–50 years old	Used	Foreign parent	FNS	600 (1)	FNS
FP3	Over 30 years old	New (TK)	Foreign eng. firm	FWS	191 (1)	FWS
FP4	50 years old	Used	Own search abroad	FWS	5 (1)	n.a.
FP5	2 years old[a]	New (TK)	Foreign eng. firm	FWS	0	
FP6	Mix of 30 years old and new	New	Foreign parent	FNS	6 (2)	FNS
FP7	About 8 years old[a]	New (TK)	Foreign eng. firm	FWS	2 000 (1)	FWS
Wood working						
WW1	8–14 years old	New	Previous work experience	FWS	n.a. (3)	FWS
WW2	Mostly 50 years old	New	Foreign parent	FNS	n.a. (1)	FWS

continued on page 114

Table 5.1   continued

| Firm | Initial investment in plant and equipment | | | | Major subsequent investments | |
| | Average age of equipment (years) | New/used equipment | Sources of information for initial investment in equipment: | | Total value of major additions since 1983 US$ '000 (number) | Sources of information: |
			Specific	General		General
WW3	5–10 years old	Used	Previous work experience	FWS	500 (1)	FWS
WW4	About 20 years old	New	Foreign embassy	L	0	
WW5	About 15 years old	New & used	Own search abroad	FWS	450 (1)	FWS
WW7	No machines, only hand tools[a]	Used	Previous work experience	L	2 (3)	L
WW8	No machines, only hand tools[a]	New & used	Previous work experience	L	0 (1)	L
Metal working						
WW1	15–27 years old	New (TK)	Foreign eng. firm	FWS	n.a.	n.a
MW2	5 years old	Used	Foreign agent	FWS	172 (1)	FWS
MW3	Mostly 2–3 years old	New	Foreign partner	FNS	n.a. (1)	FWS
MW4	Mostly 50 years old	Used	Foreign parent	FNS	18 (1)	FNS
MW5	Over 30 years old	Used	Work experience	L	12 (1)	L
MW6	n.a.	Used	Other local firms	L	3 (2)	L
MW7	30–40 years old	Used	Education and work experience	L	8 (2)	FWS
MW8	7–10 years old[a]	New (TK)	Government purchase	FWS	12 (1)	FWS
MW9	Over 14 years old	Used	Other local firms	L	1 (1)	L

[a] Founded since 1983. TK = turnkey project. L = local sources, FWS = foreign with search, FNS = foreign no search.

entrepreneur and he has the capability to use the machines efficiently (second-hand equipment does not come with the manufacturer's technical assistance, and spares may be difficult to obtain).

- There are several sources of information for the initial purchase of equipment. The column on the specific sources of information shows that foreign parents help their affiliates, while foreign engineering firms are used by locally owned firms in more complex processes. The entrepreneur's own search abroad and familiarity with sources from previous work experience are found in several instances. Other local firms have helped some of the firms starting with used equipment bought locally. A variety of other sources is also found in individual cases.

- The general sources of information on the initial investment, classified more broadly to match the data collected in the larger panel sample, are 'local' (local trade fairs, business associations, other local firms and technology institutions), 'foreign sources involving search' (independent foreign supplier of plant, foreign engineering or consulting firm, trips abroad and publications), and 'foreign sources without search' (foreign partner, parent company or buyer). For the case study sample, the sources of information are 34 per cent local, 46 foreign with involving search, and 22 per cent foreign without search. There is thus a fairly high reliance on foreign sources of information, reflecting the relatively large size of the case study firms. Again, there is a suggestion of market segmentation in access to technological information and foreign sources of technology by size of firm.

- The data on the values of subsequent investments, while not complete (23 of the sample firms provided this data), suggest that there have been relatively few significant new investments by the sample firms since 1983. Of the firms reporting this information, only 7 firms have invested (or are in the process of investing) over $100 000 each, and only 2 have invested over $1 million. The total value of new investments of $5.2 million gives an average of $227 000 per reporting firm, with only six of the 23 reaching this figure. Most new investments tended to be very small machinery purchases.

- Sources of information on the subsequent investments in the case study sample are local for 27 per cent of the firms, foreign involving search for 59 per cent of the firms and foreign without search for 14 per cent. Compared to the panel sample, the larger case study enterprises show a higher propensity to rely on foreign sources, with a much greater propensity to search by the firms.

Textiles and Garments

Firms in this industry fall into two groups. The first consists of firms sewing relatively standardised garments, aimed at local markets not competing directly with import (like army or school uniforms). The second consists of knitwear firms.

Let us start with garment manufacturers. Despite wages that are much lower than East Asia (the source of most imports),[2] the Ghanaian garment industry has been unable to withstand import competition. Some of these firms also used to make knitwear but this market has almost completely gone to imports (exceptions are noted below). The equipment in use is standard sewing machines (as opposed to the more sophisticated, programmable ones used in advanced countries), that were relatively easy to locate and buy. These were bought locally or in Europe, relying on the advice of agents, some personal search, and contacts in the trade. Two firms started by using tailors with their own machines, and added new machines later. Since there have been practically no significant new investments in this activity since import competition started (the single exception is noted below), it is difficult to assess more recent investment capabilities.

Initial start-up and training needs were met by technicians sent for short periods by equipment suppliers, experienced people hired from other garment firms (in one case by the owner's daughters who were trained in textiles), or technicians from abroad (one German stayed on after coming to install knitting machines). One firm sent two supervisors to Italy for training in embroidery and knitting (though these skills were lost when the firm closed and then restarted with school uniforms). Most of these firms did not attempt to invest in upgrading garment sewing. One exception is TG1, which kept the German engineer: this firm drew on his expertise to import and set up a computer-aided design system. This investment enabled it to carve out a niche market for customised logos (printed on imported T-shirts). This firm also attempted to set up an expensive textile finishing plant, after careful feasibility study and evaluation, but this was never commissioned.[3]

The second group of three firms in this industry manufacture knitwear (the only specialised knitwear maker left in Ghana), fishing nets and synthetic leather. The knitwear firm used a German agent to source equipment in Europe and a Sudanese engineer to set it up and train workers. The net maker searched for and bought used equipment in Germany, and a German technician helped set it up. The synthetic leather firm also bought German equipment, getting it cheaply at a trade fair; however, its installation took place some eight years later because of political instability. When installation finally took place, the owner took training in Germany and got German technicians to design the plant, install the machines and train the workers.

It seems, on the whole, that investments in this industry were reasonably well managed by the sample firms. In the nature of the industry, the demands on skill and information were not very high, and, after some search, they were met adequately by the firms. Foreign assistance was drawn upon in most cases to design, install and launch the investments, with brief training sufficing to reach the levels of operational efficiency demanded by protected local markets. Most firms were content to stay at this level of efficiency, however, and were not able to achieve world competitiveness.

Food Processing

In food processing, the sample consists of medium and large firms using modern technologies, with exclusive reliance on imported equipment. The industry is the most capital-intensive of the activities in the sample, and its investment needs are correspondingly complex. The relevant technical and engineering skills did not exist in Ghana when the firms launched production, accounting for very high reliance on foreign engineering firms (or parent companies) for the design, procurement and setting up of new plants.

The three Multinational Corporation (MNC) affiliates, FP1, FP2 and FP6, relied exclusively on their parent companies for designing, procuring, setting up and launching their investments. One of these got used equipment from the UK, the others started with new plant; each had foreign technicians staying in Ghana for extended periods to train local employees. There was no local participation in the technical aspects of these investments. It seems, some 30–40 years later, that such technical capabilities have remained underdeveloped – each of the affiliates has set up, or is planning, new investments in response to the liberalisation, with all the technical investment functions handled by the parent. The initial investments were presumably well managed, but they transmitted little information on the design and detailed engineering of the process, and the selection of the equipment, to local personnel.

Three of the local firms bought their technology in the form of turnkey projects. One of these, the state-owned cannery, got a plant (in 1960) as part of an official barter agreement . The design was by a Yugoslav

engineering firm, and, as with the multinationals, the local staff played
no role in the choice of the contractor or the design of the investment.
The equipment was sourced from several countries, creating problems
of operation which could not be solved by local staff, who were unfam-
iliar with the technologies involved (they had to be resolved by a
Yugoslav engineer). Even though ten people were taken to Yugoslavia
for initial training, this was confined to the operation of the equipment and gave no knowledge of process or plant engineering, Thus,
when the firm wanted to rehabilitate the plant in 1986 it had to go
back to the original contractor. The quotation given ($ 2.1 million)
was too expensive for the cannery, and it has had to carry on with the
old plant.

The other two turnkey projects, both more recent (1988 and 1983)
and both by Italian firms, were better executed. In the case of the
flour mill, the entrepreneurs, who were not technically qualified (though
they had worked on the management of local flour mills), found the
supplier through the local Italian embassy. They opted for Italian equipment because it was suitable for relatively small-scale production. They
negotiated a satisfactory agreement, with a ten-year guarantee and four
years of technical assistance (with four Italian engineers stationed locally
as well as regular visits by special technical teams). Though the local
staff played no role in the design of the plant, the transfer of skills and
operational routines was systematically conducted over an appropriate
period. The plant is new and there have been no major additions.

The other project, for FP7's fruit juice plant, was set up by a Ghanaian
entrepreneur, a trained chemical engineer, who was able to select the
equipment himself on technical merit. He evaluated several suppliers
before choosing the Italian manufacturer. The suppliers sent two technicians for installation and took the production manager for factory
training to Italy for a month. The foreign technicians spent only a
fortnight in Ghana, and the local production and maintenance managers participated in the design, installation and commissioning of the
plant. This gave them a thorough knowledge of the plant and facilitated efficient operation later. The firm is now going for a new Tetra
Pak (paper packaging) plant from Sweden, also on a turnkey basis
with similar local participation. This firm's local investment capabilities are the best of the food processing firms and one of the best in
the sample.

Finally, the biscuit manufacturer started 35 years ago with second-
hand equipment from the UK. The installation and startup was done
by the firm itself, drawing on the food processing experience of the

entrepreneur's family (his grandfather had started a bakery on arriving in Ghana in the 1950s, and his children now operate a food processing plant in the UK). No additions were made to the plant over time, however, and the old plant was kept running until import competition almost wiped it out (see below).

To sum up, foreign investment capabilities were tapped efficiently by the MNC affiliates, but led to little development of local capabilities in this process. The two local private firms that bought turnkey plants showed the ability to tap foreign engineering skills efficiently. The turnkey project by the state-owned enterprise was less successful, while one firm started on its own with used equipment. Only one firm (FP7) made the effort to participate in the technical aspects of investment, and was able to build up some investment capabilities in the process.

Wood Working

In the wood-working industry, the firms can be divided into three groups according to their investment capabilities (one firm, WW2, is not considered here because its plant was originally acquired by its British owners over 50 years ago and has never been updated). The first group comprises two relatively new firms (6–7 years old) that operate out of temporary sheds, using simple hand tools bought locally with minimal search. Their products are cheap and of low quality. Their investment needs are extremely simple, and the process is not complex enough to merit consideration of design and layout.

The second group consists of two firms, one small (WW6) and one medium sized (WW4), that started as micro, traditional carpentry workshops and 'graduated' to modern furniture technology and larger size. Their initial investments needed little search or special knowledge, but their graduation did involve a large jump in their technologies. Their approaches differed. WW6 bought used equipment locally (to minimise the need for search); some years later it bought used equipment abroad, drawing on contacts provided by the owner's brother in the UK. Its continued reliance on second-hand equipment meant that the owner had to use his own skills to manage the expansion, with no assistance from equipment manufacturers.

The other 'graduating' firm, WW4, opted for a new plant. In the absence of other sources of information, the entrepreneur sought advice from the local Norwegian embassy. The embassy put him in contact with a Norwegian equipment manufacturer, who also offered him credit (an important consideration in making the choice). The supplier sent engineers to install and commission the plant and provide some training. It also took 4 employees to Norway for training. However, over 20 years the firm had done little to improve on the initial transfer, and a later technical study by UNIDO found the layout of the plant and the choice of equipment to be inefficient. The firm had not invested since 1983.

The third group consists of three firms that started as medium or large modern furniture manufacturers. One was launched by an experienced and qualified Italian furniture maker who was familiar with equipment from his country, and has relied solely on Italian machinery. His experience and knowledge gave him the best investment capabilities of the sample firms in wood working. Another firm, WW3, was started by a Ghanaian without technical knowledge of furniture making but with years of experience in a furniture firm in Canada. He was familiar with the names of Italian suppliers, and went to Italy to negotiate the initial purchase of basic equipment himself. Over time he acquired information on other sources, and diversified his purchases when buying more specialised machinery (WW3 is the largest recent investor in this industry on which data are available). This suggests that the firm's investment capabilities improved over time. All purchases were supported by technical assistance from the suppliers.

The last firm started with a mixture of used and new equipment. The entrepreneur had experience in saw-milling and searched among several European suppliers. The initial layout and commissioning was done by the production manager, a technically qualified Lebanese. A substantial later expansion was carried out similarly. Investment capabilities were quite good in this case.

There is considerable variation in investment capabilities in this industry. Of the six medium and large firms, four displayed the ability to search for appropriate equipment overseas. One seems to have made a poorer choice. The smaller firms only bought simple hand tools, so did not need any special skills to start with.

Metal Working

In metal working, the firms also fall into three groups. First come two firms, both state-owned, that have relatively complex technologies. The first of these, MW1, is a 'mini' steel mill (with electric arc furnaces, continuous casting facilities and a rolling mill for making structural rods) that started in 1975. It started as a turnkey project, with a UK engineering firm supplying the plant, but with little or no receptive skills on the part of the local employees for the technology. The layout was not satisfactory and the initial transfer of technology was not successful. Large parts of the plant did not work properly and productivity was abysmal. Italian consultants were called in after some years. They modified the plant and added more complex equipment (including the continuous casting machine). The lack of local capabilities meant that the situation deteriorated further, and by 1990 only 10 per cent of the plant was operating.[4] This case is a good illustration of the risks inherent in turnkey projects where local capabilities are deficient.

The second relatively complex plant, MW8, is a foundry and machine shop, started in 1985.The foundry started with equipment that had already been purchased for another purpose. The choice had been made by the Ministry of Rural Development and Cooperatives, presumably because of the credit offered by the suppliers rather than on technical considerations. The enterprise was previously a car-servicing facility and lacked any foundry-operating skills. The foundry furnace did not work and an attempt to start it was aborted by a power breakdown. It has not been rectified and commisioned till today, so that the central element of the foundry has never worked. The machine shop has been made to work with German technical assistance, but only 5 per cent of the rated capacity is now being used.

The second group of metal working firms comprises three firms making aluminium products. Of these, one makes lightweight pots and pans from locally rolled aluminium sheets. The other two make doors, windows and other structural products, largely from imported aluminium extrusions (the local aluminium mill does not make extrusions). All these processes are simple, essentially cutting, bending and simple forming operations with low requirements of precision and skill. The pots and pans maker, MW2, started with used equipment bought through an agent by the entrepreneur, who was by training an accountant. Production skills were obtained by hiring technicians who had worked in utensil manufacture in Nigeria; this was a success and led to further purchases of used equipment (through the same dealer). This was clearly an efficient and economical investment, where the relative simplicity of the technology and the availability of skills allowed the firm to launch with little technical assistance.

The two structural products firms were started in collaboration with foreigners who transferred the initial technology. In one, MW3, an Israeli partner set up the plant and stayed for several years; later, the owner's son took over and then, in 1989, modernised and expanded the plant and is set to go into aluminium rolling (data on values of investment are not available). This later investment was carefully planned and prospective suppliers evaluated over a six month period. Installation and technical support were provided by the equipment suppliers. Training needs were, and are, systematically addressed.

The other firm, MW4, is an affiliate of a Swiss retailing firm. The plant was first set up by Swiss technicians with used equipment, and some stayed on to operate the plant for several years. For a long time the firm was the main manufacturer of aluminium doors and windows in Ghana. The initial investment, with simple bending and cutting machines, was probably well implemented. However, the old equipment was never renovated, and today the plant is obsolete and uncompetitive. The local management and the Swiss parent failed to respond positively to the liberalisation, with the result that the firm is rapidly losing market share.

The third group of metal working firms contains four smaller firms. Two of these make machines (mainly simple equipment for food processing), and two make structural products of iron and steel. The two machinery makers are interesting for several (and opposing) aspects of their TC development, taken up below. One of them, MW5, was set up by a small blacksmith who 'graduated' into the formal sector. It started with used machine tools bought locally, and added other used machines later. The owner reconditioned these machines and made a few himself. All the equipment was very simple and of old design, with little capability to make precision products. The entrepreneur made no attempt to move to more modern, higher productivity technologies. The other firm, MW7, also started with used equipment, but took a different tack. The entrepreneur was a plant engineer who could evaluate modern equipment and make an informed selection based on catalogues and visits to suppliers. Its intial purchase, in the UK, was thus of relatively high quality and modern vintage. This gave it a significantly better technological base than the 'graduating' firm.

The other two small firms differ from each other. One is essentially a welding operation with simple equipment bought used from local firms. The other is in much more advanced fabrication, and was started by an engineer who searched in Germany for used equipment. The sellers trained him and he did the layout, engineering and worker training himself subsequently.

The metal working industry in Ghana is at an early stage of development, and, with the exception of the first group (which is not representative of the industry at large), is confined to relatively 'easy' technologies with simple processes and products. In this part of the industry, the right equipment is not difficult to locate (and consists mainly of general purpose machine tools of older vintage). Used machines are generally adequate to make simple products for local consumption. However, a certain effort is required to find even such equipment and transfer the necessary skills. While many of the sample firms have been able to do this, some firms have been far more capable than others. In the case of the more complex technologies, the lack of investment and other technical capabilities has led to poor choice, transfer and absorption of technologies. Perhaps state ownership has constituted an added disadvantage.

Conclusion

In general, investment capabilities can be rated as weak in Ghana relative to those in the more industrialised developing countries. The only exceptions are the MNC affiliates, which can draw upon the highly developed capabilities of their parent companies to mount relatively complex investments. However, none have transferred their most advanced technologies to Ghana, given the low level of production capabilities there, nor have they invested in developing investment skills in their local employees. Among local firms, investment capabilities revolve around the fairly simple technologies in use in Ghana. Here, many enterprises do show adequate ability to find and transfer technologies. The needs of information, process engineering and training are met by seeking out foreign sources, and some firms devote a lot of effort to this process. At the same time, a number of firms do not invest capably even at this level. These are either small, traditional enterprises (particularly in wood and metal working) that do not know how to set about investing efficiently, or enterprises entering relatively complex (but fairly mature) technologies without adequate preparation (like the steel works). There is practically no institutional or consultancy support available locally for investors, and the smaller firms seem to come off worst in using the imperfect information market for technology.

PRODUCTION CAPABILITIES

Introduction

Production capabilities can be considered under two broad headings: process technology and product technology. Industrial engineering as a distinct discipline is so rare in Ghana as not to merit separate discussion. Process technology can be considered under various headings like maintenance, quality control (QC), plant layout, productivity monitoring, improvement in equipment and processes, adaptation to raw materials, and so on. Product technology includes design of products and changes or improvements to this design, as well as the introduction of new product designs.

Not all these categories will be considered in each case, only the ones considered significant. The technological needs of production processes vary by industry. In broad terms, for the present spread of activities, garment manufacture has the least demanding processes, and certain forms of food processing and metal working the most demanding. Each industry is now taken in turn.

Process Technology: Textiles and Garments

There are, as noted, two distinct segments in this activity, garments and other products. The four garment manufacturers operate with 14–25-year-old sewing machines. These are relatively easy to maintain and service, but only one firm (TG1) has a regular routine for maintenance and servicing; it is also the only firm with an in-house workshop with the capacity to carry out repairs and make some spares. This enables it to keep its plant running better and at lower cost than its competitors. Only TG1 has a full-time QC department and keeps track of its reject rates; the others (mainly the owners personally) do *ad hoc* checks on the finished product and do not check reject rates.

Efficient garment plants (as evidence from export-oriented plants in the NIEs suggests) need to adjust their layout every time they shift to different product patterns. None of the sample firms, with the exception of TG1, was even aware of the need to do this. TG1 had introduced computer-aided design technology for making logos on T-shirts – the only firm to do so in Ghana. Finally, it was the only firm to have a formal productivity monitoring system and a payment system based on worker productivity.

Thus, TG1 emerges as clearly the most capable firm in garments as far as process technology is concerned. It has the best quality of the sample firms, and has been able to increase its local market share and capacity utilisation in the past three years. However, its sales are essentially limited to markets where there is no direct import competition. According to its own calculation, its products are 15–20 per cent more expensive than competing products from Hong Kong, despite transport costs and the much higher wages in the latter. Using this as the technical benchmark for the best garment firm in the country gives some indication of the extent to which process technologies in the industry lag behind world levels.

As for the other textile products, the three firms concerned have fairly old equipment. Maintenance was poor in the net manufacturer, reasonable in the synthetic leather firm and good in the knitwear firm. The experience of this last firm, TG5, is worth noting. It was the only surviving knitwear firm in Ghana, the others all having caved in to import competition. It had been taken into state hands for twelve years and was badly run down when it was returned to its original Lebanese owner in 1990. His two sons (both technically trained) then managed to refurbish about one-tenth of the plant, with one in full charge of production, training, and maintenance. He looked after the old machines constantly and carefully.

In addition, various improvements were made to the equipment to raise productivity and change the process: the knitting process was adapted to make a lighter fabric; machine controls were brought up to date and settings adjusted; there was better material control and better quality; work practices were improved; and quality was carefully checked. As a result, machines per worker rose threefold, while machine productivity rose by 95 per cent. The firm was surviving the fierce import competition and was even negotiating an export order in the UK. This process of technological upgrading in TG5 is the most successful in this industry. The other textile firms had not done much to raise their productivity. The net firm was under receivership after making large losses. The synthetic leather firm was stagnating.

Process Technology: Food Processing

In the food processing industry, the technology in the sample firms is generally quite capital intensive, and needs a combination of process, food chemistry and electromechanical engineering skills. The three MNC affiliates draw heavily on their parent companies for technological inputs, with one (FP2) having a long-term technical assistance agreement for which it pays 2 per cent of sales.

Having such access does not, however, ensure technical efficiency. In this complex industry, constant local technical efforts are essential to utilise efficiently what is available from the parent company. Take, for instance, the case of FP1, an affiliate of one of the world's leading food MNCs, with operations in practically all developing countries.

During the 1980s, import constraints and slack local management in Ghana led to deteriorating quality, poor maintenance and low productivity. A worldwide comparison of productivity of a hundred-odd affiliates by the head office showed that in 1992 the Ghanaian affiliate had the lowest productivity of all FP1 operations worldwide. In addition, it found that its operations in Sub-Saharan Africa generally had lower productivity than those in other developing countries. This shows the significance of local TCs in operating similar technologies with similar levels of training and access to parent knowhow.

Similarly, poor expatriate management in the dairy products firm (FP6) prior to 1989 led to falling productivity and losses in market share. Both affiliates recently replaced their managers and were starting to invest in productivity and quality-raising measures. FP1 had introduced strict industrial engineering routines to raise productivity in every aspect of the operation, making only small new investments. FP6 brought in well-qualified new maintenance personnel, set up a good QC laboratory, improved the layout and was investing in new plant. Its market performance improved as a result.

The productivity performance of these affiliates, especially FP1, again provides a benchmark to evaluate technical efficiency in the best local firm in Ghana in food processing. Its ranking by world standards indicates how much further behind other local firms are likely to be. This has important implications for developing an export-oriented food processing industry, a likely candidate in view of Ghana's agricultural resources.

The third affiliate (FP2) still operates with 40–50-year-old equipment, with good maintenance and QC facilities and regular inputs of technical assistance from the parent company. It has, however, been content to continue to 'tick over' without upgrading its plant or making stringent efforts to raise productivity.

The flour mill, with its Italian turnkey plant, has regular visits by Italian technicians and absorbed good maintenance and operational practices. It has developed the necessary skills among local personnel to meet quality standards for flour. The new plant did not need adaptation and is almost competitive with imports: it claims to be 10 per cent more expensive because of the smaller scale of operations. It has, along with other flour mills, been able to persuade the government to grant tariff protection. If its claims are to be believed, this firm is an example of efficient technology transfer and absorption.

The two fruit and vegetable processors, FP3 and FP7, present an interesting contrast between an established state-owned firm and a new private entrant. The former owns its own plantations, and exports some ethnic processed foods (eggplant and palmnut soup). The latter has no plantations and is entirely domestic-market based. Yet FP7, with its new products (see below), and better process capabilities and QC, has been able to take domestic market share for fruit juice drinks away from FP3. The latter has done little to improve its processes over time, and claims to suffer from a lack of spare parts (though imports were liberalised in the mid-1980s). FP7 seems far more dynamic in its operations and is expanding into new packaging technology.

The last food processor, the biscuit manufacturer FP4, is technologically interesting, rather like the knitwear firm mentioned earlier. It has obsolete, 50-year-old equipment, yet is the only biscuit firm in Ghana to have survived import competition. It did this by reducing its product range to the cheapest (cabin) biscuits, sold without packaging (which is expensive in Ghana and not of good quality), and by greatly boosting its productivity.[5] Its production manager rearranged the layout, changed the electricals and generally improved the obsolete equipment in various ways. These changes reduced breakdowns and raised machine output threefold, and the firm now sells as many cabin biscuits as it can make.

There is more evidence of competent process technology in the food processing industry than in garments. The presence of MNCs partly accounts for this, but there are some local firms that also display systematic approaches to technology development.

Process Technology: Wood Working

In the wood-working industry, the situation is more akin to that in garments. Only two of the sample firms, WW1 and WW3, show evidence of reasonable mastery of process technology. WW1 now claims to be exporting one-third of its output, but this is only in the past year, and it is still a minor exporter compared to the Scandinavian firm (not in this sample), which accounts for some 95 per cent of Ghana's furniture exports.[6] WW3 is entirely domestic-market oriented. Both firms have invested in kiln-drying facilities, and have well-maintained plants. WW1, run by an Italian furniture engineer, has very good QC, and makes various efforts to raise productivity and improve finish (it is classified among the top ten furniture firms in Ghana by the export promotion council). WW3's QC is not quite as good and its production planning is weak. Nevertheless, it is relatively efficient and was identified by a UNIDO report as having export potential.

None of the other firms in the sample comes near these two in terms of process technology. It is instructive to compare WW4 with WW3. WW4 is a firm that has 'graduated' from being a micro-sized carpenter's shop, and may thus offer insights (like the metal working firm MW5, see below) into this potentially important phenomenon. Both the firms are of roughly equal size. However, process capabilities in WW4 are significantly weaker than in WW3. In comparison with the latter, the former's equipment is poorly maintained and laid out, production planning is weak, and quality is relatively low. The other large firm, WW2, has extremely old equipment that has not been rehabilitated, and has poor QC and low productivity. Its only attempts at improvement have been directed at its saw-milling operations.

The two medium-sized firms are rather like WW4, only with somewhat lower efficiency. The small-sized firms are simpler operations, using hand tools and traditional technologies that have not been improved over time.

Thus, with the possible exception of WW1 and WW3, the general level of process capabilities in the sample furniture firms is rather low. The natural protection given by transport costs, local raw materials and the pattern of local demand allows these firms to survive, though only the two better ones have registered growth in the past three to four years. Two of the firms have 'graduated' from micro traditional enterprises, but their process capabilities have not developed beyond a certain extent, and they do not match those of more 'modern' enterprises.

Process Technology: Metal Working

In the metal-working industry, the enormous differences between the technologies of the different enterprises have to be taken into account in assessing process capabilities. On the one hand is MW1 with its complex steel smelting and rolling technologies, on the other MW6 with simple welding and shaping operations.

MW1 is one of three manufacturers of rods for the construction industry in Ghana, using scrap for smelting in an electric arc furnace and rolling the billets produced into rods of different sizes and specifications. Its process is less cost efficient than a competitor with a new plant (under construction), but more efficient than another plant of similar age to itself. The initial technology transfer was, as noted, not successful; neither was a later attempt to rectify it by bringing in other foreign consultants. In about 25 years of operation, the firm managed neither to bring its facilities into full operation nor to master properly the technologies that were running. By the time new Indian management was brought in (in 1991) the plant was operating at 10 per cent capacity.

In a year the new management, using 17 Indian steel technicians and engineers, managed with very little new investment to put large parts of the plant into operational condition (see Appendix D). This is a clear example of how the lack of process capabilities can cripple a plant with complex technology, and the injection of a modest amount of such capabilities can raise productivity and efficiency without costly new plant. The changes included: bringing the second (of two) furnaces into operation; improving the performance of the first furnace so that it could operate continuously; putting the continuous casting machine into operation (by locating and installing some missing components); adjusting the settings of the rolling mill so that it suffered less break-downs and had lower costs; refurbishing motors that had been run down; starting the foundry which had never been installed; improving main-tenance, and so on. Further changes and improvements are planned, including a costly new layout to cut energy and transport costs. The firm is able to meet UK standards for its products, and was coping with import competition (though it claimed that a 15 per cent tariff would enable it to generate surpluses for reinvestment and expansion).

This sort of injection of TCs is what the other state-owned plant, MW8, seems to lack. Its foundry has not been put into operation since its start seven years ago. The firm never had the technical skills to operate the facilities, and has waited for foreign assistance to sort out its problems. The German aid agency sent two people, a technician and a student (both in mechanical rather than metallurgical engineer-ing) in 1990; they helped to activate the machine shop but could not repair and start the foundry.

In the three aluminium products firms, by contrast, the technology is relatively simple and there were experienced staff available locally (some with training in other countries like Nigeria). This enabled MW2 (making pots and pans) to start production with relatively little difficulty. However, the firm had to find an engineer within a year to maintain and improve its used machines and raise quality. The MW3 plant was started by an Israeli engineer who set up good maintenance and qual-ity procedures, and today there is an engineer in charge of mainte-nance with a supporting team. Quality was better than local competitors, spurred by the foreign construction companies that were its main cus-tomers. In 1987 the firm was taken over by the entrepreneur's foreign-trained son, who continued and strengthened the practices started earlier, and introduced incentive schemes to raise worker productivity. The equipment was renovated, and some sophisticated new machines (like a numerically controlled glass cutter) added, and the firm has become the largest manufacturer in its field in the country. This is leading the firm to start introducing ISO 9000 standards (referred to in Chapter 2), the only firm we encountered in Ghana to do so.

The third aluminium products firm, MW4, is an affiliate of a Swiss retailing firm. It has been long established in Ghana, but has been relatively stagnant and has lost its dominant market position. Its old equipment has minimal maintenance, and productivity has declined since Swiss technicians left in the late 1970s. There was no QC system and product quality was poor. This long period of technical sloth may end under a new technical manager, but so far it remains backward.

The two machinery makers specialise in simple equipment for food and wood processing, but offer interesting contrasts in technological capabilities. One (MW5), the one that 'graduated' from micro, traditional blacksmith status to medium size, remains under the control of the original entrepreneur, who has a rigid traditional approach to production and training. The other (MW7) was started by a UK-trained plant engineer who worked in the UK, taught in the University of Science and Technology in Kumasi and had good contacts with their Technology Transfer Centre.

While MW5's owner showed considerable ingenuity and skills in copying foreign products, using old equipment and building simple machines of his own (the only firm in the sample to do so), its methods of maintenance, QC, training and production remained traditional and static. As a result, the firm began to lose to import competition from countries like India that also makes simple food processing equipment, but with a better finish and design, and more powerful machines. MW7, on the other hand, had more modern (though also used) equipment, which was better maintained. The level of workmanship and training was higher, products were more reliable and better designed, manufacturing techniques were superior and after-sales service was highly regarded. As a result, MW7 was able to increase its sales and achieve full capacity utilisation. Thus, even at this level the input of higher technological capabilities made a vital difference to performance.

The other two metal-working firms are in welding and structural operations. One (MW6) is a semi-permanent activity based on simple welding techniques, the other (MW9) is a more advanced operation. The first has primitive and static process technologies. The second has not improved its capabilities sufficiently to be able to compete with imports from neighbouring countries and has been forced to give up making trailers for simpler chutes for the mining industry. Its TCs, while at a higher level, are not dynamic.

The metal-working firms thus show a mixture of process engineering capabilities. In the more demanding activities, of which there are few in the country, there are low levels of capabilities and little evidence of indigenous upgrading. However, the injection of a relatively modest number of technically skilled personnel can make an enormous difference, even without the need for large new investments. In simpler activities, some local firms do show the ability to master the processes, though they do not go further in terms of improving them. Others lack this capability and are being hurt by the new competitive environment.

Product Technology

This section can be quite brief, since there is little independent product design capability in the sample apart from the copying of imported products and designs. In garments, the markets served need little design effort – most uniforms are designed by the customer, though some school uniform designs are suggested by the firms. There is no evidence of innovativeness in design, apart from TG1's attempt to use CAD technology to design logos for T-shirts. The quality of garments is generally lower than imports, though TG1 and TG5 claim to be able to match this.

In food processing, the MNC affiliates get almost all their product technology from their parents, and after the liberalisation several new products are being introduced into Ghana. However, some adaptations have been made locally also: FP1 introduced two products in the early 1980s to compensate for the lack of imported inputs, but these were dropped later because their quality was deficient by parent-company standards. No local product development is planned, and the parent is setting up a research centre in Abidjan to serve Africa as a whole. FP2 adapted one of its main products by downgrading it to make it more affordable; this was done in the QC laboratory and is still made. The dairy product firm adapted its yoghurt to use local pineapples. These efforts are relatively modest, and the affiliates do not have any intention of developing product capabilities locally.

Of the local firms, the two fruit processors have developed new products in their QC laboratories. The private firm FP7 seems to have been somewhat more innovative in this respect, with its new formula for a mixed fruit juice-based drink. It is interesting to note that QC laboratories are the only facilities in these firms, as well as the MNC affiliates, with the facilities and skills needed to engage in product development. It is these labs that provide a focal point for (fairly rudimentary) product development effort, the nearest to formal R&D that we found in the case studies.

The wood-working industry displays practically no independent design capabilities. Most designs, whether chosen by the firms or by the customers, come from foreign magazines and catalogues. However, the ability to interpret these designs in production is also low. The designs are sketched crudely without proper technical specifications, and 'interpreted' by the craftsmen. The only firm that has better capabilities in formalising the interpretation process is WW1, with its Italian entrepreneur. The general lack of precision and training constitutes a major handicap to achieving levels of uniform quality and finish that could enable entry into export markets.

In the metal-working industry design activity at some level is inherent to production, since many of the products have to be crafted to specific needs. For this reason, the sample firms making pots, pans, doors, windows and food-processing equipment have to tailor their products to customer demands. However, this design activity is at a fairly low level, with few research or information needs, no sustained experimentation, and undemanding process specifications. Most designs are based on imported concepts, implemented without rigorous stress on tolerances and quality. The only firm that is worth noting is MW7, where the owner has introduced some (his estimate was 25) new products of his own design: even these are essentially adaptations of products that exist elsewhere. Much of the design effort consists of adding new features to older products to make them more reliable and stronger. Even this level of effort, however, marks this firm as one of the best in the sample.

In general, product engineering capabilities remain relatively poor in the sample. This is not unexpected at this stage of industrial development, and it is likely that these capabilities will start to emerge only when industrialisation has reached more sophisticated levels. There seems to be no effort on the part of foreign or local firms to build up product engineering capabilities, and there is no effective institutional assistance to firms to undertake product development (see below).

LINKAGE CAPABILITIES

Growing inter-firm and inter-industry linkages, defined as relationships that go beyond the anonymous purchase of products or services and involve exchanges of information, skills and other factors, are an essential feature of industrial development. They permit increasing specialisation, allowing firms to become more efficient. They are a very effective form of technology and information diffusion, especially from large to small enterprises. They allow for greater deepening of the industrial structure, and so less dependence on imported parts, components and services. In addition, linkages with institutions that provide training, technical information and services, and do research, can provide a valuable input into industrial capabilities, by undertaking activities with infrastructural (public goods) characteristics and filling in for deficient markets.

The Ghanaian sample has very low levels of linkages of both kinds. There is little subcontracting or local procurement of manufactured inputs and spare parts. Apart from the purchase of some repair services, large firms in the formal sector have practically no relations with small firms, especially with those in the informal sector. There is some movement of personnel across firms, more commonly among small traditional firms (see Chapter 6), but beyond this information and technology diffusion is minimal. Even the metal-working industry, normally the most linkage-intensive of all manufacturing activities, has practically no subcontracting in Ghana.

As far as linkages with technology institutions and universities are concerned, the situation is not much better. Table 5.2 shows the incidence of institutional linkages in 1991 for each of the sample firms. It also shows the firms' ranking (from 1 to 5) of the quality of service provided by each of the main institutions.

The most common interaction has been with the Ghana Standards Board. The GSB visits many of the firms on a regular basis to check the quality of their products, with the food industry having the highest incidence of contacts. The quality of the interaction is rated at the intermediate level. However, all the firms stressed that the GSB does not go beyond checking quality; it does not provide advice on how to improve quality or to prepare to meet international standards (this has been noted above, in chapter 2). It does not therefore perform the valuable function – of diffusing technological information and raising quality that good standards institutions do in more developed economies.

The other institutions used on occasion by the sample are the Food Research Institute and the Kumasi University of Science and Technology. The former is used by food processing firms primarily to do tests (for instance, microbiological tests for FP2, or quality checks for the flour firm) rather than to help with process or product technology.

Table 5.2   Linkages with science and technology institutions: frequency of use last year (A) and perceived quality of service (B)

Firm	Food Research Institute		Ghana Standards Board		Kumasi Technical University		GRATIS		Other	
	(A)	(B)	(A)	(B)	(A)	(B)	(A)	(B)	(A)	(B)
Textiles and garments										
TG1	0	–	0	–	0	–	0	–	0	–
TG2	0	–	2	–	0	–	0	–	0	–
TG3	0	–	0	–	1	2	0	–	0	–
TG4	0	–	1	3	0	–	0	–	0	–
TG5	0	–	1	4	0	–	0	–	0	–
TG6	0	–	0	–	0	–	0	–	0	–
TG7	0	–	0	–	0	–	0	–	0	–
TG8	0	–	0	–	0	–	0	–	0	–
Food processing										
FP1	2	3	1	3	0	–	0	–	0	–
FP2	52	3	1	–	0	–	0	–	0	–
FP3	1	–	2	3	0	–	0	–	0	–
FP4	0	–	0	–	0	–	0	–	0	–
FP5	4	3	12	–	0	–	2	3	0	–
FP6	0	–	1	3	0	–	0	–	0	–
FP7	2	3	4	–	0	–	0	–	0	–
Wood working										
WW1	0	–	0	–	0	–	0	–	3	5
WW2	0	–	0	–	0	–	0	–	0	–
WW3	0	–	0	–	0	–	0	–	0	–
WW4	0	–	1	2	0	–	0	–	0	–
WW5	0	–	0	–	0	–	0	–	0	–
WW6	0	–	0	–	0	–	0	–	0	–
WW7	0	–	0	–	0	–	0	–	0	–
WW8	0	–	0	–	0	–	0	–	0	–
Metal working										
MW1	0	–	0	–	0	–	0	–	0	–
MW2	0	–	2	3	0	–	0	–	5	4
MW3	0	–	1	2	0	–	0	–	0	–
MW4	0	–	1	–	0	–	0	–	0	–
MW5	0	–	0	–	0	–	0	–	0	–
MW6	0	–	0	–	0	–	0	–	0	–
MW7	0	–	1	2	1	2	0	–	0	–
MW8	0	–	0	–	6	2	0	–	0	–
MW9	0	–	0	–	0	–	0	–	0	–

A Number of times this institution was used last year.
B Rating is on a scale of 1 to 5 where 1 is very poor and 5 is very good.

Only one firm, the FP1 multinational affiliate, approached the FRI to carry out a joint research project. This was to develop an enzyme for a fermented breakfast cereal; if successful, it will be sent to the parent company for further testing.

The UST was used by one garment firm to repair equipment, by MW7 in the development of a shea-butter-kneading machine (but in this case the firm sold technical services to the UST rather than the other way around), and by MW8 (for some technical assistance). There is again little evidence of active technology development or transfer by the university to the sample manufacturing firms.

In general, therefore, the sample evidence confirms the findings of other studies that the institutional system has minimal linkages with the manufacturing sector. This may reflect deficiencies on both sides: the firms may lack the ability to identify their technical problems and formulate them into projects that can be dealt with by institutions, and the institutions may lack the skills and equipment to offer practical assistance. Both may have other reasons for hesitation in approaching each other.

Conclusions

Let us conclude this analysis of the technological capabilities of the sample firms. The general level of TCs in the sample, which is itself biased towards the larger and better firm in the country, is very low, by standards not only of developed countries but also of the industrialising developing countries of Asia and Latin America. It suggests that Ghanaian manufacturing at large has only been able to develop a rather limited range of capabilities in a few mature, simple technologies. There is little sign of dynamism in any of the main forms of capability development. The country is not in a position to launch a broad-based export thrust in response to the new incentive regime, unless new TCs are introduced by foreign investors or created by investments in local skills and technical effort.

The liberalisation has exposed these weaknesses in activities that face import competition. The evidence suggests relatively few firms have been able to withstand unfettered import competition. As noted, some firms serve niche markets where location constitutes a significant competitive advantage (uniforms in garment manufacture, structural products for building), where demand is for low income products not easily met by imports (cabin biscuits, lightweight pots and pans), or where product requirements are very specific (some food processing equipment).[7] Some have a resource cost advantage (fruit juice processing, dairy products, wood products and furniture, aluminium products). And some MNC affiliates may not be fully competitive, but may control a strong brand where import competition comes only from another affiliate of the same company, and so is unlikely to be a real threat (some processed foods and beverages).

In the case study sample, only three firms currently face the full brunt of direct import competition.[8] Most of the non-competent firms are far less able to meet import competition. Clearly the base of manufacturing competitiveness is small and narrow in the sample, and is likely to be even more so in Ghanaian industry at large where there is a much larger proportion of small, low productivity firms. What is more significant for the future growth of industry in the liberalised setting, the firms that did have locational or resource advantages showed few signs of gearing up for export markets to exploit those advantages.

Nevertheless, the case studies reveal that beneath this generally gloomy surface there are many significant differences between firms. Some are clearly doing better, and are able to deploy more technological capabilities, than others. It is firms like these that will be able to develop the TCs needed to grow in the future. It is clearly important for Ghana's industrial development to understand what has enabled some firms to be technologically more competent. This is the theme of later discussion; the identification of the competent firms is taken up in the next chapter.

6 Technologically 'Competent' Firms

INTRODUCTION

We have used the information from the case studies to draw up a list of technologically 'competent' firms. The choice is based on a combination of indicators, since much of the data reviewed above is qualitative. Most of the competent firms were easy to identify, by virtue of their clearly superior investment and production engineering capabilities. There were some where some discretion had to be exercised, but these are very few and do not distort the main findings.

The list, impressionistic though it is, is similar to standard industry analyses of industrial competence widely used by international consultants for policy analysis. In the present case, it is the first such effort in Ghana and will be used in the analysis of the determinants of technological development conducted in the next three chapters.

LIST OF 'COMPETENT' FIRMS

Table 6.1 shows the 13 firms that we have identified as relatively competent. It has to be emphasised that inclusion in this list does not necessarily mean that they are technologically capable by world standards. The evidence suggests that the level of technological mastery of the technologies in place is relatively poor. There is little or no process or product development by sample firms that can be regarded as 'innovative'. The kind of 'minor innovation' that has been found in many more industrialised developing countries, leading to the raising of machine productivity beyond its design capacity, the use of completely different raw materials, the development of technologically complex new products, and so on, are rarely found in the Ghanaian sample. In general, the best that the competent firms can do is to use imported technologies relatively well and make some adaptations to local circumstances.

Let us now look at some general features of the competent firms.

Table 6.1   Technologically competent firms in sample

Firm	Industry	Employment	Age of firm	Location[1]	Ownership[2]	Market performance
TG1	Garments	90	18	Accra	LNA	Growing
TG5	Garments	24	22	Accra	LNA	Reviving[3]
FP1	Food	650	31	Accra	Foreign	Growing
FP4	Food	200	36	Accra	LNA	Reviving[4]
FP5	Food	200	3	Accra	LA	Growing
FP6	Food	172	32	Accra	Foreign	Growing
FP7	Food	80	8	Accra	LA	Growing
WW1	Wood	267	14	Accra	Foreign	Growing
WW3	Wood	147	10	Accra	LA	Growing
MW1	Metal	430	27	Accra	Foreign	Growing
MW2	Metals	150	5	Accra	LA	Growing
MW3	Metals	71	21	Accra	LA	Growing
MW7	Metals	19	20	Kumasi	LA	Growing

[1] Accra refers to greater Accra, including Tema and surrounding areas.
[2] LNA stands for local non-American, LA for local African.
[3] Sales are starting to pick up after severe recession and handing back of firm from state management to owner.
[4] Sales started to revive last year.

Of these 13 firms (41 per cent of the sample), the largest number (5) are in the food processing industry, followed by metal working (4); textiles and garments and wood working have 2 firms each. While one should not read too much into the industrial distribution of such a small sample of firms, it is worth remarking on the fact that the two activities in which Ghana may be expected on *a priori* grounds, and on the basis of the experience of other developing regions, to have a comparative advantage are garments (which is low technology and labour-intensive) and furniture (which is local resource-based and labour-intensive). Yet these activities seem generally to register low levels of TC, not just in the sample but also in the industry more generally (see the background sections in the relevant appendices).

The food-processing and metal-working industries, with relatively more competent firms, are essentially oriented to the domestic market. In addition, many of the competent firms in metal working, normally an engine of technological development, are in relatively simple technologies. There is little sign that more advanced engineering activities are emerging in Ghana. The implications of these trends for future growth and export dynamism are not very promising.

Four of the firms are foreign controlled (two being part of large MNCs); three are owned by local non-Africans and the remaining six by local Africans. This last group will be analysed at greater length when the entrepreneurial background of the firms is discussed in the next chapter. All the competent firms are located in or around Accra with the exception of MW7 which is in Kumasi.

STATISTICALLY SIGNIFICANT FEATURES

To anticipate some of the discussion below, it would be useful to compare some of the characteristics of technologically competent and other sample firms. Table 6.2 shows the results of T-tests on the means of several features of the two groups on which data are available (the small size of the sample precluded more powerful statistical tests). The salient points are as follows.

1. **Technologically competent firms are larger than other firms.** There is a statistically significant difference between the average employment size of the two groups, with the mean for the competent firms coming to 192 employees and for the other firms 70 employees. Of the 13 firms in the Table, 8 are large (over 100 employees), 3 are medium-sized (30–99) and only 2 are small (below 30).

The correlation between size and competence may indicate one or more of three things. First, it may indicate that firms have reached large size because they were competent, i.e. they invested earlier in TC development to a greater extent, or more effectively, than other firms (this applies to foreign firms also, in that the parent companies became MNCs because they had certain 'ownership' advantages based on technology). Second, it may be due to the distribution of activities and technologies in the sample, i.e. in many of the technologies covered there were economies of specialisation and size that meant that only large firms could reach efficient levels of TCs. Third, it may reflect the existence of market segmentation, i.e. only firms above a certain size were able to gain access to the skills, information and credit needed to be competent.

It is not possible to say firmly which of these explanations has most validity, and there is probably some validity in each. The distribution of the firms in the case studies may in some cases have led to the association between size and competence, particularly in the sample food-processing firms (given the scale-intensive processes used in modern food processing, it is difficult to imagine that FP1 could be replicated

Table 6.2 T-test to compare means of technologically competent firms and other firms

	Employment (nos.)	Age in production in 1992 (years)	Capacity utilisation rate (%)	% LNA/ foreign equity	Av. wage (US$)	Entrep. edn (years)[g]	Prod. Man. edn (years)[g]	Scien., eng. & tech. (% of emp.)	Eng. only (% of emp.)	Quality control/ maint. manpower (% of emp.)
Technologically Competent Firms[a]										
Observations	13	13	12	13	13	13	13	13	13	11
Mean	192.31	19.00	66.00	35.38	64.59	17.08	15.54	6.68	1.59	6.50
Standard deviation	176.09	10.65	29.34	38.27	21.41	3.20	2.37	6.15	1.74	3.36
Other Firms[b]										
Observations	18	18	13	18	18	18	18	17	18	18
Mean	69.67	22.72	32.00	18.89	43.91	11.72	8.89	2.80	0.87	1.80
Standard deviation	81.00	14.91	16.85	34.45	15.94	3.44	6.54	2.73	2.25	3.52
T-statistic[c]	2.6*	−0.76	3.6*[d]	1.26	3.09*	4.50*	3.47*	2.25*[f]	0.93	3.15*[e]

[a] TG1, TG5, FP1, FP4 FP5, FP7, FP6, WW1, WW3, MW1, MW2, MW3 and MW7.

[b] TG2, TG3, TG4, TG6, TG7, FP2, FP3, WW2, WW4, WW5, WW6, WW7, WW8, MW4, MW5, MW6, MW8 and MW9.

[c] * denotes statistical significance at 5% level (with 29 degrees of freedom unless stated otherwise). Small sample hypothesis test.

[d] The t-test for this variable used 23 degrees of freedom.

[e] The t-test for this variable used 28 degrees of freedom.

[f] The t-test for this variable used 27 degrees of freedom.

[g] The number of years of education were computed as follows: middle school (8 years), secondary school (12 years), diploma (14 years), B.Sc. (17 years), M.Sc. (20 years), PhD (22 years).

on a small scale). Even in these technologies, however, the fact that certain firms were competent could be traced to their TC efforts rather than to size *per se*. In the case of garment, wood-working or most metal-working (apart from MW1) technologies, where the size threshold for competence was relatively low, there were still large differences in competence between firms of similar sizes.

This suggests again that technical competence was directly traceable to deliberate investments in TC development. Market segmentation may well exist in Ghana (as in all developing countries, formal credit markets tend to be biased against small firms). The analysis of the panel data above suggests that such segmentation exists, but that it does not account for the whole difference in performance between firms of similar sizes. The other factors that show up as important determinants of competence in the following chapters suggest that segmented factor markets play a relatively minor role.

2. There is no significant difference between the age in production of the two groups. **The technological learning process is not a simple function of years of experience**, but more the result of a deliberate investment in creating skills and information. The ability to undertake this investment is dependent on several factors apart from age. It is interesting to note, however, that only three of the competent firms were formed after the start of the ERP.

3. As may be expected, **performance indicators like growth and capacity utilisation significantly better** in technologically capable firms than in other firms.

4. **Ownership does not seem to matter**. The division of the sample firms by African and other forms of ownership (foreign or local non-African) fails to show statistical significance. Though the mean for non-African ownership is higher in capable firms, the T-statistic fails to reach acceptable levels. This seems surprising at first sight, since there is a general presumption that MNCs would have greater TCs than local firms in a less-industrialised country like Ghana. The reason is probably the small size and purposive nature of the sample, but it may also lie in the fact that existing levels of TCs reflect the legacy of decades of relative isolation and hardship. Even MNCs have to make do with the base of skills that is generally available: thus, in the longer term they may well develop better capabilities than local competitors but these capabilities may not match those of their affiliates in countries with higher levels of education, training and management experience.

5. **The average wage paid by capable firms is significantly higher** than in other firms (the means are $65 and $44 per month respectively).

This may be due to a number of factors, such as differences in size, capital intensity, labour market distortions, location and so on between the firms. It may, however, also indicate that capable firms employ workers with higher skill levels, give more training and then offer higher wages to retain workers, or are more productive for given skill levels for other reasons. The data do not allow these different hypotheses to be tested properly, but there is some evidence (see the next chapter) that the more competent firms do have higher skill levels that are related to their investments in TCs.

6. **There is a highly significant difference between the years of education of entrepreneurs (or managing directors) of competent and other firms.** The mean comes to 17.1 years for the former and 11.7 for the latter. This is an important point, explored further in the next chapter.

7. **There is a similar, and highly significant, difference between the education of the production managers**, with the mean being 15.5 years for competent firms and 8.9 years for other firms. This indicates that it is not just the 'vision' of the entrepreneur that matters, but that a technically competent production manager is also needed to catalyse the learning process (the role of the technological catalyst is discussed in the next chapter).

8. In terms of the employment of technical manpower, **competent firms have a significantly higher proportion of scientists, engineers and technicians** in their workforces than other firms (6.7 per cent compared to 2.8 per cent). They also have **larger proportions of employees in QC and maintenance** (6.5 per cent and 1.8 per cent) than other firms. This clearly shows the importance of having adequate 'receivers' to absorb new technologies and of paying adequate attention to certain vital process functions. However, the employment of engineers by themselves does not show any statistically significant difference.

Many of these results are expected from the literature and experience of technological development in other countries. It is nevertheless reassuring to have them show up so clearly in our sample. The following chapters explore some of them at greater length.

7 Human Capital and Technology Development

INTRODUCTION

The relevance of 'human capital' to technological competence and development is universally accepted in the literature. However, human capital may have many ramifications, each of which should be considered separately. A firm has a stock of skills given by the background and training of the entrepreneur or business leader, the production manager (who is generally the most important person, after the entrepreneur, in deciding the technical course of a firm), and other technically qualified personnel hired from the labour market (locally or abroad). In addition, it has workers of different levels of quality and education. Over time, it adds to this stock by investing in training its employees, in-house or externally (locally or abroad); it also loses skills as employees leave the firm to set up on their own or join other firms. These broad components of human capital are considered separately below.

ENTREPRENEURS

As noted in the last chapter, the level of education of entrepreneurs and managing directors of the technologically capable firms is significantly higher than in other firms.[1] This section explores in greater detail the characteristics of the sample entrepreneurs in general, and of the entrepreneurs of capable African firms in particular. Table 7.1 shows the age, education and origin of the present entrepreneurs or Managing Directors (MDs) of each sample firm. These are discussed in turn for each industry.

In the *garments* industry, the average age of the entrepreneur (excluding the two on whom this is not known) is 62, and none has had university education. Most are secondary-school graduates, while two have had vocational training in dressmaking (both in the UK). This rather simple educational background is in keeping with the nature of the technology involved, especially for garment making. It has served

143

Table 7.1   Background of entrepreneur

Firm	Age (years)	Highest level of education	Educational specialisation at tertiary level	Origin
Textiles and garments				
TG1	67	Secondary	None	LNA
TG2	62	Secondary	None	LNA
TG3	n.a.	Diploma (abroad)	Dress making	LA
TG4	60	Secondary	None	LNA
TG5	71	Secondary	None	LNA
TG6	n.a.	Secondary	None	LA
TG7	56	Diploma (abroad)	Dress making	LA
TG8	58	Secondary	None	LA
Food processing				
FP1	n.a.	University (abroad)	Chemical eng.	Expatriate
FP2	n.a.	Secondary	None	LA
FP3	n.a.	Secondary	None	LA
FP4	68	B.Sc (abroad)	Food technology	LNA
FP5	n.a.	Chartered accountancy	Accountancy	LA
FP6	n.a.	B.Sc (abroad)	Management	Expatriate
FP7	n.a.	PhD (abroad)	Chemistry	LA
Wood working				
WW1	n.a.	B.Sc (abroad)	Wood working	Expatriate
WW2	63	BA (abroad)	Management	LA
WW3	42	BA (abroad)	Management	LA
WW4	65	Primary	None	LA
WW5	n.a.	Secondary	None	LNA
WW6	36	Middle school	None	LA
WW7	26	Middle school	None	LA
WW8	44	Middle school	None	LA
Metal working				
MW1	43	B.Sc (abroad)	Metallurgical eng.	Expatriate
MW2	46	BA	Business studies	LA
MW3	35	M.Sc (abroad)	Management	LA
MW4	n.a.	Diploma	n.a	LA
MW5	65	Middle school	None	LA
MW6	45	Middle school	None	LA
MW7	46	B.Sc (abroad)	Plant engineering	LA
MW8	n.a.	B.Sc (abroad)	Mechanical eng.	Expatriate
MW9	42	B.Sc (abroad)	Mechanical eng.	LNA

as the entry into manufacturing for some of the local non-Africans who were required to invest in industry under the old regime. Four of the current entrepreneurs are local Africans (one of these took over from a non-African) and four are local non-Africans (Lebanese or Syrian).

It is difficult to relate technological performance in this subsector to anything because of the generally declining state of all the firms. For what it is worth, however, the only relatively dynamic garment firm is run by a fairly old entrepreneur of Syrian origin with secondary education, and the only knitwear firm that is surviving the blast of import competition is run by an even older entrepreneur of Lebanese origin. Both come from trading backgrounds that give them commercial rather than industrial acumen, but perhaps this is what is needed to seek out and use mature technologies.

In *food processing*, where the technology is far more demanding and the sample firms larger, the background of the entrepreneurs/MDs tends to be much more impressive in educational terms. Five have university degrees, of which three are in chemistry or food technology from developed country universities. Two are secondary school graduates, FP3 and FP2, and have worked their way up in their firms. Two are expatriates (both from multinationals) and one is of Syrian origin (his family has been in food processing for generations, and his children run an ethnic foods plant in the UK). The best firms in the sample, FP1 (for its sophistication and size), FP6 (for quality production of dairy products), FP7 (a dynamic and innovative fruit-juices maker) and FP4 the biscuit firm (for its ability to survive in a highly import-penetrated segment), all have highly trained leaders.

In *wood working*, of the seven firms on which this information is available, the average age of the entrepreneur (46 years) is much lower than in textiles and garments, but the general level of education is higher, though not as high as in food processing. There are only two entrepreneurs with university degrees – these are the heads of the two firms classified as technologically capable. The MD of WW1 has a BSc in wood working, while the owner of WW3 has a Canadian management degree. The others are primary, middle or secondary school graduates. Of these, two (the owners of WW4 and WW6) started as traditional carpenters; WW4 was started by a carpenter's son, while WW6's owner did not come from a carpentry family but was an apprentice in a carpenter's workshop.

In *metal working*, the average age of the entrepreneur (46 years) is the same as in wood working, and the level of entrepreneurial education is somewhat higher. Of the eight entrepreneurs on whom information is available, five are university graduates, all trained abroad. Four of these have engineering degrees, one has a management degree. The two who have middle-school education only are in MW5 (the blacksmith who 'graduated' but now finds it difficult to keep up with the emerging technological challenge) and MW6, which is a simple welding operation.

Does the ownership of the enterprises have an impact on the characteristics of the entrepreneur or MD? The leaders of the MNC affiliates all have high levels of education and tend to be well trained in management. However, it is interesting to note that two of the affiliates in food processing suffered slack periods of management during the 1980s that led to declines in performance and efficiency. The parent company had to send out new MDs to remedy the situation. Being part of an MNC is not by itself a guarantee of leadership quality.

As far as local non-African entrepreneurs are concerned, the best firm in garments, the only surviving knitwear and biscuit firms, and a dynamic metal working firm, are all owned and managed by local Lebanese or Syrians. At the same time, there are three stagnant firms with similar ownership. There may be two *a priori* reasons for expecting local firms with non-African entrepreneurs to have a better technological performance: first, the owner may have longer industrial experience; second, he may have better connections overseas to access capital and technology. The first applies to a few of the firms. Some of the families had been in industry for generations and may have accumulated know-how that newcomers may lack; at the same time, some moved into manufacturing from commerce and brought only financial skills with them. Access to finance and technology overseas also applies to a few of the firms, and foreign connections helped in locating and buying equipment. But this advantage seems rather marginal. In general, however, the origin of local entrepreneurs does not seem to have been a powerful advantage in terms of developing technological capabilities.

It is interesting to look specifically at the characteristics of the entrepreneurs of the six capable African owned firms, two in food processing, one in furniture and three in metal working. Of these, the flour mill shows the capability to manage well the transfer and absorption of technology, while the fruit processing firm shows more innovative capabilities based on the application of scientific knowledge by the entrepreneur. The furniture firm WW3 shows good management skills, with the ability to tap the available sources of technology and technical skills in the country and overseas. The metal-working firms MW2 and MW3 show good mastery of their process technologies and the ability to find economical sources of equipment (the latter due partly to the Israeli partner who started the firm). MW7 shows good capabilities in all these activities as well as some product design ability, though not at an advanced level that would require formal R&D.

Table 7.2 shows the age, educational and work experience of these

Table 7.2   Characteristics of entrepreneurs of technologically capable
African firms[1]

Firm	Age of entrepreneur	Highest educational qualification	Subject of qualification	Previous work experience
FP5	n.a.[2]	Chartered Act. (L)	Accountancy	In other flour mill (L)
FP7	n.a.[3]	PhD (F)	Chemistry	Standards Board (L)
WW3	42	BA (F)	Management	Furniture firm (F)
MW2	46	BA (L)	Business, Accounting	Alum. Marketing (F)
MW3	35	MSc (F)	Management	Employed (F,L)[4]
MW7	46	BSc (F)	Plant Engineering	Univ. Lecturer (L)[5]

[1] Letters in brackets: L stands for local and F for foreign.
[2] Relatively young, probably in 40s. The firm was started by a group of similar young people.
[3] Probably in his 50s.
[4] The present entrepreneur was educated and worked a short while in the US before taking over father's business.
[5] The entrepreneur was a lecturer in the University of Science and Technology in Kumasi, and has kept connections with UST. He also had work experience in the UK, where he received his university training.

African entrepreneurs. It is clear that these entrepreneurs are relatively young and highly educated. Technical education *per se* is not a distinguishing feature, though in the case where it does exist it is a valuable asset to the firm. Most of the entrepreneurs are from a business studies background, and nearly all have some experience of working in a business, three having that experience overseas (generally the same line of business as their present one).

These characteristics have interesting, and potentially important, implications for TC development. Entrepreneurial success among Ghanaians is clearly associated with high levels of education.[2] This may simply reflect that better-educated entrepreneurs have better access to segmented factor markets and official favours. It may, on the other hand, imply that education is associated with qualities that are conducive to technological acumen: like analytical and organisational skills, an appreciation of technological factors, the ability to seek out necessary information and the relevant professionals, and a willingness to try new methods and technologies. There is evidence of market segmentation, but on the whole we find support for the hypothesis that education provides real benefit to technological effort (aided in some cases by relative youth).[3]

Work experience in general has obvious benefits for the accumulation of technical know-how and institutional and marketing skills. Work experience overseas probably gives exposure to a broader range of experience and techniques. These associations are not at all surprising, but it is interesting to have them show up so clearly in this sample.

The implication is clearly not that all African entrepreneurs have to be modern, well educated, young people with work experience. There are always exceptional entrepreneurs who are 'born and not made', and rise above the constraints of low educational status to use the skills of others in building up successful businesses. However, it is still likely to be true that success in modern industry is facilitated by the cognitive, social, technical and other skills imparted by education. In this context, it is important to reiterate that there are several enterprises in our sample that 'graduated' from micro status, where the entrepreneurs had low levels of education: none of these were able to seek the technologies and skills they needed because of the limited horizons and information of the entrepreneurs.[4] This may imply that policies that seek to base future industrial development (of Africa in general) on the 'natural' advantage of its myriad micro and informal enterprises, are ill-founded. If these enterprises lack the basic educational base on which to develop the TCs needed for modern industry, they are destined to die out as modern industry emerges (if it emerges) rather than be the seed bed for the future industrial entrepreneur in Africa.

The lack of entrepreneurship has often been held up as a cause of the poor performance of African industry. Since this project focused on existing firms, it could not address this larger question, of whether the general supply of entrepreneurship was ample or not. However, the evidence of this study suggests that there was no shortage of the 'animal spirits' that drive entrepreneurs to take risks in the hope of long-term profit. The issue seems more of whether the experience, education and perceptions of the entrepreneurs equipped them for the technological challenges facing them, rather than if there was a shortage of entrepreneurs in some generic sense. There seems to be emerging a class of entrepreneurs that is so equipped, though they may comprise a small proportion of the total population of business leaders in Ghanaian manufacturing.

PRODUCTION MANAGERS

The background of the production managers is directly relevant for explaining the ability of firms to develop technologically. As with entrepreneurs, there is a statistically significant difference in the years of education of production managers in technologically capable as compared to other firms.[5] This section looks at available data on them in greater detail.

Table 7.3 shows the educational background, origin and years in the present business of the production manager of 26 of the sample firms. Five of the firms do not have a production manager, one in garments and two each in metal working and wood working, none of whom shows up as technologically capable. They are generally small firms, though in each industry there are smaller firms that do have production managers, so the lack is not merely a matter of size.

The industries are taken in turn. In *garments*, the largest and most capable firm, TG1, has an expatriate (German) textile engineer who came to Ghana to install knitting machinery and settled down there. He has been with the firm for 12 years. Nearly all the technological capabilities that exist in this firm are directly traceable to this production manager (he is the technological 'catalyst' discussed later). He has introduced a high level of discipline in the workforce and systematically developed all the necessary capabilities to run an efficient business. He introduced the CAD system to TG1, which is used by a Ghanaian trained by him and has proved a competitive advantage to the firm.

The production manager of the knitwear firm is the second son of the owner. He has secondary school training, unlike his brother who studied textile design in the UK, but is exceptionally gifted with machinery. His long exposure to the firm's equipment has given him the capabilities needed to maintain, repair, adapt and improve the machines, and is the main reason why the firm has been able to survive with its ancient capital stock. He interacts with his designer brother on adapting the fabric (making it lighter to meet standards of import knitwear).

The two production managers employed by the dress makers TG3 and TG7 have only primary education, while the manager for the synthetic leather plant (which needs some chemical skills) has a polytechnic education in electrical engineering.

In the *food-processing* industry, each production manager is university trained, one with postgraduate education in food science (FP7). Three are mechanical engineers. There are two expatriates in MNCs (FP1 and FP6), while the third operates with a local biochemist. One firm (FP4) has a local non-African; the others are all Ghanaian Africans. The noteworthy one is the production manager of FP4, who used his mechanical engineering skills to transform the obsolete machinery into a well-functioning plant.

Table 7.3 Background of production manager

Firm	Years in present business	Highest level of education	Educational specialisation at tertiary level	Origin
Textiles and garments				
TG1	12	BSc (abroad)	Textile eng.	Expatriate
TG2	n.a.	Diploma	Electrical eng.	LA
TG3	n.a.	Primary	None	LA
TG4	10	Secondary	None	LA
TG5	2	Secondary	None	LNA
TG6	None			
TG7	n.a.	Primary	None	LA
TG8	n.a.	Secondary	None	LA
Food processing				
FP1	n.a.	BSc (abroad)	n.a.	Expatriate
FP2	n.a.	BSc	Biochemistry	LA
FP3	27	BSc	Mechanical eng	LA
FP4	2	BSc (abroad)	Mechanical eng	LNA
FP5	3	BSc	Mechanical eng	LA
FP6	n.a.	BSc (abroad)	Dairy studies	Expatriate
FP7	5	MSc (abroad)	Food science	LA
Wood working				
WW1	n.a.	Diploma	Joinery	LA
WW2	n.a.	Diploma	n.a.	LA
WW3	1	Diploma	Wood working	LA
WW4	15	Secondary	None	LA
WW5	n.a.	Diploma	n.a.	LNA
WW6	n.a.	Primary	None	LA
WW7	None			
WW8	None			
Metal working				
MW1	1	BSc (abroad)	Metallurgical	Expatriate
MW2	5	Secondary	None	LA
MW3	n.a.	Diploma	n.a.	LA
MW4	2	Diploma (abroad)	Mechanical eng	LA
MW5	n.a.	Diploma	Mechanical eng	LA
MW6	None			
MW7	16	Diploma	Mechanical eng	LA
MW8	7	Diploma	Mechanical eng	LA
MW9	None			

Source: Case Studies.

In the *wood-working* industry the general level of education of production managers is not very high. The two smallest firms do not have a production manager at all. One has a production manager with only primary education. Another has a secondary graduate with no training in wood working. According to the available information, only the two technologically capable firms have production managers with diplomas in joinery and wood working.

In *metal-working*, two firms (both in structurals) have no production managers. Of the others, only MW1 has a production manager with a graduate engineering degree in metallurgical engineering, probably necessary in such a complex technology. The others all have diploma holders in mechanical engineering, except for MW2 which had a secondary-school graduate with previous experience in the industry (it had an engineer in charge of maintenance and QC). This in general conforms with the relatively simple nature of the technologies employed by these firms.

It may be relevant at this point to discuss the role of the *technological catalyst* that has been mentioned at several places above. The catalyst is an individual whose efforts and knowledge are critical to the technological upgrading of the enterprise. In most of the sample firms there was usually someone who played this role, generally the production manager or equivalent who worked closely with the entrepreneur or else was given a free hand to upgrade the technology of the enterprise. Enterprises of larger size and with more mature organisational structures do not need to rely on the (partly random) presence of a technologically gifted person to catalyse the firm. They would tend to have institutional mechanisms to identify, recruit and assign due responsibility to such persons. This is one of the advantages of large size and functionally specialised organisations that was mentioned in the analytical framework.

In small, newer, less mature enterprises, on the other hand, the existence of a catalyst seems to be essential to technological development. In some cases it is the entrepreneur himself, setting up in business to exploit his skills or innovations. In others, it is someone selected by the entrepreneur to take the technological lead: in this sense, it is a reflection of the entrepreneur's education and vision.

Technological catalysts who were entrepreneurs are found in firms like FP7 in food processing, WW1 in furniture and MW7 in metal working. Other catalysts are found, for instance, in garments (the German production manager in TG1), in food processing (the production manager in the biscuit manufacturer), in furniture (in WW3, where the production manager was important because the owner lacked technical training), and in metal working (in MW2, the engineer in charge of maintenance and QC).

A catalyst was not always needed by the sample firms. Where the technology was transferred entirely from abroad, well absorbed by the work force and has not faced major problems of adaptation, there would be no need for a dynamic leader to take initiatives that routine work cannot take care of. Good examples may be the flour mill or the aluminium pots and pans firm. The technological failures in the sample are usually firms that faced changing circumstances and could not come up with an appropriate technological response: technological activity was not routinized, and the owner could not locate a person to undertake the response.

TECHNICAL MANPOWER

Table 7.4 shows the breakdown of employment by various technical qualifications, including the entrepreneur and the production manager. The categories used are scientists, engineers and technicians (together and separately). Expatriates are also shown for interest. The last column shows average monthly wages, taken up in the next section.

The employment of scientists, engineers and technicians was found in the previous chapter to be significantly larger in technologically capable than in other firms. The firm level figures are now considered by industry, and comparisons are drawn with other developing countries wherever possible.

In *textiles and garments*, each of the firms had one technical person, with the exception of the dead firm and a small firm (TG6). Not surprisingly, none of them has a science degree, since this activity has no need for such training. However, only two firms have an employee with an engineering degree – and these are the best firms in the sample. The others have non-degree-level technicians, essentially to service the sewing machines. The total level of technical employment is low, even by the standards of this simple industry.[6]

A comparison with another developing country can illustrate this point. In Sri Lanka, a relative newcomer to the industry and not as advanced in garment quality or technology as the East Asian NIEs, two German affiliates (large operations with 900 to 1500 employees each) have 8–10 per cent of their employees in the technical category.[7] In more sophisticated operations, say, in Hong Kong and Taiwan, the proportion is likely to be higher. The technical level of the Ghanaian garment industry, as measured by its use of engineering and technical personnel, is very low.

In *food processing*, the picture is different in terms of the skill

Table 7.4 Technical manpower indicators and wages

Firm	Total employment 1991	Scientists, engineers and technicians[a]		Scientists only[c]		Engineers only[b]		Technicians only[d]		Expatriates[e]		Av. monthly worker wage in 1992 (US$)
		No.	% of emp.	No.	% of emp.	No.	% of emp.	No.	% of emp.	No.	% of emp.	
Textiles and garments												
TG1	90	1	1.1	0	0.0	1	1.1	0	0.0	1	1.1	55.6
TG2	73	1	1.4	0	0.0	0	0.0	1	1.4	0	0.0	48.3
TG3	42	1	2.4	0	0.0	0	0.0	1	2.4	0	0.0	41.1
TG4	30	1	3.3	0	0.0	0	0.0	1	3.3	0	0.0	48.5
TG5	24	1	4.2	0	0.0	1	4.2	0	0.0	0	0.0	53.0
TG6	15	0	0.0	0	0.0	0	0.0	0	0.0	0	0.0	36.2
TG7	13	1	7.7	0	0.0	0	0.0	1	7.7	0	0.0	25.0
TG8	(g) 0	0	0.0	0	0.0	0	0.0	0	0.0	0	0.0	0.0
												Weighted av. monthly worker wage 48.2
Food processing												
FP1	650	130	20.0	n.a.	n.a.	n.a.	n.a.	n.a.	n.a.	4	0.6	120.8
FP2	246	10	4.1	4	1.6	1	0.4	5	2.0	0	0.0	96.6
FP3	228	8	3.5	1	0.4	1	0.4	6	2.6	1	0.4	34.2
FP4	216	2	0.9	1	0.5	1	0.5	0	0.0	0	0.0	43.5
FP5	200	11	5.5	1	0.5	1	0.5	9	4.5	0	0.0	48.0
FP6	172	15	8.7	2	1.2	3	1.7	10	5.8	4	2.3	80.5
FP7	80	4	5.0	3	3.8	1	1.3	0	0.0	0	0.0	43.5
												Weighted av. monthly worker wage 81.7
Wood working												
WW1	267	7	2.6	0	0.0	2	0.7	5	1.9	1	0.4	60.4
WW2	225	2	0.9	0	0.0	2	0.9	0	0.0	0	0.0	40.3
WW3	147	3	2.0	0	0.0	0	0.0	3	2.0	0	0.0	65.0
												Weighted

continued on page 154

Table 7.4 continued

Firm	Total employment 1991	Scientists, engineers and technicians[a]		Scientists only[c]		Engineers only[b]		Technicians only[d]		Expatriates[e]		Av. monthly worker wage in 1992 (US$)
		No.	% of emp.	No.	% of emp.	No.	% of emp.	No.	% of emp.	No.	% of emp.	
WW4	135	2	1.5	0	0.0	0	0.0	2	1.5	0	0.0	36.2
WW5	65	3	4.6	0	0.0	0	0.0	3	4.6	1	1.5	48.3
WW6	41	0	0.0	0	0.0	0	0.0	0	0.0	0	0.0	43.5
WW7	16	0	0.0	0	0.0	0	0.0	0	0.0	0	0.0	29.3
WW8	10	0	0.0	0	0.0	0	0.0	0	0.0	0	0.0	31.4
Metal working												
MW1	430	17	4.0	0	0.0	3	0.7	14	3.3	17	4.0	85.3
MW2	150	5	3.3	0	0.0	1	0.7	4	2.7	0	0.0	51.2
MW3	71	10	14.1	0	0.0	0	0.0	10	14.1	0	0.0	72.5
MW4	30	1	3.3	0	0.0	0	0.0	1	3.3	2	6.7	41.5
MW5	28	2	7.1	0	0.0	0	0.0	2	7.1	0	0.0	36.2
MW6	28	0	0.0	0	0.0	0	0.0	0	0.0	0	0.0	39.0
MW7	19	3	15.8	0	0.0	1	5.3	2	10.5	0	0.0	60.4
MW8	16	3	18.8	0	0.0	1	6.3	2	12.5	2	12.5	63.4
MW9	13	1	7.7	0	0.0	1	7.7	0	0.0	0	0.0	51.2

av. monthly worker wage 50.0

Weighted av. monthly worker wage 70.9

[a] All degree and diploma holders.
[b] BSc degrees (and above) in food technology, chemistry or biochemistry.
[c] BSc degrees in different types of engineering.

composition of the employees. FP1 claims to have 20 per cent of its employees technically qualified (unfortunately a breakdown between scientists, engineers and technicians is not available), the absolute number exceeding the rest of the sample put together. Of these, there are four expatriates in key technical and marketing positions. The dairy products affiliate comes next, with nearly 9 per cent of its employees with technical qualifications. It is followed by the flour mill and FP7, the fruit drinks firm. FP2 is relatively low considering the nature of its technology (which is very similar to FP1's). The lowest is the biscuit maker, due to the simpler nature of its product. The number of scientists is highest in FP2 (FP1 excluded), but as a percentage of the workforce it is FP7 that takes the lead. The dairy firm has the largest absolute numbers of engineers and technicians.

In general, these data correspond with the relative performance of the firms within their respective technological segments. FP1, for instance, is distinctly a better performer in the market than FP2, and the two multinationals show very different propensities to invest in human capital. FP7's dynamism compared to FP3 may be traced to the superior quality of its high-level technical resources. FP4 does not really need any highly qualified technicians, but its access to an engineer (the production manager) allows it to perform very well.

In the *wood working* industry, none of the firms has any scientists, and only two have any engineers (WW1 and WW2, the latter using its engineers in saw-milling rather than furniture manufacture). Technicians are found on the staffs of four firms, with WW1 leading in terms of absolute numbers. The three smallest firms do not have a single technically qualified person (including the entrepreneur). WW5 has the highest proportion of its employment as technicians, but has no engineers. In the absence of data on other countries, it is difficult to assess how Ghanaian firms fare in relative terms.

In *metal working*, there are again no scientists, and relatively few engineers. Of the seven engineers in total in the industry, three are in MW1, all recently imported from India. The others are distributed over four firms, including 'capable' firms like MW2 and MW7. MW3 does not have an engineer (though one of its founders was an Israeli engineer, and set up its processes); however, it has a relatively high proportion of technicians. One of the firms, MW6, has no technical personnel at all.

In the very small firms, again, the figures are difficult to interpret, because the presence of one person shows up as a large percentage. If these are ignored, the employment of engineers in the Ghanaian metal working firms is under 1 per cent of total employment. This may be compared to some figures for the employment of engineers by large firms in engineering products in India, Korea, Malaysia and smaller firms in Sri Lanka.[8] These are as follows:

India[9]

Associated Babcock (1982): total employment 5000, engineers 10 per cent.

Hindustan Machine Tools (1981): total employment 25 600, engineers 5.1 per cent.

Tata Engineering & Locomotive Company (1982): total employment 39 500, engineers 4.3 per cent.

Korea[10]

Daewoo Heavy Industries, Diesel Engine Branch (1978): total employment 1181, engineers 14 per cent.

Kolon (1984): total employment 4132, engineers 5.6 per cent.

Malaysia[11]

Eng Group (1993): total employment 230, engineers 4.3 per cent.

Inventec Corporation of Malaysia (1993): total employment 2300, engineers 5.2 per cent.

National Panasonic Malaysia (1993): total employment 996, engineers 8.0 per cent.

Motorola Malaysia (1993): total employment 5000, engineers, 4.4 per cent.

Sony Malaysia (1993): total employment 4900, engineers 12.7 per cent.

Sri Lanka[12]

Acme Aluminium (1989): total employment 177, engineers 2.8 per cent.

Brown and Co. (1989): total employment 1200, engineers 3.3 per cent.

Elsteel Ltd. (1989): total employment 150, engineers 2.7 per cent.

Metalux Engineering Co. (1989): total employment 160, engineers 2.5 per cent.

These figures should not be taken as direct indications of skill gaps in Ghanaian firms, since the technological level of the firms in the other countries is generally far higher than those of the Ghanaian sample. However, this is less true of Sri Lankan firms, which are relatively small and in simple technologies, and so more comparable to the Ghanaian sample. This comparison is particularly revealing, since it is difficult otherwise to establish if Ghanaian firms have adequate technical manpower to achieve efficiency. Moreover, even the data on India, Korea and Malaysia are useful to illustrate the kind of skill upgrading that may be needed by Ghanaian industry if it is to enter more complex engineering activities.[13]

WORKER SKILLS

Ideally the skill levels of workers employed by the sample firms should be measured by their years of education and training, broken down by job categories and length of stay in the firm. Such data are not available for the Ghanaian sample. In their absence, skill levels may be indicated by average wages paid by firms. While using wages as indicators of skill suffers from a number of well-known handicaps (in particular, it assumes perfectly functioning labour markets), it is the best measure that is available. If used carefully, it may reveal something about relative skill levels. The last column of Table 7.4 shows the average monthly wage for each firm, and the weighted average for each industry and the sample as a whole.

The last chapter showed that technologically capable firms paid higher average wages than other firms. This may have indicated, among other things, that they employed more skilled labour than other firms. We now look at the wage levels of each industry separately, to assess if the competent firms within each pay higher wages than comparable firms.

The weighted average wage for the sample as a whole is $69.3 per month (or $58.6 if FP1, an outlier in terms of its wages and its large size, is excluded), and the mean in $50.3. In general terms, the food and metal-working industries have higher weighted average wages ($81.7 and $70.9 respectively) than wood-working and garments ($50.0 and $48.2 respectively). If the largest firm in food processing (FP1) and in metal-working (MW1, also a special case in terms of its technology and size) are excluded, their averages fall to $59.4 and $53.5 respectively.

Whether or not these two large firms are excluded, the ranking is in line with the technological characteristics of these industries. Garments requires the lowest levels of skill of the four activities, while large-scale food processing requires the highest. Metal working may be highly skill-intensive where difficult processes (steel making, as in MW1) or complex equipment are concerned, but is not very demanding for the manufacture of many simple products. Furniture making is generally not a very technically skilled activity, at least in the form that it takes in Ghana. This suggests that wage levels are not too distorted, and relative wages can serve as a good proxy for human capital.

Within textiles and garments, the highest wages are paid by TG1 and TG5, the two firms found to be technologically capable. The latter is in a different (more demanding) technology from garment sewing, so its wages are expected to be higher. TG1, however, makes the same product as firms whose average wages are significantly lower, ranging from $41.1 to $25.0. There are therefore grounds for believing that it has a more skilled workforce.

In food processing, the three MNC affiliates pay far higher wages than the average. This is a tendency found in MNCs the world over, and may be traced to their more complex technologies, established brand names and, because of this, stronger market positions. It also reflects their more selective recruitment and better training. The state-owned cannery pays the lowest wages in this industry, which accords with the relative technical slack found there. The biscuit maker pays relatively low wages, but this is in line with its technological processes, which are much simpler and less capital-intensive than in the other firms in the industry.

In wood working, all the firms make similar products (with the exception of WW2, which is essentially in saw milling). Yet the wages paid by WW1 and WW3, the two competent firms, are significantly higher than for the other large- and medium-sized firms (the two small firms pay expectedly lower wages). It is interesting to note that WW4, the firm that 'graduated' from traditional carpentry, is almost the same size as WW3 but the latter's wages are nearly 45 per cent higher. This suggests that the difference between them in terms of attention to worker skills is partly responsible for the resulting difference in TCs.

In metal working, MW1 is, as noted, exceptional in terms of its production processes, and it is not surprising that its wages are relatively high. To some extent this also applies to MW8, though its foundry has yet to start operations. There are two sets of comparisons between firms in similar activities that are of interest. First, between MW3 and MW4: both are aluminium-structural-products firms that compete directly with each other, yet the former's average wage is 75 per cent higher than the latter's. Similarly MW5 (another 'graduating' firm) is in the same line as MW7, but the latter's wage is 55 per cent higher. In both cases, the higher wage firm is technologically more competent and in market terms more successful.

It does seem, therefore, that there is a relationship between skill levels and wages paid, and that worker skills are positively related to technological competence.

TRAINING, RECRUITMENT AND TURNOVER OF LABOUR

The level of employee skills of any firm is affected by its recruitment and training strategies, and by the turnover of its employees. Recruitment policies determine the initial quality of the workers taken in, while training is a crucial element of capability-development thereafter. The departure of employees constitutes a possible leakage of skills created by the firm. This section discusses the available information on these aspects of capability development in the sample firms.

Many of the skills that are needed to operate specific technologies are not imparted by formal instruction and have to be learnt on the job. Training can take three main forms. The first is apprenticeship, which generally refers to training given to a young entrant who knows little about the skill in question, and who learns by working alongside an experienced worker. The second is on the job training, which generally refers to further hands-on skills imparted to a person who already has some theoretical knowledge of the work. The third is formal employee training, where experienced employees are given formal training to refresh, increase or alter their skills.

The apprenticeship system is particularly important in Ghana (and most African countries), since it is the main way in which traditional activities and crafts transmit their technical knowledge to workers.[14] It is useful to distinguish between this form of apprenticeship and what goes under the same name in highly industrialised societies (like Germany). In the traditional African systems the apprenticeship system is directed at primary or middle school leavers, and involves little or no further formal education with it. It is thus geared to transferring relatively low-level manufacturing skills which do not change much with time and which do not require numerical abilities. There is usually no formal certification at the end of the training, though the firm involved may give a testimonial. Generally some allowance is paid to the apprentice, but at a much lower rate than the market wage.

On the other hand, apprenticeship in countries like Germany starts after fairly lengthy schooling, and incorporates a great deal of continuing higher education in technical subjects. The qualification is formally certified, and the content of the training is upgraded constantly in line with technological requirements. There are strong incentives for undergoing such training, and the level of skill acquisition is considerable (the German system is the envy of the developed world). The apprenticeship system in Ghana is discussed below for the sample firms that have this system.

Let us start with some general data. It was possible to collect information on the numbers of employees sent by firms for external training, within Ghana and overseas. Table 7.5 shows these numbers for 1991, as a percentage of total employment, and labour turnover rates in that year. Table 7.6 shows the use of apprenticeship training by the sample firms.

External training is undertaken by very few firms (9 in total), and seems to be very low in relation to the skill needs of the activities undertaken. Again, a comparison with Sri Lanka shows that there was considerably less sustained external training by garment and metal working firms in Ghana.[15] The data are presented in Table 8.3 in the next chapter. Of the training offered by Ghanaian firms, most seems to be in management courses[16] rather than technical skills, and is sporadic rather than sustained. There are few institutions available in the country to provide industry-specific training in activities such as garments and textiles, or furniture making.[17] It is therefore difficult to judge the contribution of the external training that does take place in the sample.

There are no data available on training conducted internally by the sample firms. Few of the firms have separate training departments with separate budgets. However, it is possible to review qualitatively recruitment and internal training by the firms. These findings are reviewed by industry.

The *garment* end of the textile and garment industry in most developing countries does not require high levels of education among its shopfloor employees, and as a consequence normally experiences high levels of labour turnover. It does, however, have to invest in training its workforce, especially where export markets, with very demanding standards, are served.[18] In the Ghanaian sample, the garment makers hire a mix of primary-school leavers and experienced workers, except for TG1, which has a policy of hiring secondary-school graduates.[19] The knitwear manufacturer hires a mix of O (Ordinary) level and A (Advanced) level graduates.[20] In general, hiring policies seem to be casual and not related to skills, except for supervisory or technical staff.

Only two firms have training programmes in this group: TG1 and TG5, the two technologically capable firms. In TG1, training was provided in its early years by the owner's daughters, and later, under the close supervision of the German production manager, by senior employees. New recruits get 3–4 weeks' training. All staff get occasional half-day courses by the production manager on quality control, clearly an important input into the quality edge that the firm enjoys over local

Table 7.5 Personnel sent on external training and labour turnover rates

Firm	Personnel sent on external training in Ghana & abroad in 1991 (% of emp.)[a]	Personnel sent on external training abroad only in 1991 (% of emp.)[b]	Labour turnover rate in 1991 (%)[c]
Textiles and garments			
TG1	0.0	0.0	5.6
TG2	0.0	0.0	n.a.
TG3	0.0	0.0	7.1
TG4	0.0	0.0	3.3
TG5	0.0	0.0	4.2
TG6	0.0	0.0	n.a.
TG7	0.0	0.0	15.4
TG8	0.0	0.0	0.0
Food processing			
FP1	1.2	0.9	n.a.
FP2	2.4	0.4	n.a.
FP3	3.5	0.4	0.0
FP4	0.0	0.0	1.4
FP5	0.0	0.0	n.a.
FP6	0.6	0.0	5.2
FP7	5.0	0.0	n.a.
Wood working			
WW1	0.0	0.0	2.2
WW2	0.0	0.0	n.a.
WW3	0.0	0.0	0.0
WW4	1.5	1.5	3.0
WW5	0.0	0.0	n.a.
WW6	0.0	0.0	4.9
WW7	0.0	0.0	12.5
WW8	0.0	0.0	20.0
Metal working			
MW1	0.0	0.0	2.3
MW2	0.0	0.0	11.3
MW3	4.2	2.8	8.5
MW4	3.3	0.0	3.3
MW5	7.1	0.0	7.1
MW6	0.0	0.0	0.0
MW7	0.0	0.0	5.3
MW8	0.0	0.0	12.5
MW9	0.0	0.0	23.1

[a] Number of employees leaving during 1991/average number employed during 1991 (* 100).

Table 7.6 Traditional apprenticeship system

Firm	Current apprentices No.	% of emp.	Apprentices' entry qualification	Apprenticeship period (months/years)	Apprentices' monthly allowance (% of master's monthly wage)	Apprentice turnover rate (% of emp.)
Wood working						
WW3	20	13.6	Secondary	2 years	19	n.a.
WW4	12	8.9	Less than primary	6 months – 1 year	21	negligible
WW5	12	18.5	Most primary, odd KTI	3–6 months	24	n.a.
WW6	14	34.1	Primary	6 years	16	4.9
WW7	13	81.3	Less than primary	3 years	21	18.8
WW8	2	20.0	Less than primary	2 years	30	negligible
Metal working						
MW5	5	17.9	Primary	4 years	40	n.a.
MW6	24	85.7	Less than primary	3–4 years	31	10.7
MW7	5	26.3	Secondary, odd KTI	3–4 years	0[a]	0
MW9	3	23.1	Less than primary	2–5 years	39	n.a.

[a] Apprentices do not receive monthly allowances.

competitors. In TG5, many employees were fired after the firm was returned from government to private management, to get rid of 'bad habits' and 'troublemakers'. New recruits were intensively trained personally by the production manager (the numbers involved were fairly small), who had intimate knowledge of all the machines and processes. This sort of personal and systematic attention to training is lacking in other firms.

In *food processing*, FP1 pays the most attention to recruiting well-qualified staff, while FP2 has the strongest policy of placing Ghanaians in top management positions. Recruitment seems to be carefully conducted in all the firms with the exception of the biscuit firm, that has an existing core of experienced workers and is not hiring new workers (in any case its skill needs are lower than that of the other firms in the sample).

All the food firms provide on-the-job training for employees. Both FP1 and FP2 have formal training programmes, but the former has a more comprehensive system, probably the best of all the sample firms. Apart from the programmes for new recruits, FP1 has annual training for all employees coordinated by an expatriate training officer. Technical training is conducted on the job by expatriate trainers. Upper management is sent to FP1's training centre in the parent's home country for courses in management and marketing. FP2 gives one week formal training to production workers and two weeks to supervisors, both followed by several weeks of on-the-job training. Managers and technical staff also go on external courses, while the production manager and chief engineer get training in the parent's plant.

The dairy multinational gives on-the-job training for production workers by the expatriate production manager and maintenance managers. A technician was sent to the parent company for training in 1991 in relation to the planned expansion of capacity. Data processing staff are being trained in a local firm. The flour mill got its workers trained by the Italian plant suppliers, but has not instituted a formal training programme thereafter. Of the two fruit processors, FP7 used its Italian suppliers of plant to train workers, and since then conducts on-the-job training for new recruits under the supervision of a senior employee. The government cannery provides on-the-job training. It planned a proper skill-upgrading programme, but did not implement it for lack of resources. Its quality manager has twice attended courses in Sweden.

In general, the level of investment in human capital development seems to be geared to meeting basic production needs rather than to upgrading the stock for coping with technical change and competitiveness.

The only exception seems to be FP1, which invests in continuous training and uses foreign professional training personnel. FP2's policy of training high-level Ghanaians is commendable, but it is not clear that the operational workforce has skill levels comparable to FP1's. The others seem to be content with training for immediate production needs.

In *wood working*, WW1 sets high standards of recruitment and training. It has recently introduced a minimum recruitment level of a vocational training certificate as well as a test set by the firm itself. It does not take apprentices, but has an extended in-house training programme that runs over three years and covers each stage of production (this is the only specialised training programme of the wood-working sample firms). There are presently 31 trainees in this programme. In addition, foreign consultants will provide QC training periodically over the next two years; this project is promoted by the Ghana Export Promotion Council as part of its effort to boost furniture exports.

By contrast, WW2 has no recruitment standards and there is no in-house training programme (there is no apprenticeship system). This indicates a disregard of skill needs, though when its saw mill was rehabilitated the German technicians who had implemented the programme instructed some local staff.

WW3 provides training by the apprenticeship system. It recruits fresh trainees from the Industrial Training Centre, as well as apprentices who have been trained at smaller carpentry workshops. Both sets of entrants are given further apprenticeship training for two years. Though no testimonial is given at the end, the firm claims that its reputation allows many trainees to get jobs elsewhere. There are currently 20 apprentices and 50 master carpenters. Apprentices are paid Cedis 15 thousand per month, compared to Cedis 80 thousand for the master carpenters. This firm is unusual in taking apprentices with previous training, and paying relatively high salaries (see below on other firms). The owner feels, however, that this system does not meet the firm's skill needs adequately, and is considering changing to a more formal on-the-job training system.

WW4 used to hire mainly primary-school leavers for apprenticeship training in the firm. It found that primary school recruits did not have the skills to read technical drawings, so it changed to recruiting graduates in wood working from the Kumasi Technical Institute. It found, however, that these graduates were 'too theoretical' and continued to give apprenticeship training. The training is relatively brief, six months to a year, with a testimonial provided at the end. It pays an allowance of Cedis 7400 per month, compared to Cedis 35 thousand for a foreman.

Currently there are twelve apprentices but no new ones are being taken because the firm is not doing well.

WW5 also hires mainly primary-school leavers and some graduates from the Kumasi Technical Institute. It offers apprenticeship training for three to six months, and pays apprentices Cedis 6 thousand per month (compared to Cedis 20–39 thousand for a master and 40 thousand for a foreman). There is no other form of training given.

The three remaining firms (WW6, WW7 and WW8) all take recruits with minimal levels of schooling and give them apprenticeship training. The training period varies between two and six years, with allowances ranging from Cedis 4 to 7 thousand per month, compared to the masters' pay of Cedis 20 to 28 thousand per month. These firms also try to hire apprentices trained by other firms. They expressed no dissatisfaction with this system of recruitment and training, perhaps reflecting the low levels of skills that had to be imparted.

In *metal working*, MW1 is in too complex an activity to rely on apprentices. It has to take recruits with some education and give considerable on-the-job training. The previous management had given very little training to workers. The new owners kept about half of the former workforce when they took charge, and got rid of the rest. New recruits were taken from middle schools, and provided with intensive on-the-job training by the expatriate personnel. There was currently an unfulfilled need for metallurgical engineers as well as for skilled workers like fitters and electricians. The level of skills was found to be well below that in India, and it is felt that more formal on-the-job training systems need to be installed after the task of refurbishing the plant is completed.

None of the three aluminium firms has an apprenticeship system. MW2 takes mainly primary-school leavers, and does not regard formal educational qualifications as very important. For its needs, on-the-job training for two to three months provided by experienced operators is sufficient.

MW3, by contrast, felt that it had to upgrade its recruitment standards. It recently introduced a minimum requirement of vocational training for its new shopfloor recruits and a technical diploma for higher-level recruits, and pays a correspondingly higher wage (above) to ensure that it attracts good-quality applicants. Recruits have a six month probationary period when they are trained on each aspect of the firm's operations and their progress is evaluated. This systematic approach is unique among the metal-working firms in the sample. In addition, two technicians are sent to Israel for about a month to the plant of the former partner to learn specialised tasks like computerised glass cutting (the Israeli firm provides the training for free but MW3 bears all the travel and subsistence costs).

MW4 has also recently switched to hiring vocationally trained workers, and provides on-the-job training for new employees supplemented by occasional sessions on problems like QC. The owner of this firm said that a new recruit with vocational training had higher productivity than an untrained worker with 25 years of work experience. This is an interesting claim, which we could not substantiate. Even if it is partly true, however, it implies that raising productivity in large parts of Ghanaian industry will involve boosting the vocational education of workers rather than relying on traditional apprenticeship methods.

Both the food processing machinery makers, MW5 and MW7, recruit from primary schools and give apprenticeship training along traditional lines. MW5 also tries to hire trained apprentices from other firms. Interestingly, it does not want technical-school graduates for higher-level skills; its owner is suspicious of technical-school graduates, and finds their training 'too theoretical' and their wages too high. This may be a reflection of his own lack of formal training and his background in traditional blacksmithing. The owner of MW7, by contrast, hires technical-school graduates for supervisory work.

Both firms train their apprentices for three to four years, and provide testimonials at the end. MW5 pays apprentices about half the salary of a qualified worker, while MW7 pays nothing (but gives much higher salaries to its qualified workers). MW7 also provides further on-the-job training to its workers, with the owner taking personal charge of this activity.[21] MW5 provides no further training, with the apprenticeship system having imparted all the skills considered necessary. Part of the technological difference between the two firms may be traced to the relatively static approach of MW5 to recruitment and training.

The two structural product firms, MW6 and MW9, both give apprenticeship training. MW6 only takes primary-school leavers, while MW9 also takes vocational-school trainees. MW6's apprenticeship lasts for three to four years, and apprentices receive allowance of Cedis 5 thousand per month (depending on-the-job to be done). MW9's apprenticeship lasts for two to five years, and the allowance is Cedis 11 thousand per month, compared to Cedis 28 thousand for a master. The owner himself trains workers in the use of new equipment. MW9's recruitment standards and salary levels (the remuneration of apprentices is the highest of the sample firms) suggest higher levels of skill than MW6.

Finally, MW8 has been recruiting only for the machine shop rather than its foundry. It takes only technically qualified personnel, who are given on-the-job training by the foreman and the German technician sent by the aid agency. There is, however, no formal on-the-job training system.

To sum up on the apprenticeship system, there are ten firms in the case study sample (six in wood working and four in metal working) that use it for training their workforces. Only two of these, WW3 and MW7, have been classified as technologically competent. Both of them have made adaptations to the traditional system to enhance its training potential. WW3 takes graduates from technical schools and other firms' apprentices and gives them further training rather than relying on recruits with minimal educational qualification; and it pays them relatively high salaries. More importantly, it is finding this system inadequate to its skill needs and is contemplating a move to a more formal method of training. MW7 recruits some workers with technical training for supervisory work along with primary-school leavers for the shopfloor; it supplements apprenticeship with follow-up on-the-job training.

In general, the apprenticeship system seems to be well suited to the transmission of fairly simple manufacturing skills to workers with minimal formal education, with little change over the generations. It is less suited to training for the skills needed for modern manufacturing, where completely different types of skills from those possessed by traditional craftsmen may be required, and where a considerably higher level of education is necessary to operations.[22] Even in activities where there is a role for traditional skills like metal and wood working, an upgrading of the apprenticeship system to encompass more formal education would seem to be called for.

As far as labour turnover is concerned, Table 7.5 shows that the rates were quite variable in 1991, with no consistent pattern by industry (except that food processing generally had low turnover). There was some propensity for the higher rates to be concentrated in the smaller enterprises, but this pattern does not hold for metal working. It is possible that the 'leakage' of skills through turnover constituted a barrier to investments in training, but this cannot be ascertained without further investigation.

SUMMARY

To conclude on human capital, the broad picture that emerges for the sample firms is as follows:

- There is a clear relationship between the education of the entrepreneur and the propensity to invest in capability development. There are several indications that poorly educated entrepreneurs lack the 'vision' and competence to appreciate the needs of modern technology, even at fairly simple levels, and to undertake the effort necessary to meet those needs.
- The education of the production manager is also an important element in the technological success of enterprises.
- In most small and medium firms, as well as some large ones, technological success is related to having a 'technological catalyst' present, who can introduce the practices, systems and information needed to upgrade operations. This catalyst may be the entrepreneur (if he is technically qualified), or the production manager; the ability of the firm to locate and use a good catalyst is itself an indication of entrepreneurial acumen. While a catalyst is obviously desirable, the need to depend on one person indicates the lack of the ability systematically to organise for technological development.
- The high-level skill composition of the employees varies, as expected, by the nature of the technology. The most demanding activity in the sample, food processing, tends to have the largest numbers of scientists and engineers; garments the least.
- In general, the use of formal technical skills in the sample is relatively low, and is likely to be even lower for the larger population of enterprises. This partly reflects the generally low level of technologies in use, but it is also likely to reflect the scarcity of technical manpower in the country and the lack of awareness of firms (especially smaller ones) of the need for technical skills.
- There is no clear connection between size as such and the relative use of technical manpower. This does not conflict with the fact that certain kinds of technological activity have minimum thresholds for firm size and need large firms to be managed efficiently: in the sample, this is particularly true of some food processing and metal working activities.
- The gaining of technological competence is clearly related to the employment of technical skills at managerial and supervisory levels.
- While worker skills are difficult to measure, it appears that technologically competent firms pay higher average wages and employ more skilled workers.
- In training, there is a mixture of the traditional system of apprenticeship and more modern on-the-job training. The former is confined

to wood and metal working, and even there is not ideally suited to providing modern operational skills.

- On-the-job training is carried out with varying degrees of effectiveness by different firms. Some firms have created the base for absorbing technologies (especially in food processing) by getting training from equipment suppliers, others by investing in their own systems. Affiliates of foreign firms, or firms run by technically trained expatriates, seem to have the best systems. In many other firms, on the other hand, the training systems are weak and ineffective.

- There is very little use of external training conducted by institutions or by firms overseas. A few of the large firms send managers on courses, but the basic skill needs of operatives, especially in the smaller firms, is not met by any existing institutions.

8 Technical Effort

INTRODUCTION

There are several ways to examine the technical effort of manufacturing enterprises, none of them entirely satisfactory. On the input side, the most common measure used is R&D expenditures. This is not relevant for our purposes, since none of the sample firms conducts what is normally understood as formal research and development. Even the large MNC affiliates do not claim to do R&D in Ghana. Another measure of technological effort may be the employment of technical personnel, which has been discussed above. In any case, this is a very imperfect measure of effort, since two firms with the same numbers of technical personnel could invest quite different amounts of effort on improving their technologies.

The more correct measure would be the actual engineering or technician time spent in purposive technical work directed to raising the productivity of the technologies in use. This sort of data was impossible to obtain, though we did get one or two indications of the sums spent in improving equipment. However, these are not very helpful in constructing proper indices of technological effort.

In the absence of better measures, therefore, this analysis has to be based on three aspects of the sample firms' operations: the use of foreign licensed technologies and technical assistance contracts; the distribution of enterprises' workforces in identifiable technical functions like QC and maintenance; and firm relations with the technology institutes.

TECHNOLOGY LICENSING AND TECHNICAL ASSISTANCE

The import of technology is an indicator of one aspect of technology input, which may or may not be related to internal technological effort by the firm. In most developing countries, however, the import of technology by licensing and other contracts tends to be positively correlated with internal technological effort, and it may be assumed that this is also true of the Ghanaian sample. Data on technology contracts by the sample firms are shown in Table 8.1.

Table 8.1   Technological indicators

Firm	No. of foreign licences in 1992	Technical assistance contract (TAC) in 1992	Expenditure on TAC in 1991 (% of sales)	Expenditure on technology institutions in 1991 (% of sales)
Textiles and garments				
TG1	0	No	0	0.04
TG2	0	No	0	0
TG3	0	No	0	n.a.
TG4	0	No	0	0.07
TG5	0	No	0	0.14
TG6	0	No	0	0
TG7	0	No	0	0
TG8	0	No	0	0
Food processing				
FP1	1	Yes	n.a.	n.a.
FP2	1	Yes	2	0.02
FP3	0	No	0	0.13
FP4	0	No	0	0
FP5	0	Yes	n.a.	n.a.
FP6	0	Yes	1.5	n.a.
FP7	0	Yes	n.a.	n.a.
Wood working				
WW1	0	Yes	0.06	0.06
WW2	0	No	0	0
WW3	0	No	0	0
WW4	0	No	0	0.03
WW5	0	No	0	0
WW6	0	No	0	0
WW7	0	No	0	0
WW8	0	No	0	0
Metal working				
MW1	0	No	0	0
MW2	0	Yes	0.6	n.a.
MW3	2	Yes	n.a.	0.01
MW4	2	Yes	n.a.	n.a.
MW5	0	No	0	0
MW6	0	No	0	0
MW7	0	No	0	0.2
MW8	0	Yes	n.a.	1.4
MW9	0	No	0	0

The table shows that only four firms in the case study sample took foreign licences, two each in food and metal working. Of these, three were foreign affiliates (FP1, FP2 and MW4), and one (MW3) was a local firm. The food multinationals licensed their technology as well as brand names from their parent companies. The metal-working firms only licensed some designs for doors and windows. In these cases, there may have been some transfer of process technology, but it did not affect the rest of the firm's technology. The impact of the new technologies transferred through licensing was marginal for the sample.

Purchases of technical assistance by the sample firms were more widespread. In 1992, ten firms had technical assistance contracts overseas, mainly in food processing and metal working.[1] Four of these firms were affiliates of foreign firms. Data on the expenditure on these contracts are only available for four firms. The two affiliates (FP2 and FP6) spent 1.5 to 2.0 per cent of sales on technical assistance provided by their parent companies. The local firms spent less: WW1 spent 0.06 per cent and MW2 0.6 per cent. In general, the use of this channel of technical information and assistance was rather limited.

In general, therefore, very few Ghanaian firms were trying to improve their process technologies, or their product range, by getting know-how from abroad. This is surprising, especially in the food-processing and metal-working subsectors, where licensing is very widely used the world over. The sample Ghanaian enterprises are clearly well behind international, even most other developing country, levels in their technology, and their lack of contact with international technology markets suggests that they were relatively static in their approach to technological upgrading. None of the local enterprises expressed the intention to seek new foreign technologies or joint ventures.

MANPOWER IN QC AND MAINTENANCE

One indicator of the ability of firms to launch technological effort, partial and limited though it may be, is the distribution of its workforce in certain essential technical functions like quality control and maintenance. It was noted in Chapter 6 that there was a significant difference between technologically competent and other firms in their employment of full-time QC and maintenance personnel as a proportion of total employment. The mean for the former was 6.5 and for the latter 1.8.

Table 8.2 shows full time personnel in the sample employed in these two functions, individually and together as a percentage of total

Table 8.2   Full-time personnel in quality control and maintenance[a]

Firm	Quality control manpower (% of employment)	Maintenance manpower (% of employment)	Quality control & maintenance manpower (% of employment)
Textiles and garments			
TG1	3.3	4.4	7.8
TG2	0.0	0.0	0.0
TG3	0.0	2.4	2.4
TG4	3.3	0.0	3.3
TG5	0.0	4.2	4.2
TG6	0.0	0.0	0.0
TG7	0.0	0.0	0.0
TG8[b]	0.0	0.0	0.0
Food processing			
FP1	2.0	7.8	9.8
FP2	2.8	10.2	13.0
FP3	1.8	4.4	6.1
FP4	0.9	0.9	1.9
FP5	2.0	3.5	5.5
FP6	2.9	7.0	9.9
FP7	5.0	5.0	10.0
Wood Working			
WW1	n.a.	n.a.	n.a.
WW2	0.0	0.9	0.9
WW3	0.7	3.4	4.1
WW4	0.0	0.0	0.0
WW5	0.0	0.0	0.0
WW6	0.0	0.0	0.0
WW7	0.0	0.0	0.0
WW8	0.0	0.0	0.0
Metal working			
MW1	n.a.	n.a.	n.a.
MW2	0.0	1.3	1.3
MW3	1.4	5.6	7.0
MW4	3.3	3.3	6.7
MW5	0.0	0.0	0.0
MW6	0.0	0.0	0.0
MW7	0.0	10.5	10.5
MW8	0.0	0.0	0.0
MW9	0.0	0.0	0.0

[a] Full-time personnel employed in these functions. Includes all employees regardless of qualifications. Does not include part-time personnel or technical visits from abroad.
[b] Dead firm which retains a few employees for tasks apart from production. It employed employees at its peak in 1986.

Table 8.3   Full-time personnel in quality control and personnel sent on external training in firms in Sri Lanka

Firms	Total employment 1989	Ownership structure (%)	Quality control manpower in 1989 (% of employment)[a]	Personnel sent on external training in Sri Lanka & abroad in 1988 (% of employment)
Garments[b]				
Dial Textiles	1500	100 Foreign	5.9	1.0
Cadillac Garments	1000	100 Sri Lankan	9.5	3.4
Kundanmal Garments	1000	15 Foreign, 85 Sri Lankan	8.4	1.7
Eskimo Fashion	900	100 Foreign	4.5	2.2
Alliance Garments	330	100 Sri Lankan	4.6	1.5
Average for garment firms			6.6	2.0
Metal working				
Acme Aluminium	177	53 Foreign, 47 Sri Lankan	5.6	7.9
Metalux Engineering Co.	166	100 Sri Lankan	3.1	0.0
Elsteel Ltd	150	100 Foreign	5.4	5.3
Agro Technica	75	100 Sri Lankan	4.0	4.0
Swedlanka	40	49 Foreign, 51 Sri Lankan	3.6	5.0
Average for metal working firms			4.3	4.4

[a] Full-time personnel employed in these functions. Includes all employees regardless of qualifications. Does not include part-time personnel or technical visits from abroad.
[b] Total number of employees sent on external training courses in Sri Lanka and abroad during 1988.

Source: G. Wignaraja, 'Manufactured Exports, Outward-Orientation and the Acquisition of Technological Capabilities in Sri Lanka', Doctoral thesis in progress, Oxford University.

employment. The data illustrate clearly the difference between the firms classified as technologically competent and others.

It may be interesting to compare QC employment (this refers to full-time personnel) between this sample and some Sri Lankan firms in garments and metal working. The Sri Lankan data are shown in Table 8.3.[2] They give the employment size of the ten firms, the percentage of employment in QC, and the personnel sent overseas on training. The latter set of figures pertains to the discussion of training in the previous chapter.

The firms in Sri Lanka have significantly higher proportions of their employees in QC than the Ghanaian sample. It is notable that a large locally owned garment firm in Sri Lanka, with 1000 employees, has 9.5 per cent of its workforce in QC; even the smallest, with 330 employees, has a figure of 4.6 per cent. The best Ghanaian firm, TG1, only has 3.3 per cent, and most other firms have zero. The differences are equally striking in metal working.

LINKAGES WITH TECHNOLOGY AND OTHER INSTITUTIONS

Technological and other linkages have already been discussed in Chapter 5 under the heading of linkage capabilities, and the available data on recent use of technology institutions were presented in that context. It was shown that linkages with the science and technology infrastructure were very low, and this discussion need not be repeated here.

However, the question may be addressed in a different way. One of the most important causes of poor technological response by Ghanaian firms is the sheer lack of information on the part of enterprises on a variety of tasks. The main items on which sample firms need information are:

- What technologies are appropriate to survive, grow and (in the longer term) export in the new competitive environment.
- What equipment to buy, how to evaluate its capabilities, where to buy it and what prices to pay.
- Where and how to negotiate the best technology-transfer deal.
- How to participate in project engineering, and to persuade foreign technology suppliers to impart elements of process technology to local engineers.
- How to train workers to the necessary skill levels, initially and on a continuous basis, with in-house and external inputs.
- How to establish suitable quality-control procedures, standardise products and get them certified, so that they can have market acceptability.
- How to optimise production processes, adapt them to local scales of operation, materials, components, and market conditions, by in-house engineering effort and troubleshooting, or by getting technical assistance and consultancy.
- How to establish industrial-engineering procedures, to schedule production, control inventory, keep track of productivity, set up procurement procedures, and so on.

- How to reduce costs over time and adapt to changing factor conditions, by conducting (or contracting) research into processes and keeping a watch on international technological developments.
- How to improve products and diversify the product range, again by conducting or contracting design, research and development.
- How to source materials and components locally, by establishing linkages with potential suppliers and subcontractors, and rendering them technical assistance.
- How to establish supply or sales contracts with overseas companies.

This is a list of the main technological tasks that manufacturers have to perform to become technically efficient (there are many others related to management and marketing). Many of these are not performed satisfactorily by many sample firms, or are not performed in a manner that is conducive to competitive growth and diversification. One of the main reasons is that the enterprises lack the necessary information, or ready access to sources of this information. They do not often know what they need, nor how to go about finding out. If they have some idea of their needs, they may be unable to define them properly. To use external technical assistance effectively a firm has to be able to explain what its problems are in technical language, otherwise the consultant or technology institute has to spend considerable resources in finding out what to address. It is unlikely that most of the local firms in the sample could frame their technological needs in this way. In other words, they have to be taught to 'learn' in the broad sense of the term.

Even if firms could define their technological needs, there are few institutions in Ghana to which they can turn for effective and economical help. The existing institutions related to industry, in the S&T network or in other ministries, lack the skills, technical resources, incentive and organisation to attempt this kind of education/assistance for industry. Thus, the sample firms that have been able to undertake technological activity on a systematic basis are only those that have internal sources of information (the educated entrepreneur or technological catalyst) or links with other sources overseas. The former suffices for relatively simple and low-level technological activities, which is what most of the observed effort in Ghana consists of. The latter becomes necessary for larger-scale and more demanding effort, the nearest approximation being the type of systematic plans being launched by FP1 to raise productivity. This requires external training resources, new technologies and equipment and better management control. The parent company of an MNC affiliate is geared to providing this, but few if any of the local firms have the resources or connections to tap a similar source of information and skills. Foreign licences or joint ventures are crucial ways of supplementing local information, but, as noted, these are extremely rare and show few signs of increasing among the established local firms.

While it is difficult to establish this firmly, the lack of local institutional support for TC development may be a significant determinant of the weak technological performance of Ghanaian firms. It is certainly the case that the best performing industrialisers, the East Asian NIEs, noted the market failures that existed in the functions noted above, and provided a diverse set of institutions to support their firms. This was, of course, a small part of the process of creating technological capabilities that included massive investments in education, training, research and local linkage creation. In addition, these countries also had a much stronger tradition of industrial entrepreneurship. Their export activity, once it was started, provided its own inputs into information flows. Nevertheless, the array of support mechanisms that were set up in the form of institutions for research, training, technical extension and marketing is likely to have made a significant contribution to TC development. This contribution is signally absent in Ghana.

As far as other technological linkages are concerned, foreign affiliates obviously drew upon their parent companies for all sorts of technical information. Of the local firms, some drew upon foreign equipment suppliers as the most important source of technical information when they purchased new plant. These technological linkages were limited in duration, and were generally not maintained after a period of three to four years. Many firms did not have this linkage at all because the technology was too simple or because the plant had been purchased second-hand. There was little of the constant search for foreign technical know-how that characterised the NIEs.

Not surprisingly, there were very few technical linkages within the country in the more modern sectors of industry. In traditional technologies (like parts of wood working or simple metal working) where the technology is largely embodied in worker skills, a lot of informal exchange of information did take place in the form of apprentice training (many apprentices left after training, carrying the master's know-how to other firms). However, as discussed in the previous chapter, this was not particularly useful in handling modern technologies, and firms like MW5 illustrate the technological limitations of traditional metal working firms.

9 Incentives and Other Influences on TC Development

INTRODUCTION

This chapter briefly deals with some of the other factors that may influence the development of technological capabilities in the Ghanaian sample firms. Some of these, like financial markets, labour markets and regulations, were not designed to be covered by this study, so will not be discussed. This does not imply, of course, that they are not important for TC development, though their influence is less direct than that of the factors included here. However, the most important indirect influence on TC investments, the incentive structure facing firms, does need some discussion.

INCENTIVES

The incentive structures facing Ghanaian industry have been described in Chapter 2. Let us briefly reiterate its main features and connect them to the findings from the case studies. The incentive structure that existed in Ghana before liberalisation – import substitution, with heavy regulations and a strong role for the state – gave considerable protection to all local industries. There was a mixture of positive and negative incentives for industrial development. On the one hand, the infant industry protection offered the chance for firms to enter difficult activities and invest in developing capabilities. On the other, the unselective nature of the protection, the lack of offsetting pressures to invest in TCs and enormous gaps in skills, industrial experience, information and supporting institutions meant that the opportunity for learning could not be exploited to deepen the industrial structure and build up competitive capabilities.

Resource allocation in Ghanaian industry was not guided by a strategy of what the country could realistically achieve in industry, though

178

it does not appear that there were gross errors in terms of setting up huge white elephants. The ideological predilection in favour of public ownership, the suspicion of private enterprise and the uncertain economic climate further reduced the incentives for healthy TC acquisition.

After the liberalisation, the incentive structure improved enormously for the raising of operational capabilities in existing industries. The initial impact, around the mid-1980s, was to ease access to foreign equipment, inputs and technology. This raised capacity utilisation and improved profitability. Thereafter continuing liberalisation started to compete with domestic production. The pace of liberalisation accelerated towards the end of the decade, and by 1992 the bulk of protection for manufacturing had been dismantled.

The exposure to import competition was sweeping, with little selectivity exercised in terms of offering different rates of transitional protection to different industries. There was, in other words, no attempt to reform gradually the protectionist structure to take account of the time and effort involved in restructuring enterprises and improving their technological capabilities. Thus, the requirements of the 'learning' and 'relearning' processes were not taken into account.

At the same time, no strategy was designed or adopted to help firms improve their competitive position by improving their access to information, advice, skills or technical extension. The resulting incentive structure thus had two effects: intensified competitive pressures for firms whose products were directly importable and it helped industries that had 'natural' protection from import competition in that were able to use their new access to imports and improved demand in the local market to expand production and, in the better managed firms, to raise efficiency.

Many of the activities devastated by liberalisation were entry-level activities that usually form the first stage of industrial development. They are labour intensive, and use relatively easy technologies that are embodied in relatively inexpensive equipment. The low base of existing capabilities and the speed and nature of the liberalisation meant that they could not display the kind of export surge that has been witnessed in the new NIEs of South-East Asia. Thus, the new incentive structure, while giving strong signals for investing in improved TCs, failed to give the breathing space or provide the sort of supply-side measures that were needed for a strong supply and investment response. There were activities that benefited from the liberalisation (as well as individual firms that could muster the technological wherewithal), but a large proportion did not.

The emerging incentive structure, with low effective protection for most industrial activities, also offers little protection for new infant industries. Any sustained industrial growth in the future will thus have to depend on 'natural protection' to offset the costs of overcoming infancy: a local resource advantage (apart from cheap labour), protection given by high transport costs, or a niche local or export market. In the absence of a more positive industrial strategy, this may not be enough to allow domestic enterprises to diversify the industrial base and lead to dynamic growth of manufactured exports.

It is mainly foreign investors that can undertake such diversification in the absence of protection, because of their greater financial, technological and marketing resources, and because of their experience of capability building in other developing countries. However, MNC affiliates also face learning costs in new locations and need a base of skills and capabilities to work with. With its small base of skills and poor infrastructure, Ghana is not likely to provide an attractive location over many others in the developing world for non-resource-based activities that aim for world markets or face intense import competition. If Ghana is to emulate the foreign investment-led growth of countries like Malaysia or Thailand (or even Sri Lanka), it would need to improve considerably its physical, human and technological infrastructure. Foreign investment in Ghana is likely to continue for the foreseeable future mainly in activities with 'natural protection', or those that can tap regional markets.

Coming now to the individual industries, there are wide differences in the incentive regimes between them. It is interesting to review the entrepreneurs' own perception of the competitive situation facing them since import liberalisation. The sample firms were asked to rank their perceptions of the degree of competition faced from domestic firms and imports since 1986 on a scale of 1 to 5. The individual scores were normalised on a scale of 0 to 1, with increasing competition shown by scores closer to 1. Table 9.1 presents the results of this exercise for each of the four industries.

The table suggests that import competition was felt most severely by the textile and garment industry and least by wood working. Some metal-working firms also felt the import pressure, as did some food-processing firms, though both gave somewhat higher weight to domestic competition. These perceptions are in line with what our previous discussion suggested, drawing on general considerations of technology and comparative advantage.

The *garments* subsector offers perhaps the clearest example of the impact of import liberalisation on an entry level industry that should

Table 9.1   Entrepreneur's perceptions of the degree of competition faced
since 1986 from local producers and imports

	Competition from local producers	Competition from imports
Textiles and garments (average)	0.43	0.91
Food Processing (average)	0.57	0.40
Wood working (average)	0.63	0.20
Metal working (average)	0.57	0.53

Entrepreneur's scores were normalized along a scale of 0 to 1, in which the degree of competition ranked close to 0 are least intensive and those ranked close to 1 are most intensive. The figures are averages for all firms surveyed. This procedure was adapted from Levy (1993). The number of firms in this sample was 25. Textiles and garments had 7 firms while the other industries each had 6 firms.

be able to survive, export and do well in a low wage country like Ghana (this industry accounts for the largest share of the increase in manufactured exports from the developing world in the past three decades). The combination of cheap and relatively good-quality new clothes from Asia and even cheaper second-hand clothing from the developed countries has wiped out any local producer that is in direct competition. The firms that survive are in markets that are non-tradeable till now because of transactions costs involved in making customised uniforms or designs.

Within these markets there is competition among Ghanaian producers though it is very localised, and those that are able to improve their capabilities are gaining market share. However, all firms are operating at very low levels of capacity utilisation. There is a possibility that the best of these firms (TG1) may be able to develop sufficient capabilities to attract foreign buyers, though none of the others seem to be near this possibility.[1] On the other hand, Ghanaian customers may be able to overcome transactions cost barriers and themselves start ordering uniforms abroad (from East Asia), in which case the local industry would collapse completely.

In the *food processing* industry, the impact of incentive reforms is more mixed. Some manufacturers of processed foods are affected by import liberalisation, but the income and demand patterns of Ghana mean that highly processed and sophisticated food imports have a relatively small market. The exceptions are items like biscuits, where the FP4 case illustrates the impact of import competition, or mass-produced foods like flour, where local producers have survived by getting protection from the government. In the beverage sector, soft-drinks concentrates are being imported for local bottling rather than the final product, so that the impact on production does not appear so drastic. In products where multinational affiliates already have an entrenched market position, imports are restricted by the parent firm even if local production is more expensive. Small food processors are not included in this sample, but they are likely to be fairly well insulated from direct import competition, at least until incomes rise and consumer tastes become more sophisticated.

For those sample food processors not threatened by imports, the liberalisation has improved incentives for technological upgrading. However, this is primarily by making inputs easier to obtain for selling to the local market rather than by opening up large export opportunities. Despite the resource base in Ghana for food exports, there were few signs (except from the state-owned FP3-Cannery, which has been exporting for some time) that the new incentive structure was the prelude to a significant shift to export orientation. The technological and marketing capabilities needed for this are evidently missing.

In *wood working*, there seems to have been little direct import competition. The availability of local raw materials, local tastes in furniture, and the tradition of having furniture made to order, have served to help local manufacturers (though local competition has increased). The industry depends on imported equipment, chemicals and accessories, and liberalisation has helped local firms. The incentive climate is thus conducive to technological upgrading and entry into export markets. While some upgrading is taking place, however, the significant upgrading in skills, work practices, management and technology that are needed for export activity are still extremely rare in the furniture industry.

In *metal working*, there is increased import competition in intermediates (iron and steel), certain kinds of equipment and tools, and also a range of assembly products like motorcycles (which are not in the case study sample, but are apparently suffering badly). This is inducing technological upgrading in a few cases or driving firms out of business in others: the case study has instances of both reactions. Other products that serve niche markets face little direct competition, and are doing well from the access to equipment and inputs. These firms also face stronger incentives for TC development than before, because local competition is growing, and their products may become subject to import competition as customers become aware of imported alternatives.

In general, therefore, the changes in incentives brought about by the post-1986 reforms have had a mixed impact on the TC development of sample firms. Import competition, access to imported inputs and equipment, and the growth of local competition have greatly increased the pressure and ability to undertake technical upgrading. At the same time, the speed of the liberalisation and weaknesses in local TCs and institutions, together with an absence of supply-side measures to boost capabilities, have meant that many firms have been unable to respond in an appropriate manner. At the present level of development of Ghanaian industry, improved incentives provide a necessary but not sufficient condition for TC development to happen.

ACCESS TO INPUTS AND FINANCE

The technological performance of firms may be affected by segmentation in factor markets, especially for materials and credit. As far as the raw material and other physical input markets are concerned, access to imports is likely to have been segmented in the pre-liberalization period when foreign exchange was tight. Large firms, and perhaps state-owned enterprises, may have found it easier to get foreign exchange allocations from the Government than small firms. Thus, activities that were less import-dependent may have found it easier to operate than others, and may have been able to invest in TCs to a greater extent.

After liberalisation, however, this discrimination seems to have disappeared, at least as far as official policy is concerned: none of the sample firms complained of difficulties in getting access to imported inputs. There may still exist inherent segmentation in import markets, however, arising from the disadvantages of buying in small lots or from markets on which local information is difficult to get. It is not clear how important these were for the sample enterprises.

As far as access to local credit is concerned, a separate study in Regional Programme for Enterprise Development (RPED) deals in detail with problems of capital-market segmentation. What appears from our research is that there does seem to exist capital-market segmentation, combined with credit stringency that makes TC investments very difficult, especially for smaller firms. A number of firms complained of the financial squeeze imposed by the adjustment programme, including some which (like MW7) were performing relatively well in the market. What is worth noting, however, is that investments in TC at the level of the Ghanaian sample are not particularly demanding of finance, and that lack of technological competence *per se* cannot be blamed on credit stringency or segmentation.[2]

CONCLUSIONS

The incentive framework in Ghana for technological development has improved greatly since liberalisation. Both domestic and foreign competition have increased, and access to imported inputs and technology has improved. However, the speed of the liberalisation and its lack of coordination with capability building measures has imposed costs on Ghanaian enterprises, including those in activities in which the country may be expected to have a comparative advantage. It is difficult to decipher from the case studies if segmentation in markets for finance and other inputs have held back TC development or distorted its incidence across different groups of firms. The analysis of the panel data in Chapter 4 suggested that it had, but that a significant proportion of firm-level differences in technology could not be explained by segmentation. The case studies confirm this finding: the factors discussed in the last three chapters, the components of TC building, do seem to account for a very substantial part of firm-level technological performance. Thus, much of the explanation for technological development would appear to lie there rather than in factor-market imperfections.

Part C

Policy Implications

10 Lessons of the Case Studies

INTRODUCTION

This chapter draws the main policy conclusions that emerge from this analysis of technological development in Ghanaian enterprises. The discussion deals first with the incentive regime (trade and industrial policies) before going into human resource, infrastructure and support service issues.

TRADE POLICY

The opening-up of the Ghanaian economy as well as the ensuing adjustment programme have had important impacts on the industrial sector. While the new trade regime offers some incentive for Ghanaian enterprises to enhance their technological capabilities and to reallocate resources to more competitive activities, the evidence suggests that so far the supply response in manufacturing has been weak. Relatively few activities have improved their technological performance and raised their international competitiveness, while many have closed down or are in serious trouble. The activities that have benefited, and in some cases expanded exports, are those that already had a resource-based comparative advantage, were specialised in market niches (like very simple products for low income consumers) or were protected by high transport costs from direct foreign competition.

Some industries set up in the earlier trade regime in Ghana were inherently inefficient and did not deserve to survive, and the liberalisation raised economic efficiency by releasing resources from them. However, others that are in difficulties are potentially competitive and should have been able to survive and grow by upgrading their physical and human capital. The fact that they have not done so may be traced to various causes, eg. the speed of liberalisation, the scarcity and/or the cost of investible resources (or the inability of the financial system to assess and support worthwhile technological effort), the extra risk and uncertainty created by the change in policy regime, lack of information and knowledge on feasible strategies (or on their own requirements of technologies and skills) on the part of firms, deficiencies in the supply of the necessary skills in the labour market, poor institutional support for the restructuring and technological upgrading by individual firms, and so on.

For many industrial enterprises the lifting of protection has implied the need to change the composition of their output to nontraded products or close shop. Sample firms in the garments industry provide good illustrations. Several clothing makers reported shifts to the production of school and other types of uniforms, instead of the products they were making before, as a result of the rapid influx of imports of new and used clothing. In the case of simple steel products such as construction bars, the need for a limited extent (15 per cent) of protection was raised because of the disadvantages inherent in Ghana's poor industrial infrastructure facilities.

These considerations raise the possibility that import liberalisation by itself may not be sufficient to evoke a dynamic technological response from a majority of manufacturing firms. Rapid exposure to import competition may, on the contrary, deter firms from investing in restructuring that takes time to bear fruit. However, slowing down the liberalisation process *per se* will not be sufficient to ensure efficient restructuring and resource allocation: it would merely provide a breathing space for certain actions to be taken. To ensure that the granting of a grace period will be useful, certain conditions must be met:

- The activities supported must be economically viable (that is, able to survive without protection) in a relatively short period.
- The support provided (e.g. protection against imports) must be limited in extent and duration and its future progress must be pre-announced, to ensure that firms have a strong incentive to invest in their upgrading.
- Entrepreneurs must be able to gain access to capital to finance the restructuring process.
- Entrepreneurs should have access to the technologies, skills and other inputs they need to operate competitively (market failures in factor markets must be addresses).
- Technology, training, marketing, and other institutions should be available to 'fill in' the capability gaps within enterprises that they cannot remedy on their own.

The ideal trade regime for the transition period may thus be one that gears the phasing of exposure to world competition to the speed at which industry can achieve efficient restructuring and integrates it with measures to remedy supply-side weaknesses. While optimal phasing and support may be impossible to achieve in practice, it is not difficult to differentiate the pace of liberalisation among broad groups of activities according to their technological complexity (more difficult activities getting a longer 'grace period', easier activities a shorter one), and to mount measures to meet the most critical skill, informational and technological needs. A selective use of the limited resources, material and human, that the government has may still yield better results than leaving matters entirely to free markets.

So much for existing activities. A good case could also be made for the granting of infant industry protection to new manufacturing activities in Ghana. Given the cost, duration and risk associated with entry into more complex industries, full exposure to import competition may 'freeze' Ghana's comparative advantage in its existing mould, which is largely based on its natural resource endowments. The granting of limited protection, again if accompanied by supportive factor market policies, may be a necessary condition for the diversification and growth of industry. The pursuit of such selective but integrated interventions enabled countries like Korea and Taiwan to achieve rapid industrial growth and entry into new and difficult activities. The need for support would be lessened if foreign investments could be induced to come in and bear the learning costs, but, as noted, this is not likely in the foreseeable future. And even the promotion of foreign investments would require selective interventions in factor markets to allow affiliates to be internationally competitive.

Given the dangers inherent in giving protection, it is important that the process should be carefully set up. It should not be granted by non-transparent methods, but based on a detailed analysis by private and public committees or consultative groups. The extent of protection granted should be in all cases: (i) low, with a range, say, of 10–40 per cent in effective protection terms; (ii) limited in time, to a maximum of five to seven years, and with declining values for the protection during that period; (iii) as a *sine qua non* productivity and export targets should be negotiated at the time of granting the protection. It is vital that the effects of protection and the productivity performance of industries be continuously monitored, with shortfalls subject to penalties.[1]

INDUSTRIAL POLICIES

Past industrial policies in Ghana, promoting public ownership and favour-
ing protected activities, have distorted the pattern of technological learning
in Ghana. The new regime has improved the competitive environment
for industrial enterprises. It has liberalised entry of local and foreign
investors, though improvements to the foreign investment regime are
still needed.[2] It has launched measures to divest itself of some public
enterprises and improve the performance of those that remain in state
hands. This will release resources and raise productive efficiency in
the economy. An improved regulatory framework, with fewer bureau-
cratic requirements and faster processing, will pave the way for healthier
business strategies by private enterprises.

These reforms to industrial policy may, however, be permissive rather
than compelling inducements to technological upgrading. While increasing
domestic competition would be a stimulus to investments in TCs, the
response of private enterprises may be weak if rapid liberalisation de-
ters the entry of enterprises into more demanding industrial technologies or activities, or if the institutional and education/training system
fail to produce the information, know-how, skills and finance needed
for such upgrading. Apart from setting the stage for private enterprise
to grow and compete freely, therefore, the government should adopt a
more forceful strategy of promoting activities that are in the country's
medium-term technological and competitive interest.

This is what the government seems to have in mind in naming a list
of 'priority industrial areas' in its new *Industrial Policy Statement*.[3]
However, the present list is too wide and unselective, and there does
not seem to exist a coherent set of policies on import competition,
R&D, institutional support and skill creation geared to promoting effectively the priority industries.

A new industrial policy should also examine how small-scale enterprises could best be stimulated and helped to become technically efficient. There is a clear role for efficient SSEs in activities that do not
have scale economies and yet enjoy competitive advantages, either as
competitors to large-scale enterprises or as suppliers and subcontractors to them. In the medium to long term, SSEs could contribute significantly to Ghana's comparative advantage in manufactures, as they
have done in the new NIEs of South-East Asia.

The kinds of policy and infrastructure support needed for SSE promotion are well known, and lie beyond the scope of this study. It
should also be noted, however, that supply-side measures to promote

African SSE in modern industry have not had an impressive track record in recent years.[4] The tendency has been to blame all the problems of SSEs on the lack of finance and to 'throw money at them'. The lack of access to credit markets is only one of the problems of small enterprises, and this strategy can be extremely wasteful. The experience of Kenya, which has had the largest programme for promoting African entrepreneurship, shows that extensive financial support, when technological and managerial capabilities are lacking, does not succeed in creating competitive enterprises.

HUMAN RESOURCE DEVELOPMENT

It is evident that human resource improvement has to be an integral part of any industrial development strategy in Ghana. This is widely accepted for most African countries, and the evidence of the present sample reinforces the belief strongly. An evaluation of the existing education and training system is outside the scope of this study. However, it is important to note that there seem to be serious deficiencies in skill availability at practically all levels of industry, from the shopfloor and supervisory levels to the highest levels of technological and managerial manpower. Few specialised training facilities exist to meet the specific needs of particular industries (for instance, for better quality control, improved designs, preventive maintenance, and so on), and most firms have no recourse but to meet these needs as best they can in-house. Some of the larger and better-informed firms indicated that the content of the technical education curricula is unsuited to modern industrial needs, and there is insufficient emphasis on practical, hands-on experience.[5]

The balance between elementary, secondary and vocational, and university and other tertiary education should be carefully evaluated in Ghana. Preliminary examination of the data, as well as direct impressions, suggest that while the labour force is generally literate, there is a great shortage, except in the case of large firms and foreign subsidiaries, of university-trained technical professional personnel – particularly engineers and scientists.[6] Institutions such as Kumasi University of Science and Technology and the Kumasi Technical Institute are very few in number and their output is still limited in relation to the country's needs. Apart from adding to the educational facilities for technical skill creation, it may be desirable to involve industry in determining the nature and content of the courses and practical training to be given.

There may be room for private–public cooperation in setting-up and running the required institutions. There is also a clear need for policies to induce skilled Ghanaians resident overseas to return to their country.

Despite the shortage of technically trained manpower in the country, few manufacturing enterprises seem to regard the shortage of skilled labour as an important constraint on their growth or survival.[7] This suggests that many industrial enterprises (particularly medium- and small-scale firms) are unaware of the need to utilise higher skills. This is a major problem in itself, which has to be tackled before investing in skills and education. As a part of skill-upgrading policies, it may therefore be necessary to launch a campaign to inform and persuade Ghanaian enterprises of the need to use higher levels of skills to attain greater competitiveness.

Enterprises may also have to be helped in using effectively, rather than simply employing, skilled manpower. The temporary use of foreign experts as 'teachers' that can demonstrate the practical ways of upgrading production methods with better skills may be an efficient way of doing this. The case of MW1 shows how the induction of a group of experienced personnel from another developing country can not only raise dramatically the production efficiency of a complex operation but also transmit the necessary skills to the local workforce.[8] However, the use of foreign skills cannot be a complete solution to the effective use of local skills; domestic 'teachers' must be developed over time. The growth of local consultants and technical extension services is a solution to be aimed for in the long term.

Apprenticeship programmes are only prevalent in certain activities with traditional technologies such as wood and metal working. As they exist at this time, they do not seem to constitute a solution for Ghana's training needs. They are geared to the transmission of traditional technologies and work practices and, unlike the apprenticeship system of Germany which is now the envy of most developed countries, have no formal education or higher skill content. Thus, the technical knowledge needed for new industrial activities, or even the modernisation of many existing ones, cannot be imparted via these programmes. They may be modified to meet these needs, but it appears that the modifications will have to be very substantial, with vastly increased inputs from the formal education system.

Finally, one of the main findings of this study is the strong link between technological capability and the level of education and work experience of the entrepreneur. This seems to determine the firm's capacity to undertake the technical and human capital development efforts needed to cope with modern technology. It would seem that the prevalent model of entrepreneurial development in Africa, driven by the graduation of traditional small and micro enterprises, may not in fact be conducive to Ghana's industrial development. There is a need for a new breed of enterprises (of all sizes) that are more in tune with the needs of TC development, and this calls for an entrepreneurial class with a more informed and modern outlook than traditional enterprises can provide.

This is one of the strongest reasons for investments in education and training, and for assiduous efforts to attract back skilled and experienced Ghanaians from other countries. It may also be beneficial to launch training programmes for entrepreneurship development directly, but our study offers no clues on the effectiveness of such programmes.

INDUSTRIAL INFRASTRUCTURE

A close relationship exists between productivity at the plant level and the quality of available infrastructure services. Of particular significance are the transportation (especially the availability of roads), energy (especially the supply of electric power), and telecommunications (in particular telephone services). While this has not been treated in this study, several firms in the sample describe the pernicious effect of deficits in infrastructure facilities. Some emphasised breakdowns in electric power supply, others the poor quality of the telephone service, and the lack of good access roads. In the Suame Magazine in Kumasi (an industrial zone) the almost-total lack of infrastructure services, in particular roads, was evident. A similar situation was apparent in a woodworking area where a number of small operators have created a large concentration of primitive shops equally lacking in most infrastructure facilities.

SUPPORT SERVICES

Under this heading we include access to information, the S&T infrastructure and the provision of extension services to industry. The *import of technology* into Ghana was tightly regulated during much of the import substitution period. The Ghana Investments Centre was required to check each technology transfer agreement.[9] It laid down maximum royalty rates (5 per cent of sales for domestic sales), the duration of contracts, and clauses that were permissible. The procedure was long and cumbersome, and the GIC was supposed to ensure that local alternative technologies were utilised whenever possible. This framework for technology transfer was inefficient and counterproductive. To quote a World Bank study,

> The tight control by the Government perhaps reflected a concern about local firms' limited capabilities in concluding agreements that are fair in terms of the use of technology, and that inappropriate agreements could lead to a loss of valuable foreign exchange to Ghana. Whatever may be the justification for the restrictions and conditions that are presently imposed on technology transfer agreements, their implementation raised some difficulties. Some of the controls, such as the evaluation of the appropriateness of technology, are hard to implement, given staff constraints. The problem is compounded by the ambiguity of many regulations, which are vaguely worded and leave the interpretation wide open and at the discretion of authorities. Furthermore, the regulations do not have a clear legal status as they have not been formally adopted.[10]

These regulations seem to be more relaxed now, at least according to official statements (our sample firms had older foreign licences, it was not possible to evaluate this issue). New regulations are in the process of being drafted. The more realistic exchange rate and the more competitive environment probably induce firms to negotiate agreements more carefully. Perhaps because of this, and because of the general difficulties confronting the manufacturing sector, the number of technology agreements has dropped in recent months. However, the policy framework for technology transfer does not appear to be an important handicap any more.

The most important need with respect to technology imports is to improve the provision of information support to enterprises in locating and buying technologies in international markets. SMEs even in advanced industrial countries face market failures in buying technology, because of the fragmentation of the market and the large fixed costs inherent in building up a base of information and negotiating skills at the firm level.[11] In countries like Ghana, the gaps are much larger, raising the costs of upgrading technology and keeping in touch with international technological trends.

Apart from gaining access to foreign technology, policies should be devised to encourage *in-house technical activity* by Ghanaian enterprises. At this stage this is going to consist of shopfloor engineering and improvement rather than formal R&D activities. However, as industry develops the larger firms may be encouraged to set up R&D facilities as a way of absorbing new technologies. Formal research and development is practically non-existent in Ghanaian industry. At the most, a few of the larger and better-managed enterprises, mostly multinational affiliates, conduct some adaptive technological activity, but all serious technological effort is referred to parent companies or joint-venture partners abroad. Small- and medium-sized firms do very little even of basic process and product engineering.

There are no specific incentives for R&D in Ghana, beyond the normal tax deductibility of expenditures. The Government's new draft *Science and Technology Policy Statement* mentions the need to encourage the private sector to take advantage of the existing tax deductibility. This suggests that the provision remains unutilized. It does not seem at this stage, however, that the lack of financial incentives *per se* is a significant deterrent to the undertaking of private R&D in Ghana. The deficiencies lie elsewhere, in the skill and capability gaps noted above, and, perhaps to a lesser extent, in the poor quality of the research institutions in the public sector.

In general, there is a lack of awareness on the part of Ghanaian enterprises of the importance of research and experimental development effort for assimilating technologies. As with investments in skill development, there may therefore exist a strong need to inform and persuade enterprises of the benefits of technological investments, both in-house and in collaboration with research institutes and universities.

Coming to the *S&T infrastructure*, the evidence of the sample suggests that there are serious deficiencies that policy needs to address to enhance the technological capabilities of Ghanaian industry. Of the three CSIR institutes concerned with industry, only the FRI has provided some modest inputs into the technological efforts of sample firms, mainly by conducting tests. Practically none of the technologies developed by the institutes has evoked interest on the part of industry. This is so for several reasons: the nature of the work undertaken by these institutes, the poor quality of their facilities and skills, the lack of marketing the technologies to industry and of seeking to understand their technological needs, and the lack of knowledge or dynamism on the part of the enterprises themselves.[12]

The Government is aware of many of these problems. Its *Technology Policy Statement* has several comments on the need to upgrade the

CSIR facilities, including their management and linkages with industry. It even proposes that the institutes be required to earn a significant proportion (30 per cent) of their revenues from the sale of services. These measures are clearly in the right direction. However, it is not clear that such an objective is realistic. The *Statement* still shows a 'top down' approach. The CSIR institutions are still seen as a primary source of industrial technologies, and technological 'self reliance' is still mentioned as an objective of policy. The driving force of technological change is still seen as being located in research institutes rather than manufacturing enterprises.

Since Ghana will, for the foreseeable future, remain a user of imported, relatively simple, mature technologies from the developed countries or the NIEs, its very limited technological and human resources should all be focused to this end − to make technology imports as effective as possible and to master the imported technologies as rapidly as possible. The technology institutes should play their part in helping enterprises to obtain and absorb the relevant technologies: this itself would require a considerable strengthening of their capabilities, along with a reorientation of their objectives and management.

As far as information networks relevant to technology are concerned, Ghana has two that are worth noting: Ghana National Scientific and Technological Information Network (Ghastinet) and the GSB's Scheme for Technical Assistance to Exporters. Ghastinet seeks to establish a national capacity for the provision of scientific and technological information to assist national development. At this stage, it is considerably under-funded, and would need substantial infusions of skilled manpower and financial resources to enable it to make a positive contribution. The GSB's Scheme aims to provide prospective Ghanaian exporters with information on standards and other technical regulations in foreign markets. This is still in an embryonic stage and needs a great deal of skilled staff and equipment to function effectively. It is not clear if all these skills requirements can be met within the framework of the existing education and training structure in the country, or if there would be a further need for upstream investments in skill generation.

The need to strengthen the standards services has been noted through this study. This is an essential infrastructure service that every industrialising country needs, regardless of the composition of its manufacturing sector. A liberalising economy that wishes to expand its export base, like Ghana, needs it even more urgently, especially in the context of tighter quality rules in major developed country markets. Moreover, the Standards Board should take on the task of introducing industry to quality control management systems (like the ISO 9000 series) rather than simply helping them to check the final quality of their products. This will increasingly become a necessary condition for export-oriented industry, and countries like Malaysia are already far advanced in implementing the series.[13]

There is little point in strengthening S&T institutes if linkages with industry remain weak. It is essential to have policies encouraging manufacturers to establish linkages with the institutes, by providing matching funds or subsidies for firms that buy services from them.[14] In the initial stages, the government may provide a very substantial part of the funds (say, three-quarter or more), with the proportion falling as the mechanism gets better established. In conjunction with the provision of matching funds, firms may be given access to a special line of credit to fund projects at the research institutes and universities. At the same time, technical personnel at these institutions should be encouraged to consult for industrial enterprises, and to commercialise their findings by setting up their own enterprises. For the latter purpose, the government may consider an incubator scheme for technology-based entrepreneurs.

Finally, there is a pressing need to provide *extension services* to industry, especially to SMEs which are prone to suffer the most market failures in getting technical information and assistance. The existing services for small-scale industry in Ghana seem inappropriate because they are more interested in advocating a 'small is beautiful' philosophy than in surveying the actual production and technological needs of small enterprises.

CONCLUSIONS

Let us summarise the main policy conclusions of this study. The promotion of industrial technology and competitiveness in Ghana will require policy support and new initiatives over a wide front. Some progress has already been made, with the reforms to the incentive regime wrought under the liberalisation. This is not, however, likely to be enough. There is a case for retaining some instruments of infant industry protection to encourage enterprises to enter new activities with long and difficult learning periods. The granting of protection entails several difficulties and has to be carefully designed and implemented, with measures to offset its deleterious effects on incentives to invest in technological capabilities.

More important, protection by itself is unlikely to lead to industrial dynamism when there are widespread shortages of skills, technical know-how and support services. These are market failures that have to be addressed at source. Their remedying has to be part of an integrated strategy to promote industrial growth, since addressing one set of problems (like incentives) cannot compensate for gaps elsewhere (say, in skills). However, just creating more skills and services cannot succeed if manufacturing enterprises are unaware of their value or of how best to utilise them. Thus, informing and educating enterprises is likely to be a central part of industrial strategy in the early stages of development.

In any integrated strategy for industrial development, there will be a need to build up a variety of educational, training, technology and infrastructural institutions to carry out the tasks that the government has to perform. Ghana has an array of such institutions in existence, but their effectiveness is limited. The government is well aware of these limitations and is attempting to overcome them. What it seems to lack is a clear and comprehensive vision of the components of a proper strategy, and of how to integrate its incentive measures with policies on the development of capabilities.

Appendices

There are four appendices to this study, dealing with each of the industries studied in Ghana. They provide background information to the industry in the country, and provide some of the more detailed material from the case studies here. However, instead of going through each of the cases studied, they highlight the more interesting cases. The essence of the findings has been reported in the main body of the book, but those interested in the details of capability development will find these appendices of interest.

Appendix A: Textiles and Garments

BACKGROUND

The textiles and garments subsector is the largest manufacturing activity in Ghana in terms of the number of enterprises, the second largest (after wood working) in terms of employment, and the third largest (after food processing and wood working) in terms of value added. Since the adjustment programme was launched, it has shown modest signs of growth, mainly because of improved access to imported parts and inputs. However, growing import competition over the period (particularly of second-hand clothing) has caused considerable distress. The value of output (in constant cedis) in 1990 was only 39.4 per cent of that in 1970. The index number of production of textiles, apparel and leather products in 1990 was 37.7 compared to 63.5 for the whole of the manufacturing sector.[1]

Table A.1 shows the size and employment distribution of enterprises in the subsector in 1987, the year of the last available census.[2] The subsector comprises two very different types of technologies. Modern textile production is a large-scale, capital-intensive activity, with correspondingly high requirements of engineering and technical skills. Garment manufacture, by contrast, remains a largely labour-intensive operation with low capital and skill needs (though there are segments of the industry that use sophisticated computer-aided techniques). The structure of the industry in Ghana reflects these characteristics: the average employment size of the enterprises in the two activities and the concentration of employment across the different size classes reflects the differences in their capital intensity.

It should be noted, however, that within each activity the size of enterprises in Ghana is relatively small. In garments, for instance, there is only one firm with over 100 employees, and its workforce of 195 is small by the standards of garments' producers in the developing countries of East and South-East Asia (where employment is often in the thousands).

Technological advance in textile production (the technology of spinning, weaving and finishing, the three main stages of manufacture) is determined mainly by advances in the design of equipment. Much of modern textile equipment is very complex and expensive, and operational efficiency depends on plant-level capabilities to operate, maintain, repair, adjust, and improve upon these machines. Given the low wages in Ghana, the appropriate level of mechanisation is at the intermediate level: ring-spinning, semi-automatic or automatic weaving and largely manual finishing. Such technology is very well diffused, and the equipment is not difficult to locate (the major producers are concentrated in Switzerland, Germany, Italy and the UK, with second tier producers scattered in many NIEs); second-hand equipment is available from various developed and newly industrialising countries.

Table A.1   Characteristics of textile and garments enterprises by
employment size (1987)

	Micro (1–4)	Small (5–29)	Medium (30–99)	Large (>100)	Total
Textiles					
No. of Enterprises	26	110	25	16	177
No. of Employees	75	1 092	1 411	10 247	1 225
Empl. per Enterp.	2.9	9.9	56.4	640	72.5
Garments					
No. of Enterprises	982	1 398	36	1	2 417
No. of Employees	2 275	12 091	1 537	195	16 098
Empl. per Enterp.	2.3	8.6	42.7	195	6.7

Source: RPED Background Paper on Ghana, 1992.

Many of the NIEs started their export drive with older or second-hand textile equipment, which allowed them to lower their capital costs and use their abundant supplies of labour. However, the production of textiles with older, less automated equipment is extremely demanding of worker, supervisory and technical skills if world class quality is to be achieved. Labour in East Asia was skilled, and was complemented by an ample supply of technicians and managers. The NIEs quickly upgraded to modern equipment, and their production facilities are now practically as capital intensive as those of advanced industrial countries. However, in some areas of textile production older technologies (at least in their current versions, like ring spinning) are capable of producing very high quality output if used at best-practice levels of efficiency.

In garments, technical efficiency is determined less by the equipment than by operator skills, layout, and an ability to meet rapidly changing product-design requirements. Equipment technology has not changed much, except in very high-wage countries where cutting and pattern making have been automated and design is becoming computerised. The most skill-intensive task remains product design, but in most exporters of garments in developing countries, design is undertaken in the developed countries and communicated to the manufacturers by buyers. Most developing countries specialise in the export of low end, standardised garments, but even this has strict requirements of worker discipline and skill, and technical needs related to production planning, layout and quality control.[3] Garments are an "easy" industry to enter, but a core of TCs is required that takes effort to acquire.

Ghana does not appear to be an efficient producer of textiles. The machinery installed is not of the latest design, which may be considered appropriate to its factor endowments. However, technical evaluations of its firms shows that it lacks the technological capabilities to operate the equipment efficiently. To quote: 'machine efficiencies in spinning and weaving are on the lower side and range between 50 and 79 per cent'.[4] Moreover, despite having one of the world's lowest wage levels in this industry, its cost advantage is 'undermined by low labour productivity which is only 10 per cent in spinning, 20 per cent in weaving and 12 per cent in processing compared with the developed countries'.[5] Thus, one comparison puts the Ghanaian cost of grey cloth at 1.73 times higher than in the East Asian NIEs.[6] An estimate of effective rates of protection (ERPs) in this industry places it at 75 per cent in 1990, compared to 54 per cent for garments.[7] The quality of textile output is very low, constituting a major handicap to local downstream users like garment makers.[8]

In garments, the equipment employed is largely manual, but operational efficiency is 31 per cent of European levels in garments and 37.5 per cent in knitting, while wages are only 3.6 per cent of German levels.[9] The resulting processing costs are consequently higher in Ghana than in Germany. The product range is at the low end, and quality tends to be poor by international standards. There are shortages of technical skills like cutting, pattern making, designing and so on, apart from the poor quality of local fabrics used.

Exports of garments to the developed world are negligible.[10] The high ERP noted and an unfavourable domestic resource cost ratio of 1.99, denoting a lack of international competitiveness (presumably because of the low levels of process efficiency[11]), reinforces the more technical evaluation that the industry is largely inefficient. Import liberalisation appears to be hurting the industry seriously, especially since 1990 when tariffs were reduced sharply. Thus, the capacity utilisation level of the industry, estimated at 20 per cent in 1990,[12] is likely to be lower today. In view of the lack of competitiveness of the industry, this is not surprising. The purchase of second-hand clothing, which would devastate even very efficient garments producers, has greatly exacerbated the situation, but it is not, as noted, the only cause. The case studies illustrate the experience at the micro level, and point to the non-traded niche of the domestic garment market as the reason for the survival of many Ghanaian firms.

The sample consists of 8 firms, of which 5 make (or made, since one folded up some 5 years earlier) sewn garments, while the others make a variety of textile products: 1 makes knitwear, 1 fishing nets and polyester fabrics, and 1 synthetic leather. It did not prove possible to collect usable data on a textile-printing enterprise which was visited. Thus, the following analysis does not apply to the textile industry in the usual sense of the term.

It is useful to distinguish between the garment-sewing and knitwear parts of the industry, though the two are often found in the same firm. Knitwear is more capital-intensive and demanding than sewing garments, and it may be more difficult to reach international levels of competitiveness in the former than in the latter. Of the garments firms, TG1, TG3 and TG6 (and the dead firm TG8) produced knitwear earlier, but closed down this operation because of foreign competition, and only make sewn garments now. TG5 is the only local firm in Ghana specialising in knitwear that has survived import competition till now. The net and synthetic-leather firms are in speciality products.

All the enterprises but one are wholly locally owned. The exception is the net manufacturer (TG4) which had some Syrian capital. Another four were started by other local non-African entrepreneurs; of these, one was started by a local non-African but is now under an African. The remaining three firms were started and operated by African Ghanaians. Only one of the eight can be classified as growing: TG1, which is the largest of the sample firms in this subsector. Apart from the one that has folded up, the others are surviving at very low levels of capacity utilisation.

INVESTMENT CAPABILITIES

Most of the firms in the sample started with both sewing and knitting of garments, but only one has survived as a knitwear maker after liberalisation. The investment capabilities of the firms in this industry are assessed separately for those specialising in sewing of garments from those involved in knitting and other special fabrics.

Garment firms. The largest firm in this sample, TG1, has an interesting record of investing in a variety of technologies, and is worth describing at some length. It was originally in both sewing of garments and knitwear. It started in 1974–5 with 80 new machines bought from a local dealer. The dealer installed the machines, while the owner's two daughters (who had technical training in textile production) designed the layout and trained the workers in sewing. The technical skills provided by the daughters were significant to the initial growth of the firm (the daughters left the firm in the early 1980s to get married and so ceased to be a source of skills). In 1979 the entrepreneur bought some knitting machines from Germany, visiting several suppliers before making his choice. The supplier sent an engineer to install the equipment and train the workers in the new technology. This German engineer stayed on in Ghana with the firm and became the technical manager (his role as technological 'catalyst' is elaborated on below). This investment was a success in the sense that the knitting plant worked well until 1987, when the liberalisation knocked it out of the market and the firm withdrew into making military uniforms and civilian overalls (which were less exposed to import competition).

In 1984 the firm purchased a finishing plant, financed by a $1.2 million loan from the African Development Bank. Textile finishing is one of the more complex of textile technologies, and the firm went about the investment carefully. It used a major international consulting firm to do a feasibility study, and negotiated the purchase of new equipment from the UK. However, TG1 claims that the plant supplied was defective and never worked; the matter is still under litigation. It is impossible to decide without further evidence whether the fault lay with the purchase and transfer of technology, the lack of local technical skills, or defects in the plant.

In 1987, when imported inputs and equipment were available but finished products still faced tariffs, the firm bought a computer-aided design (CAD) system from Germany for $60 000 (the system is the only one in the industry in Ghana). The German engineer was familiar with the technology and conducted the search and negotiations, and subsequently trained a worker (with secondary education) to use it. The CAD system proved an important competitive advantage as import competition grew, because the firm could design logos for local customers and print them on imported T-shirts; this activity now comprises 5 per cent of sales. The investment was thus well-conceived and properly executed.

Of the other four sewing firms in the sample, two started without their own equipment: TG7 and TG8 (now dead) hired tailors and seamstresses who brought their sewing machines. Over time, new machines were bought from a variety of sources. TG7 had eight machines by 1992, while TG8 had 48 machines at its peak. TG3 bought new Italian and German machines (25 sewing, 8 knitting, and 1 each for pleating and embroidery), based on advice from a UK cloth supplier. Two supervisors were sent to Italian suppliers for training in embroidery and knitting, while the suppliers' engineers came to Ghana to set up the plant. The knitting part of the operation came to a halt after liberalisation, and the firm now survives on school uniforms. TG6 was set up by a businessman of Indian origin who got new sewing and knitting machines and imported a textile engineer from India to do the installation and commissioning. A German technician was brought to train workers in cutting and sewing techniques. This gave the firm a good start and it worked well till the original entrepreneur left Ghana in 1976. He sold the plant to an employee, who subsequently added nothing to the plant. Most of the machines had been sold off by 1992, and a small rump of the original was still in operation by the time of the interviews.

Other firms. The knitwear firm TG5 was started in 1970 by a Lebanese trader forced to move into manufacturing by government policies on non-African traders. He drew on the advice of a relative who had a textile factory in Syria on how to start. He used a German agent to import the equipment, and was guided by him in locating suppliers, mainly in Germany, but also in Italy, US and UK. The layout and initial training was done by a Sudanese engineer, and appears to have been efficiently carried out. However, the firm was taken under state management from 1979 to 1990, and was badly run, with no additions to the equipment stock. The original entrepreneur took over again after all other knitwear manufacturers in Ghana had caved in to import competition, and was trying to refurbish the old plant (with some success, as discussed below).

The net firm (the largest of three Ghanaian net makers), TG4, was started in 1976 by three Syrians who were already manufacturing textiles in Ghana. They were able to search for used machines in Germany. The seller's engineer came to install some of the machines, while the local production manager installed the rest. A group of experienced textile workers were hired away from other firms to train workers. This was a promising start, and the firm added a knitting machine in 1983. However, this was its last investment. The firm could not develop competitive capabilities (see below) and so could not compete with imports when liberalisation started. Capacity utilisation declined drastically in the late 1980s. The firm went into receivership in 1989, and is now being run by the receivers.

The synthetic-leather firm TG2 was started in 1984 by a Lebanese trader. He initially bought the equipment cheaply from a trade fair in Germany in 1976, but did not install it until 1984 because of political instability. Prior to the installation he went to Germany for some training, then got two engineers from the equipment manufacturer to come to Ghana to design and set up the plant and train the workers. Liberalisation started soon after and sales declined sharply with cheaper imports from other developing countries. There were no further additions to the plant, and the owner is trying to diversify into ceramics with second-hand equipment bought from an auction of a bankrupt firm in Ghana.

PRODUCTION CAPABILITIES

Garments firms. Garment sewing has relatively simple processing technologies (cutting and sewing), but differences in technical capability with respect to maintenance, operation, layout, quality control, and inventory and stock control can make important differences to firm-level competitiveness. Process and product technologies are taken in turn.

As far as process technologies are concerned, the main equipment in the sample firms, manual or power sewing machines, is around 14 to 25 years old. It is relatively simple to use and maintain. It needs regular overhaul and a ready supply of spare parts. However, only TG1 has a well-established routine for maintenance, with daily, monthly and yearly servicing; it also has an in-house workshop with four employees that can carry out repairs and make some spares. This is a major advantage over the other four firms, which do not have a similar servicing routine or in-house repair and workshop facilities (one of these firms, TG8, closed down some time ago). In the absence of a well-functioning service industry, this raises their operating costs and 'downtime' (the period for which machines are idle), because machines are run till they have problems, and spares and repairs have to wait for outside supplies.

Quality control is a critical function in garment manufacturing. Again, only TG1 has a full-time quality control department (three employees) and keeps track of its reject rates (1-2 per cent). It sells only on the domestic market, so it is difficult to assess whether its standards are up to international levels. It has the reputation of having the best quality on the local market, but has been forced by foreign competition to go into niche markets (army uniforms). The other firms have no quality control teams, no idea of their reject rates and so no feedback into production from mistakes made. In each of these, *ad hoc* checks are done by the owner or production manager on random pieces of the finished product.

None of the enterprises with the exception of TG1 was even aware of the need to adjust plant layout to different products and manufacturing sequences. TG1 experimented with different layouts and adjusted it to changing product patterns. None of the enterprises had made any process improvements. With TG1's exception none of the enterprises had any system to monitor productivity or formal methods of inventory control. TG1 used a piece-rate payment system to keep track of worker production and to give incentives for higher productivity. Other firms also used piece-rates, but without trying to use it as a measure to raise productivity.

In sum, the general level of capabilities in the garments firms was very low in all cases except for TG1, that stood out in practically all respects. TG1 had good process capabilities and some beginnings of product design capabilities. It would seem, however, that these process capabilities were not on a par with those of new entrants in garment exporting countries in Asia.

Other firms. All the firms in this group have fairly old equipment. The fishing net manufacturer had knitting machines over 30 years old that were not well maintained; there was no maintenance routine or workshop. The knitwear firm (making T-shirts) had no maintenance routine, but this was after a period in which the firm had been managed by the state and had recently (in 1990) been returned to its owners, and its run-down machines were being nursed back to health. The tenth of the plant that was in operation was under constant repair and upgrading. The synthetic-leather firm had a maintenance routine and an in-house workshop, and seemed reasonably capable in this.

Quality control (QC) is variable among these firms. The net firm has a QC manager but lacks the equipment needed for testing or trained personnel. The knitwear firm had a QC system at the start, but quality deteriorated during the period of state management and was now being improved by the former owner and his sons. The synthetics firm's QC was exercised by the owner. The chemicals used were checked against an international standard, though there was no laboratory in-house.

The layout of the net manufacturer was poor, and it estimated that an improved layout would reduce time required for production by 15 per cent. The firm had nevertheless made no layout changes, and had made no improvement to the production process. It had adopted a piece-rate system that raised labour productivity in 1989–91, when the firm went into receivership, but this was the only discernible attempt to improve its operation. Its technological response was very weak, which is not surprising in view of the fact that the receivers are accountants rather than industrialists. There was no sign of any technological assistance from its foreign equity holder.

In contrast, the knitwear factory had made numerous efforts to raise productivity and cut costs since repossessing the plant. The owner's two sons changed the process of knitting to make a lighter fabric to match importers' T-shirts. They improved the settings of the knitting and cutting machines. They fired many of the workers who had got into 'bad habits' and retrained the remainder as well as hiring new young workers. The improvements in work practices meant that the number of machines per worker rose threefold. Better material control meant lower waste and a better quality product. The controls on the machine were changed to electronic controls, raising the efficiency of the equipment by 95 per cent.

The resulting improvements in cost efficiency account for its survival, and for its attempts (apparently promising) to win an order to sell to the UK. This was the most sustained and successful attempt at TC development in this subsector. It should be noted that knitting technology is more complex than garment sewing, and the processes involved are more skill- and capital-intensive (note that many of the other firms, even TG1, had to shut down their knitting operations).

The synthetic-leather firm adjusted the layout when capacity utilisation declined and only one line instead of two could be used. Otherwise there seemed to be no process adaptation or improvements.

LINKAGE CAPABILITIES

Linkages tend to be low in garments unless there is an efficient local textile industry, a system for 'putting out' (subcontracting) of garment sewing or a lively fashion industry. None of these existed in Ghana. None of the sample garment firms had any subcontracting (TG3 had tried once but found the quality too poor to persist). They had no linkages with textile firms, and practically all the fabrics were imported. There were no design linkages. The only linkage was an involuntary one among the garments firms themselves, via the movement of workers and managers. Since there is very little investment in specialised training, this does not seem to be of much economic significance.

There were no linkages of the garments firms with any official institution, for training, technology, standards, or design. The Ghana Standards Board (GSB) did visit TG1 occasionally, but did not offer any technical assistance.

The other firms in this subsector also had minimal linkages. They noted that the GSB paid regular visits to check on standards, but that it was unable to offer technical advice on how to improve quality or meet import competition. The other CSIR institutes had no contact whatsoever and were regarded as valueless for technological purposes. The net manufacturer commented on the overly academic nature of the training given to textile engineers by the University of Science and Technology, and on the lack of training of other kinds in the country.

Appendix B: Food Processing

BACKGROUND

The food-processing industry encompasses a large range of processes and products, from traditional rural technologies for simple processing and preservation of produce and beverages, to large-scale modern technologies for making more complex convenience foods.[1] In developing countries, small-scale, localised activity, like baking, coexists with capital, skill and marketing intensive activities (mostly under the control of giant multinational companies), addressing different markets and using radically different technologies. The balance between the small and simple activities on the one hand and large-scale, complex activities on the other depends largely on levels of income and industrialisation.

In Ghana, much of the subsector is concentrated at the simple end of the spectrum. In 1987, food processing had the third largest number of enterprises as well as employment in manufacturing (after textiles and wood). It had, however, the largest value-added of manufacturing subsectors. As Table B.1 shows, a high proportion of the employment was accounted for by large enterprises. Thus, a relatively few large food-processing firms accounted for the bulk of the industry's activity, though even the largest (with 650 employees) was small by international standards.

The subsector has experienced steady growth since the launch of the adjustment, though its index of production in 1990 (57.5, with 1977 as the base year) was lower than the average for all manufacturing (63.5). Given its heavy reliance on local materials and its orientation to local markets and tastes, it is less subject to direct import competition than most other parts of manufacturing. There are, however, several processed foods and drinks that do suffer such competition, and have been hurt by imports, but in general this impact has been relatively small and confined to products consumed by high-income Ghanaians.

The subsector has relatively low exports of a non-traditional variety, despite Ghana's agricultural resource base (partly-processed cocoa is the country's main traditional export). According to the Technology Transfer Centre (1990b), the technologies in use in the larger enterprises are entirely imported from the developed countries, while those in simpler local activities (first stage processing of raw materials, baking and so on) rely on a mixture of imported and local equipment.

In the absence of independent technical studies it is difficult to comment on the efficiency of food processing. ERP calculations suggest that food processing, despite reductions in protection, is still relatively inefficient (46 per cent in 1990, down from 81 per cent in 1987), an impression reinforced by the domestic resource cost (DRC) figure for 1990 of 1.25.[2] However, these calculations should be treated with caution. Apart from the inherent methodological problems of assessing efficiency from ERP or DRC calculations, the

Table B.1 Characteristics of food processing industry by employment size (1987)

	Micro (1–4)	Small (5–29)	Medium (30–99)	Large (>100)	Total
No. of Enterp.	675	550	86	50	1 361
No. Employed	1 731	5 329	4 325	15 000	26 385
Empl. per Enterp.	2.6	9.7	50.3	300	19.4

Source: RPED, Background Paper on Ghana 1992.

level of aggregation is very high, and may be misleading for such a diverse industry.

It is likely that small-scale food processing activities in Ghana are generally quite proficient in using their simple technologies to meet local demands with little packaging and product differentiation. They would, however, find it difficult to grow out of the confines of their present activities because of the large jump in technologies and scales involved. The more capital-intensive activities, making more highly processed foods, are likely to face greater technological challenges. The technologies and equipment involved are quite sophisticated, and the production process involves a variety of technical skills. The marketing of many such processed foods involves considerable investment in brand-name promotion and sales networks. If the requisite production and marketing skills have not been built up by the larger firms, they may be uncompetitive by world standards.

The case study sample has 7 firms, all medium to large sized (employing over 30 people). This was a deliberate choice to concentrate on enterprises of medium or large size where the technological development process could be better investigated (the smaller firms were mainly bakeries). As for ownership, three of the firms are partly or wholly foreign owned, one is state owned (but is being divested), and the others are local private (two indigenous Ghanaian and one non-African). With the exception of the state-owned enterprise (which has some exports of speciality fruit juices), the others have rising sales (all aimed at the domestic market) even though significant underutilization of capacity still exists in most.

INVESTMENT CAPABILITIES

All the equipment used in the sample food-processing firms is imported. The three foreign affiliates in the sample got their equipment through the parent companies, which provided the plant design, engineering, initial training and start-up services. The technologies provided were all new to Ghana at the time of introduction, and complete dependence on the foreign partner seems inevitable.

The parent organisation of FP1 has a separate company to provide technical services, including plant procurement and engineering, to affiliates worldwide. This company engineered the firm's plant in Ghana in 1961. There was no local participation in the investment process. The parent company sent twelve expatriates to give on-the-job training in Ghana, and some managers were sent to the parent company for training. Production supervisors from Ghana were also sent to FP1's plants in various parts of the world for training. The company has not undertaken any significant new investments after the liberalisation, though its output and productivity have been raised by better use of existing facilities. New investments are planned in the future; these will be handled, as before, by the parent company and its engineering offshoot.

FP2 started in Ghana in 1969 with used equipment from the parent. A team was sent from the head office to engineer the plant, train workers and operate the facilities for several years. This reliance on the parent company continues till today, and the Ghanaian affiliate pays 2 per cent of sales as a technical assistance fee. The affiliate has continued to operate with old equipment till now. It is now planning a new investment to manufacture a new line of candies. The equipment will be new, and the parent company will again fulfil all the investment functions.

FP6 started to make dairy products in Ghana in 1960, the first modern plant of its kind in the country. The equipment, design and engineering services were all provided by the parent company. This firm responded more quickly to the liberalisation than the previous two, and launched a major new project in 1989. The investment was entirely managed by the parent, with new equipment sourced in France and Germany. One Ghanaian was sent to the parent company for training.

Three of the remaining firms, the state-owned FP3, the private flour mill FP5, and FP3's private sector competitor FP7, bought their initial technology in the form of turnkey projects. Turnkey projects are a convenient way to transfer new technologies, especially in process industries. They can, however, be an expensive way of buying technology, since the package is put together by the foreign contractor and the buyer may lack the price and technical information to make the optimal choice concerning the various elements of the package. More importantly, if the buyer lacks the relevant technical knowledge and skills, this form of investment may have hidden costs.[3] Where the buyer cannot evaluate and monitor the design of the plant, it is possible to get the wrong equipment. Where the processes involved are new and complex, the short and limited commitment of the technology seller may mean that the recipient is unable to develop quickly the necessary capabilities to handle the technology. The lack of local participation in the engineering and construction of the plant may deprive the owner of the plant of the understanding needed to master the technology and improve upon it.

Some of these costs show up in the case of FP3, as noted in the main text. The lack of local participation and understanding of the plant meant that if was unable to rehabilitate its plant even after 30 years of operation. The second turnkey project, for the flour mill FP5, was better selected and executed. The prime contractor was an Italian firm, which was found through the local Italian embassy. The supplier guaranteed the plant for ten years and provided four years of technical support (this came to an end in 1991). Under this agreement, four Italian engineers were stationed in Ghana to provide technical services and training, and visiting teams provided other technical support with QC, servicing and maintenance. Though local personnel played no role in the investment, the subsequent heavy foreign involvement ensured that the plant operated efficiently. There was a rigorous training programme to ensure that local operational capabilities were created.

The third turnkey project was for FP7, the fruit-processing firm, which was started in 1983 by qualified scientist who searched for the equipment and evaluated several suppliers before making a choice. Italian equipment was found to be best suited to the scale and product needs of FP7. The suppliers sent two engineers to install the equipment and provide the initial training. These engineers stayed for only two weeks, but FP7's production manager had earlier spent a month in Italy at their plant for training. The entrepreneur, production manager and maintenance manager of FP7 participated in the design, layout, installation and commissioning of the plant, which gave them the capability to operate it efficiently afterwards. FP7 is now setting up a new $2 million project for Tetra Pak (paper packaging to replace cans for fruit juices). This technology, also to be provided on a turnkey basis in 1992–3, was chosen because the supplier has a regional office in Nigeria, with engineers who could install the plant and provide technical services. The firm hopes that its technical staff will again participate in the investment.

FP4, the biscuit maker, started 36 years ago with second-hand equipment. The original entrepreneur located the plant in the UK, where Huntley and Palmer, a leading biscuit manufacturer, was about to scrap it. He was able to buy it cheaply and bring it to production in Ghana (no information is now available on who provided technical assistance and training initially). The old plant was kept operational over the years, but was badly hit by the liberalisation (see below). No new investment has been undertaken since 1986.

In sum, there is some variation in the investment capabilities of the sample firms. None of the firms had such capabilities to start with in Ghana, and depended on foreign partners, contractors and equipment suppliers for most of the technical skills involved. The foreign affiliates used their parent companies' investment capabilities and did a competent job of selecting the technology, setting up the plant and training the workers. Over time, FP7 and FP5 seemed to have done a more systematic job than FP3, and FP7 in particular has been able to add to its production capabilities by some participation in the investment process.

PRODUCTION CAPABILITIES

Process engineering. All food-processing technologies are highly 'embodied' in the process equipment, but the skill and technological needs of efficient operation vary with the level of processing and the specific technologies involved. All the large-scale food-processing activities included in the sample need a combination of chemical process, chemical laboratory testing, electromechanical engineering and maintenance skills, but differences in product specialisation exist among the sample firms.

The two affiliates of major multinationals (FP1 and FP2) produce infant cereals, evaporated milk, malted drinks and the like, all products requiring fairly high degrees of chemical processing skills. The dairy-products affiliate, making ice cream and yoghurt, needs some of these skills, but less advanced processing know-how. Two of the local firms are involved in fruit juices and fruit canning, which call for a moderate level of processing and quality-control skills. One is in flour milling, a capital-intensive but technically relatively undemanding task, and one makes biscuits, again a relatively simple operation.

There is a difference in the reliance on foreign technology, via licensing and technical assistance contracts, between the three foreign-owned and the four local enterprises. The FP1 affiliate draws on the parent organisation for technical assistance on practically all aspects of manufacturing activity, and for the purchase of equipment and the use of brandnames. The parent operates a separate company to take care of the technical problems of all affiliates and handle their investment needs. FP2 and FP6 have technical assistance agreements with their parents which give them access to continuous technical assistance. The four local companies, by contrast, do not have technical assistance agreements, apart from the flour mill's initial technical support contract.

As noted in the main text, access to foreign technical assistance (or being part of a large multinational) does not by itself ensure technical efficiency. During the 1980s the FP1 affiliate, subjected to constricted imports of spares and materials, suffered a deterioration in performance and productivity. This was exacerbated by poor management. The local management at the time allowed quality standards to drop, equipment maintenance to deteriorate and poor work practices to creep in. Though easier access to imports allowed production to rise in the latter part of the 1980s, poor productivity persisted until the end of the decade, when a new managing director from the head office took over. Similarly, the dairy products firm was poorly managed prior to 1989. As liberalisation took hold, the firm failed to respond to growing competition, and started to lose market share. A new managing director was brought in. He recruited new, qualified maintenance personnel, set up a well-equipped QC laboratory with a graduate chemist and several technicians (able to conduct microbiological tests), improved the layout of the plant, launched proper production scheduling, and was investing in new plant and computerisation.

Clearly, certain 'entrepreneurial' qualities made all the difference in these two cases with respect to the decision to invest in technology, when other requirements, such as access to skills and capital, were met by the parent company.

The third affiliate, FP2, is a good but not outstanding performer in its process technology. It operates with very old equipment (which was brought in second hand, and is now 40–50 years old), an indication that the parent company was not very interested in this affiliate until now. It has good maintenance and QC facilities, with well-qualified personnel in charge: the chief engineer in charge of maintenance has 24 technicians under him, and a well-equipped workshop (necessary to keep the old machines operational). The QC lab has three graduate biochemists and four secondary-level chemists; it is moving into microbiological testing. The factory layout is poor, since the plant was built as a warehouse rather than a manufacturing plant. The operational efficiency of the plant is satisfactory, given the age of the plant and the layout, with experienced and trained staff and inputs from headquarters-staff visits (there were three technical visits in 1991 and four in 1992). It is interesting to note that, unlike the other two affiliates, the higher management is wholly Ghanaian.

Of the local plants, the best-embodied technology is possessed by the flour mill, with its new Italian plant. The turnkey project was carefully designed to suit the needs of relatively small-scale production, and to provide training and follow-up technical services. Maintenance and production routines were established by Italian technicians. Maintenance has been taken over by a mechanical engineer, with six technical-diploma holders under him. The Italian firm continues to send technical personnel, who help with difficult problems if they arise. There is a well-equipped laboratory with a graduate biochemist and three secondary-graduate science assistants. The quality requirements, not very demanding by food-industry standards, are met satisfactorily. There has been little need to adapt the plant so far.

The biscuit manufacturer FP4 is an interesting case for technological purposes. It almost went bankrupt, but was able to find a market niche for the simplest and cheapest of its products ('cabin' biscuits, eaten with tea or coffee), which it expanded by selling the product in plastic sacks, initially as broken biscuits. This marketing tactic was not, however, the only reason for its survival. It invested in process improvement, and enjoyed significant increases in productivity as a result. A local consultant, with the help of supervisors, was responsible for the design and implementation of these improvements. The process changes included: complete change in the layout of the machines, so that production could continue if one broke down; complete renovations of machines, including the replacement of single-speed motors by variable speed motors, and so on. The result was fewer breakdowns, less downtime and higher productivity. The total cost of the improvements was Cedis 3–4 million (about $7–10 thousand), and machine output rose by 300 per cent as a result. The consultant now manages the intensive maintenance that the equipment requires. The firm now sells as many of its cabin biscuits as it can make.

Of the two fruit-juice processors, FP3 (state owned) and FP7 (private), the former is relatively old, and has declined in production and employment while the latter is new and is planning an expansion. Yet the older firm exports over a quarter of its output, while the newer is entirely oriented to the domestic market where it has gained market share at FP3's expense. Both use local raw materials, and FP3 has its own pineapple plantations. In terms of process technology, FP3 claims to suffer because it has not had the resources to buy spare parts. It has a good workshop that can do repairs and make some spares, and a QC laboratory with a graduate food technologist and qualified assistants. However, there is a distinct lack of attention to process improvement and optimisation, and a 'wait and see' attitude with respect to the future, presumably because of its impending privatisation.

FP7 has an efficient maintenance system headed by a graduate mechanical engineer, with three mechanics and electricians. Its QC system appears more comprehensive and better than FP3's, with the owner, a former Standards Board scientist with a British chemistry doctorate, in charge. He is assisted in process functions by two sons, also well qualified. The plant operates well, but, with the planned expansion to use the Tetra Pack packaging system, the owner is aware that it will need better production scheduling and inventory control.

Product technology. The product technology in the three foreign affiliates comes mostly from the parent companies, and quality conforms to international standards. However, various adaptations have been made to local tastes and material availability. In FP1, two new products were introduced in the early 1980s because of the lack of imported materials. These did not meet the parent company's standards, and were dropped in 1988 when imports became available. The affiliate now depends wholly on the head office for new products. FP1 is setting up a research centre in Abidjan (due to start in 1994) to serve the whole of Africa, but there are no plans to undertake product development in Ghana. Clearly, the level of capabilities in Ghana are not thought to be up to the necessary level.

FP2 has also introduced product modifications since 1983, essentially to downgrade its main product and make it cheaper.[4] The formula was developed in the firm's QC lab and approved by the parent company, and is still in production. Other new products continue to come from the parent. There is thus some product capability, but it is at the low end (not based on research) and probably of the same order as FP1.

The dairy-products company has drawn on the parent company for new flavours and better-quality products. It has also adapted its original formula to use local pineapples in its yoghurts. Apart from this, there is little investment in product development capabilities.

The two fruit processors have introduced new products. FP3 developed canned palm nut cream soup and eggplant, both of which are popular locally and in ethnic markets in the UK and the USA. The development came from the QC manager, who, as in the affiliates, was the only person with the expertise and the equipment to specify ingredients and additives and test them. In FP7, the owner (also the QC manager) developed the formula for an orange/pineapple drink in his laboratory.

LINKAGE CAPABILITIES

None of the foreign affiliates has local supply linkages. This seems surprising at first sight, since both FP1 and FP2 use local cocoa, but they buy in bulk and have no special linkages with suppliers. They rarely use local producers of spares and components since their technology is not up to the requisite standards. The same applies to the dairy-products firm. The Standards Board pays regular visits but there is no element of technology transfer. FP2 uses the Food Research Institute (FRI) for some testing. FP1 is working on a joint project with the FRI to develop an enzyme for a fermented breakfast cereal. Once this is done, it will be sent to headquarters for laboratory testing. This is a rare case of a large firm attempting to use a CSIR institute for research purposes. FP2 uses the Management Development Productivity Institute (MDPI) training courses for its managers and QC staff.

The flour mill uses the FRI to verify the quality (fat and moisture content, protein analysis) of its maize flour and the wheat purchased from a government agency. It also uses the services of GRATIS to obtain spare parts in Tema. This is also unusual, and may show promise for the future of small-scale metal-working. The biscuit firm has no contact with the technology institutes, and does not even deal with the Standards Board since it moved into cabin biscuits. Its only local supply linkage is the attempt to get local flour mills to produce the special flour it needs, and now imports; its attempts have not been successful till now.

FP3 also uses MDPI courses occasionally for its managers, and expressed the need for more technical training in food processing. It has very limited contact with FRI, and feels little confidence in its capabilities. FP7 sends managers for courses to MDPI, and has sought FRI's advice on testing procedures (which it was happy with). It feels that FRI had good services to offer the food industry; this may be due to the fact that the owner is on the Board of FRI.

Appendix C: Wood Working

BACKGROUND

The wood working industry is the second largest in the country in terms of the number of enterprises and output, and the largest in terms of employment. The industry falls into two main parts, furniture making and 'other' (mainly sawmilling). The case study sample firms are all in the furniture manufacturing part, and the discussion here will concentrate on this.

Table C.1 shows some features of the furniture industry in 1987. Manufacturing activity is largely concentrated in micro and small enterprises, which together accounted for 93.3 per cent of the number of enterprises and 66.5 per cent of employment. There were only ten firms in the country with over 100 employees, with an average of 203 employees each (of which four are in the sample). At the other end of the spectrum, micro enterprises had 2.6 employees each on average, and small scale enterprises 8.1 employees (there are two small-scale and no micro enterprises in the sample): these enterprises were essentially semi-permanent roadside operations using very simple tools, making low quality cheap furniture largely to customers' designs. Exports of furniture (most of the growth in wood exports is in saw milling rather than furniture) are small, and mainly concentrated in a few large firms with the equipment and organisation needed to meet the quality and design standards of European markets.

The wood-working subsector as a whole, including sawmilling, has fared relatively well after liberalisation. Its index of production in 1990 was 74.2 compared to 63.5 for all manufacturing, though it is not clear how much of the growth was coming from sawmilling rather than furniture. Capacity utilisation for the subsector was 70 per cent in 1990, which was better than for textiles and garments or food. This performance is due to Ghana's large resource base in timber; and the fact that the local furniture industry, because of high transport costs and its design features, does not suffer from direct import competition.

As noted in Chapter 2, exports of wood products rose from $ 1.5 m. ($1.0 m. furniture and $0.5 m. other wood products) in 1986 to $ 6.2 m. ($3.6 m. and $2.6 m. respectively) in 1991. Of this threefold increase, furniture accounted for 64 per cent and other wood products for 36 per cent, with the former enjoying an increase in export earnings of 260 per cent and the latter of 420 per cent. However, 96 per cent of furniture exports came from one enterprise alone.[1] The rest of the furniture industry is almost entirely oriented to the domestic market, and with one or two exceptions (one is in the case study sample), is failing to compete effectively abroad.

ERP calculations show that while furniture is less protected in 1990 (39 per cent) than it was in 1987 (108 per cent), the rate of protection is still high.[2] Though its domestic resource cost ratio of 0.9 suggests that the activity is potentially competitive, the fact that only one firm has been able to

216

Table C.1   Characteristics of furniture enterprises by employment size
(1987)

	Micro (1–4)	Small (5–29)	Medium (30–99)	Large (>100)	Total
No. of Enterp.	417	799	36	10	1 262
No. Employed	1 090	6 468	1 783	2 026	11 367
Empl. per Enterp.	2.6	8.1	49.5	202.6	9

Source: RPED, Background Paper on Ghana 1992.

exploit this in export markets suggests that technological lags are holding back the industry despite its strong resource base, low labour costs and favourable incentive climate for entry into export markets.

The technology of furniture making remains essentially labour intensive, but high quality imposes requirements of precision, craftsmanship and design. For export markets, the product has to be made in series, with a need for production planning, order processing, strict quality control of materials and processes, machine and tool maintenance, materials handling, wood drying, dust extraction and compressed air facilities, inventory control, costing and pricing, transport and so on. Some processes in furniture manufacture (like wood drying)[3] are capital intensive, and a number of delicate finishing operations call for expensive tools and rigorous training. The skill and equipment needs of large-scale manufacture for the world market are therefore quite different from those of traditional furniture making for the domestic market.

There are considerable lags in the capabilities of most Ghanaian firms *vis-à-vis* the minimum requirements of production for world markets. These lags are documented by a study of the furniture industry by UNIDO (1988). Some of its findings are worth noting. Most Ghanaian firms had their origins in small carpentry workshops, and remained in their original sites and with their traditional work practices. The machinery, all European, was of mixed ages, but purchased without proper study of what was to be produced and how, inadequate knowledge of modern production technologies and based on partial advice from the equipment suppliers. Layout tended to be poor and space inadequate. Few had dust extraction or compressed air systems. Equipment maintenance was poor, especially in the grinding of cutters and blades (a necessary function for high-quality work). There was a lack of technical know-how in the choice of tools, leading to excessive waste and poor finish.

The UNIDO study was particularly critical of the management of furniture firms. To quote:

Almost all of the factories visited are managed by the owners who have started their businesses as small workshops. Having no experience in performing such vital functions as business planning (financial and operational), business control and personnel management of any significant magnitude, the problems associated with a weak management are clearly visible. The machines and workers are standing idle, the low productivity, high rates of timber waste, poor quality, accumulated parts and components from past production runs, general attitude to take things easy, delays in meeting deadlines, aimless drift of the company towards various unrelated product lines, little or no delegation of work to subordinates, are some of the symptoms.[4]

In addition, the study found that skills were inadequate. Artisans with some joinery and carpentry skills did not know how to operate modern equipment properly, so that a lot of new machines were idle or under-utilised. The lack of production-planning skills led to delays and waste. Technical drawings were hardly ever used, with a consequent lack of standardisation and loss of quality. Quality control (though sufficient for the local market) was totally inadequate for export markets. Product designs were mainly supplied by the customers or taken from foreign catalogues, with no independent capability for design. Equipment maintenance was 'a total catastrophe', with badly kept machines and tools, leading to inaccurate dimensions and loss of quality in the product. Management showed a lack of awareness of the importance of proper maintenance and gave little guidance on this, while maintenance personnel were poorly trained. This was exacerbated by poor motivation and discipline in the maintenance staff.

The UNIDO study highlights many of the technological problems that were also observed in furniture firms by our team. Its findings are fully supported by the analysis of the GEPC's 1991 export development plan. In the section on production problems in the furniture industry, it says that the four main problems are: obsolete and inefficient production methods; poor maintenance and improper tooling;[5] lack of skilled labour (machinists, kiln and saw operators, jig and template makers, and so on) due to inadequate training facilities; and poor management, leading to inadequate production planning, costing, design and quality control.

Our sample comprises four large firms, two medium and two small firms (by the Ghanaian census definition). All but one of the firms in the present sample (the exception being the largest, WW1) is locally owned, though half of WW5's equity is held by a local non-African businessman. WW1 is a joint venture between an Italian (who has a minority share) and a Ghanaian economist, with the former (an experienced furniture maker) being the effective entrepreneur. Thus, the sample does not have an instance of 'real' foreign investment in the sense of a large multinational company with an affiliate in Ghana.

All but the two smallest were founded before the liberalisation, while one of the large firms is 65 years old. The two smallest firms have, with some fluctuations, stayed in the same size and technology range through their lives. The three largest firms started as large enterprises with modern technologies, while the Lebanese firm started and stayed as a medium-sized enterprise. The remaining two firms, WW4 and WW6, are firms that started as traditional micro enterprises in the informal sector and 'graduated' to the modern formal sector, the former into a large-sized and the latter into a medium-sized firm. These are part of a small group of firms in the present sample that achieved 'graduation', and their experience is of special interest.

INVESTMENT CAPABILITIES

The industry has a mixture of simple and complex investment needs, depending on the segment of the market and the level of technology aimed at. The sample firms fall into three groups in these terms. These groups exclude one firm, WW2, which is *sui generis:* it acquired its machinery under its original British owners over half a century ago, and has not purchased new equipment for furniture making in its recent history.[6] The issue of investment capabilities does not really arise in its case, since it carries on with its ancient machinery. The other firms are as follows:

a. At one end are the two most recent firms, which are also the smallest, WW7 and WW8. They started with simple hand tools acquired locally (but mostly of foreign origin), and have stayed with this equipment. They had no need for special information on sources and characteristics of the equipment, nor for any interaction with equipment suppliers. The layout of the plant was not relevant to this level of manufacturing (both operate out of temporary sheds). These simple investment needs were met with minimal information and skills, and investment capabilities were basically non-existent.

b. At the other end are firms that started as medium or large operations with new or used equipment from overseas. They had to locate the right suppliers for the kind of machines they needed, negotiate the price and arrange for installation and initial training by the suppliers. Three firms fall in this category, ranging in size from 267 to 65.

WW1's entrepreneur, with years of training and experience in Italy, was able to find the appropriate equipment (in Italy) himself. Over time, as the need arose, he added new Italian machines. His background gave him the information and skills needed to invest rationally and economically, and enabled him to build up what the UNIDO study found to be 'one of the best equipped and versatile plants to produce furniture, joinery and their components' (p. 10) in the country. Given his stock of information, he had perhaps the best investment capabilities of the sample firms in this industry.

WW3 started with used basic woodworking equipment, also from Italy. The entrepreneur, a Ghanaian, had become familiar with the Italian machinery in his earlier job in a furniture firm in Canada, and himself went to Italy to negotiate the purchase from the supplier. When the firm moved to new purpose-built premises some five years later, he had learnt enough about the business to diversify his sources. He bought expensive special purpose machines (including a large drying kiln), which needed longer search and more information on prices and specifications, from Germany and the UK as well as Italy. The kiln was installed by an engineer sent by the UK supplier. The process suggests that the entrepreneur had been able to develop his investment capabilities with experience.

WW5 started about 15 years ago with a mixture of used and new German equipment. The owner, a local of Lebanese origin with experience in sawmilling, travelled to several suppliers in Europe before choosing the machines he needed. His production manager, another Lebanese with a technical diploma, carried out the layout, installation and commissioning. There was an expansion in 1985, mainly with six new German machines. It seems that the owner conducted a search of potential suppliers and made an informed choice, though his specific experience was in sawmilling rather than furniture making.

c. Finally, there are the two firms, WW4 and WW6, that 'graduated' from simple hand tools bought locally to power machinery. Both were started by local Africans who were carpenters in the traditional sense. The initial investments required little investment capability. The subsequent expansions into power machinery took place in 1962 for WW4 and around 1980 for WW6.

WW4's owner lacked the knowledge and resources to search foreign markets for the appropriate equipment, being unaware of the specifications of available machines and the best sources of supply. As described in the text, he sought information from the Norwegian embassy and bought Norwegian equipment. The supplier provided credit and new machines, and sent engineers to install and commission the plant. It provided some local training and took four Ghanaians to Norway for some instruction. No new machines have been bought since then. The layout of the factory is poor and the UNIDO study found that there was a lot of excess production capacity because of the duplication of particular machines combined with the absence of some basic items of equipment. This suggests that weak investment capabilities led to inadequate search, over-reliance on the supplier for specifications and poor choice of equipment.

WW6 started its move into modern technology by buying used equipment locally. It then started to buy used equipment abroad, drawing upon contacts provided by the owner's brother, who lives in the UK. The accumulation of equipment was gradual, and reliance on second-hand machinery meant that there was no technical assistance from foreign suppliers. The graduation of WW6 was thus less pronounced than WW4's. Its employment stayed much smaller than the latter's, and its plant never reached the level of sophistication of WW4. This does not mean that its investment capabilities were poorer (perhaps the reverse, since the process was based on a more careful search of the market), but its aims were more modest and its expansion more gradual.

In sum, investment capabilities in the wood-working firms vary, as expected, by the entrepreneur's strategy, his familiarity with the equipment market and his ability to search for the best deal. The transactions costs inherent in setting up in a new technology were overcome in different ways by the sample firms, apparently with different degrees of success. It is difficult to assess in a technical sense how good the choices were (apart from the few insights provided by the UNIDO study), but the most successful investments would seem to have been by WW1, WW3, WW5 and WW6.

PRODUCTION CAPABILITIES

Process engineering. None of the sample firms had foreign licenses or technical consultancy. The only foreign skill input has been into WW1 in the form of the Italian entrepreneur. Production capabilities may be considered first for the four large-scale firms.

WW1 has 8- to 14-year-old equipment that is well maintained, with kiln-drying facilities. There is an established routine for preventive maintenance, with a full-time maintenance engineer and a well-equipped in-house repair shop. Layout is reasonably good, and was improved in 1987 to save significantly on production times. Nevertheless, the plant needs more space to operate efficiently. Quality control is the best of the sample firms (and also the best of the firms studied in the UNIDO report), with the owner himself taking responsibility for checking all stages of production.[7] There are efforts to monitor productivity and undertake work scheduling, with workers being given incentives to improve productivity. These efforts to raise quality and operational efficiency have enabled the firm to enter the export market, though it is not a major exporter on a scale comparable to Scanstyle. There is still a heavy reliance on manual rather than machine finishing, which reduces its ability to produce in large volumes for the export market. Nevertheless, its performance has led it to be classified by the Ghana Export Promotion Council as one of the ten best firms in the country, and so to be eligible for assistance offered by the EC to help develop export capabilities.

WW2 has extremely old furniture-making equipment and most of its maintenance and rehabilitation efforts have been directed at its sawmilling operations. The layout of the furniture plant appears to be poor, and the quality of the output is low. Little attention seems to have been given to raising productivity and quality in recent years.

WW3 has satisfactory maintenance procedures, with a small but adequate workshop. Its relatively new plant is well laid out, though some of the new machines need to be relocated to cut production time. It has invested in adequate kiln-drying equipment, which could be a major competitive advantage. The firm does not export at all, though it was identified by UNIDO as one of the firms that had export potential. This may be due to the fact that its quality control is still unsystematic, addressed to finished products rather than to the production process itself. It does not have preventive maintenance, and machines are repaired as the need arises. There is no production planning because the firm mainly produces to order; this is a major competitive barrier for export markets. The firm has no system for monitoring or improving productivity. These gaps may constrain it from raising its efficiency to levels needed to compete abroad. However, it seems to be a good 'learner', in that it responded rapidly to UNIDO advice and upgraded several of its functions. The entrepreneur is aware of the need and significance of TC development, but his lack of technical know-how seems to be a handicap (he expressed the desire to hire a production engineer if he could find one).

WW4's stock of 20-year-old Norwegian equipment, not renovated or added to, is in poor condition and obsolete. It is badly laid out, cramped and with a large number of unusable machines. The firm is handicapped by not having kiln-drying facilities, and has to use air-dried timber, which is unacceptable in western markets.[8] There is no preventive maintenance and parts are only changed when machines break down. Repairs are carried out by other firms, which may reduce the effectiveness of operations. Nevertheless, the plant has tool maintenance facilities; and it is the lack of trained management that prevents it from achieving greater efficiency. The firm has exported in the past, but the sale (to Cuba) was not on open markets; its attempt to sell to the UK and Germany met with the response that its quality was too low. There are no attempts to improve quality or productivity, and a general lack of dynamism in efforts to raise production capabilities.

The two medium-sized firms, WW5 and WW6, have most of the features of the less dynamic large firms.There is no preventive maintenance and no in-house repair shop. Quality control is *ad hoc* and not of very high standards. Layout is poor and rarely or never changed. There is no attempt to monitor or improve productivity.

The two smallest firms operate in a lower market segment than the others, using hand tools to make low-price furniture. They have all the deficiencies of the medium-sized firms, but magnified because of the informal and semi-permanent nature of the activity. It becomes irrelevant to apply concepts of maintenance, layout, quality control and so on to these firms in any formal sense. The technology is essentially static, learned by the owner through apprenticeship in a similar operation (one of the entrepreneurs comes from a carpenter family), and kept at that level for the life of the enterprise. There is no attempt on the part of these entrepreneurs to move up the technology ladder.

In general, with the exception of WW1, the level of production capabilities is fairly low by world standards. Low wages and cheap raw materials do not compensate for the lack of these capabilities. However, they do serve to protect domestic sales, aided greatly by the ability to produce to consumer demands at the expected quality level. Even WW1 has not developed the capabilities to become a major exporter. However, its systematic approach to quality, maintenance, productivity and training gives it far better capabilities than its counterparts in the sample. Next comes WW3, which has a less comprehensive technological strategy but is fairly well equipped by local standards and has better quality control and other operating capabilities than other sample firms.

The cases worth remarking on are the two firms that 'graduated' from micro-scale and traditional technologies. It appears that they could muster the capabilities to grow in size and enter the next stage of technology with a certain level of competence, but they could not develop beyond that level. In the new outward-looking regime they have little chance of dynamic growth. The two enterprises that have stayed at the small-scale level seem to have no ambitions to grow much larger or adopt higher levels of technology.

Product engineering. There is practically no independent product design capability in the Ghanaian furniture industry. All the sample firms copy designs from imported catalogues, or make to designs suggested by customers (also from catalogues). The owner is generally in charge of this function, and makes drawings that are interpreted by the craftsmen. None of the sample firms uses technical drawings with precise measurements, such as would be necessary for high-quality volume work for export markets. Apart from the absence of design skills, it appears that none has the shopfloor skills to interpret the technical drawings with the accuracy needed to carry out very precise operations and finishing. There is thus little to analyse in this category of technological capabilities, a reflection on the long-term ability of the industry to exploit its resource advantages in world markets.

LINKAGE CAPABILITIES

None of the furniture manufacturers has any links with the Government technology institutions. There seems to be nothing on offer that could help the firms to raise their productivity or use facilities that they could not afford themselves (the small cane furniture firm felt that common facilities for cane splitting, weaving and finishing machines could be useful on a fee-paying basis). The only official help came from the Export Promotion Centre, that has offered training and foreign travel facilities to the ten best firms in Ghana: as noted earlier, this only includes WW1 in this sample. One of the small firms, WW7, pays a larger firm for machining its wood, but there are no other production linkages between large and small firms. There is little sign of the specialisation and subcontracting which may be necessary for a more efficient furniture industry.

CONCLUSIONS

The furniture firms in the sample generally conform to the poor picture of technological capabilities painted in the UNIDO report, but there are exceptions. Investment capabilities are not at world class for any of the firms, but they are reasonable for those that have some direct contact abroad. Much the same applies to production capabilities, which are at rather low levels by international standards. Only two firms, WW1 and WW3, have reasonable capabilities by local standards, with WW1 clearly further ahead in terms of the range and extent of its efforts. Both still need to upgrade their production capabilities considerably before they become fully competitive in world terms. Product design capabilities are almost non-existent in all the firms, but this may not be a handicap if foreign buyers provide designs. What is really needed is the range of skills and technologies to produce in large volume at the high quality needed for world markets.

Appendix D: Metal Working

BACKGROUND

By international standards, the Ghanaian metal working industry (defined here to include simple equipment manufacture) is at an early stage of development.[1] Ostensibly, there are enterprises in each of the five major sub-groups of activities (fabricated metal products, non-electrical machinery, electrical machinery, transport equipment, and scientific and measurement equipment). However, there is essentially a dualistic structure of production. Large foreign-owned or foreign-related firms dominate the formal part of the industry, mainly undertaking the final assembly of imported parts and components at very high cost (many of these have now closed down as a result of liberalisation). The small-scale and informal part of the industry comprises a large number of blacksmiths in the rural areas and small workshops in the urban centres. These make a variety of simple food-processing and agricultural equipment, hand tools and simple machine tools like wood lathes, pedestal electric grinders, wood-planing machines and so on. They also make parts and spares for transport equipment.[2]

The numbers of micro and small enterprises that appear in the census of industry, and the numbers in sole-ownerships or partnerships (as opposed to corporate ownership), suggest that the bulk of activity is in the low end of the technology scale. Table D.1 gives some relevant data from the 1987 census.

The bulk of Ghana's metal working is concentrated in the simplest category, fabricated metal products, and, within that, in micro and small enterprises that are sole proprietorships or partnerships. The large numbers of such firms that appear in transport equipment are mainly in repairs rather than manufacturing – the most advanced end of this activity is in the assembly of bicycles and motorcycles. Thus:

> The picture that emerges from a scanning of domestic production is of a very limited range of products, fewer than five or ten years ago, virtually all of them of a relatively simple kind and not requiring high levels of precision. The only prominent product groups are machinery and equipment for food processing and agriculture, light metal consumer goods, hand tools, some woodworking equipment, and spare parts for many types of machines and vehicles, plus structural items for the construction industry. The list is sparse by comparison to the range of products included in the engineering industries. Metal working machinery of even a simple kind is absent ... and all machine tools are imported.[3]

The micro, small and medium-sized sector of the industry has few linkages with the large-scale sector, since subcontracting is minimal and the level of technology utilised is far below that required for the more demanding, precision needs of the large firms. The smaller firms also have very few techno-

224

Table D.1   Distribution of metalworking firms by activity and
employment size (1987)

	Micro (1–4)	Small (5–19)	Medium (20–99)	Large (>100)	Total (%)	% Sole Prop. or Partners	% Corporate
Fabricated Products	205	410	38	15	668 (57.3)	82.6	17.4
Non Elect. Machinery	33	85	12	5	135 (11.6)	74.8	25.2
Electrical Machinery	3	18	11	6	38 (3.3)	36.8	63.2
Transport Equipment	57	121	25	12	315 (27)	83.2	16.8
Scientific Instruments	3	2	3	2	10 (0.9)	30	70
Total	**301**	**736**	**168**	**89**	**1166**	**78.5**	**21.5**
Percent	25.8	63.1	7.6	3.4	100		

Source: Moore (1989).

logical links overseas, for the same reason – they operate at a level below
that needed to license advanced technologies. There is no standardisation in
the use of materials and tools. Product specification is rough. Skill acquisition is largely through apprenticeship in the traditional sense, with little or
no formal instruction. There is little mechanisation, 'with virtually no participation of engineers and very few skilled workers.'[4]

However, the TTC's study (1990a) notes that there are emerging a few
enterprises with better capabilities able to produce machinery for local markets. However, it found that these capabilities had seldom (probably only in
one or two cases) been developed to more sophisticated levels than the manufacture of food processing machinery and implements.[5] Apart from the lack
of inter-firm linkages, the accumulation of TCs in the smaller firms is also
held back by the absence of institutional assistance for testing, design or
training. Basic engineering support in the form of foundries, forges, heat
treatment shops, tool rooms and so on is largely absent.

The capabilities that have been developed indigenously are therefore modest, for the manufacture of implements, food processing equipment, simple
machine tools and some parts: 'the technologies for the production of this
equipment has largely been that of intermediate technology'.[6] The more modern
large-scale operations have not graduated beyond assembly, the maintenance
of ships and railroads and some foundry work.

The liberalisation has had mixed effects on the engineering sector. Large
sections of the industry are not exposed to direct import competition, because they serve local markets for goods and services of a kind not readily
provided by foreign producers. Most of these are in the traditional, small-
scale sector, but there are some in the modern sector, making products that
are not easily imported, like lightweight pots and pans not made in the developed countries, structural fittings like window and door frames that have

to be custom-made, or heavy simple products like tanks and vessels. Other parts of the industry are facing more direct competition. Of these, some are doing badly, like assembly activities, while others are surviving because of cost advantages or product designs adapted to local needs.

This experience of the present sample of 9 metal-working firms illustrates these different cases. There are two large, two medium sized and five small firms, making a range of products. Of the two large firms, the first, MW1, was for a long time state-owned. It now has over 400 employees smelting steel from scrap in electric arc furnaces (a 'mini' steel mill) to make billets and rods for the construction industry. This is the second largest firm in the sample, and is the most complex and 'heaviest' of the metal-working firms. It is 27 years old, and is now a joint venture of the state with an Indian firm, with the latter providing the management and direction. It faces increasing import competition, since its products are undifferentiated intermediates that are in excess supply in world markets. The second, MW2, a private firm, is the largest manufacturer of aluminium utensils in the country. The technology is, by contrast, relatively undemanding and its products are effectively non-traded, with the main input locally available at competitive prices.

Two more firms are medium sized, both fairly long-established, making aluminium structural products, one (MW3) wholly African owned and the other (MW4) a joint venture with a Swiss firm (which is in retailing rather than manufacturing in its home base). Both are essentially cutting and shaping operations, using a mixture of imported and local raw materials (imports are needed because the local aluminium rolling mill cannot make some of the more complicated shapes and strengths needed). Neither faces direct import competition because of transport cost advantages and the need to custom-make the structurals, but there is fierce local competition.

The other five firms are all 'small' by the census definition. There are two wholly African firms, again long established, that make machines for food processing and wood working (MW5 and MW7). These are the only capital-goods makers in the sample, thus in the relatively more advanced end of the industry but with a specialisation in fairly simple equipment. Some of their products are subject to competition from other developing countries with similar processing needs (e.g. India), while others are more localised. One African firm (MW6) with considerable experience makes tanks, gates and doors, heavy simple products that are mainly non- traded. A state-private joint venture of relatively recent origin (MW8) makes spares for the auto industry, both by foundry work and by machining. It faces some direct import competition. Finally, a private joint venture, MW9, between a local Lebanese and an African used to make trailers for nearly a quarter of a century, and now, under import pressure, has switched completely to making simple structures like chutes for the mining industry-a cutting and welding operation.

Of the 9 firms in metal working, there is a fairly even distribution of growth performance: for are growing, four are stagnating and one is reviving after a long period of decline. The poorly performing firms are concentrated in the smaller-size end of the sample.

INVESTMENT CAPABILITIES

Large firms. The largest of the sample metal working firms, MW1, started with turnkey plant. There were two major investments, both of which were conducted without local capability to evaluate the technology and to absorb it.[7] The initial turnkey plant was purchased around 1975 from a UK supplier, who designed the plant, procured the equipment and did the commissioning and initial training. However, there were various problems with the transfer of the technology and the design of the plant that the firm could not remedy. One of the two furnaces was not successfully commissioned and left inoperative. The training was insufficient to ensure the smooth operation of the technology, and operating efficiency was always very low. The design of the initial layout was inefficient, and involved high in-plant transport and re-heating costs, but the nature of the plant made it very expensive to alter and the poor layout carries on to this day. The company lacked the capabilities to bring the second furnace into operation, raise operating efficiency or adapt the plant to local demand.

Some time later, MW1 asked some Italian consultants to improve the initial technology, apparently again on a turnkey basis. The Italians provided an expensive continuous casting machine (an efficient but complex technology) and a new foundry. Neither was ever brought into production, and the equipment lay idle till the enterprise came under new management (below). The Italian consultants also made several changes to the original technology, altering the dimensions of the rolling mill machinery to produce different dimensions of bars and rods. This made the plant even more difficult to operate without a thorough grasp of the technology, and lowered further its operating capacity.

By the end of the 1980s the plant was only working at 10 per cent of capacity, and the government decided to sell part of the ownership by tender. An Indian firm bought 60 per cent of the equity in 1991, and invested in some items of machinery to raise the capacity utilisation and efficiency of the plant (reviewed below). The capabilities that a relatively small group of experienced steel men was able to apply to the plant made an enormous difference with the same basic equipment.

The other large firm, MW2, is a very different story. The firm (making lightweight pots and pans from locally rolled aluminium sheets) is in a very different, far simpler, technology. It is relatively new, starting production in 1987 at the beginning of the liberalisation process. The entrepreneur, a trained accountant, was involved in marketing aluminium in Ivory Coast. On a trip to the UK he met someone who bought and reconditioned used equipment for export to developing countries. This person helped him to buy good reconditioned equipment of 1950s vintage (with credit provided by relatives living in the UK).

The equipment was designed to work on much heavier grades of aluminium, but could easily be used for the light grades popular in Ghana. There was little competition in Ghana at that time, and imports were not a serious threat (developed countries do not make this grade of utensils). Neighbouring countries like Nigeria did make similar products, but cheap local raw materials and closeness to the market were substantial advantages to the Ghanaian entrant. The investment was not preceded by a detailed study of the technical feasibility of the project, though the entrepreneur had a good 'feel' for the industry in the region.

The access to the specialised information that the UK contact provided was invaluable to MW2 in setting up the initial plant, since the background of the entrepreneur was not technical enough to enable him to locate good used machines quickly. The equipment was some 15–18 per cent of the price of new equipment. The layout and training needs at the start were simple, and were met by hiring 3 Ghanaians with experience of the technology who had returned from Nigeria. The initial success of the purchase led the firm to add to its stock of used equipment through the same dealer. The purchase of new, more automated equipment was considered but still found too expensive.

The MW2 case is an example of economical and efficient investment, made possible by a reliable source of information and equipment supply and the availability of skilled workers who had been exposed to the technology abroad. The relative simplicity of the technology made it possible to launch a viable activity with relatively little preparation. Nevertheless, the ability of the entrepreneur to locate and utilise the source of information and skills successfully was a critical element.

Medium-sized firms. The other two aluminium manufacturing firms in the sample, MW3 and MW4, are in a different product range from MW2. Both the medium-sized firms make structural products like doors, windows, partitioning and blinds for the construction industry. Both are long established in Ghana, MW3 for 21 years and MW4 for 30 years. Theirs is essentially a cutting, shaping and assembly operation, customised to individual needs and not subject to direct import competition. The market for construction has boomed since the liberalisation, and domestic competition has grown apace. However, MW3 is doing well and MW4 badly, mainly because of their relative investments in TCs.

The technology is labour intensive and relatively simple, with the information needs of investment confined to the choice of cutting, milling and bending machines that are widely available in world markets. Nevertheless, for a newcomer it is not easy to locate the right equipment, and both firms had foreign assistance in choosing it at the start. MW3 was started as a joint venture between a Ghanaian who had three other metal-working firms and an Israeli engineer (the joint venture ended in 1983 when the Israeli partner left). The foreign partner planned the investment, selected the equipment (new cutting machines from Israel), and trained workers in their use. He supervised the plant during his stay, and the Ghanaian owner's son took over in 1987.

The son was responsible for the two major new investments that took place after 1989. The first was to retool the plant with new, more advanced, cutting machines (including a computer numerically controlled machine for glass cutting). These were purchased from Italy and Germany after a six-month search in trade journals and foreign material suppliers by the son. The investment was studied and there was a careful evaluation of the final candidates, which also included US suppliers. The installation and initial training was provided by the suppliers. These investments introduced a measure of automation into the manual process.

The second investment was to integrate backwards into aluminium rolling.

The firm studied the feasibility of an extrusion plant but decided against it because of its large-scale requirements. Instead, it purchased roll forming and slitting machines from Europe after careful search and evaluation, with prices playing a decisive role. The suppliers sent technicians for 2–3 months, with further training to be provided by local rolling mills (the investment is still to become operational). Both investments point to systematic planning, search, and evaluation, with good follow-up to ensure that the necessary skills are transferred. Thus, investment capabilities were good in this case.

The MW4 plant was set up by Swiss technicians sent by the parent company in 1957. The parent company, a Swiss retailer, had been in retailing and trading in Ghana since the 19th century. It was not in aluminium products in Switzerland. However, the firm had an affiliate in Nigeria also involved in making aluminium products, and the design of the Ghanaian investment was based on the Nigerian plant. There was thus some relevant experience for the initial investment to draw upon.

The machines used were second-hand, and a few Swiss technicians stayed to work them until the end of the 1970s. Unlike MW3, the MW4 plant still continues with its old (now over 40 years) machines, and the only expansion, in the late 1980s, has been a new manual machine for making venetian blinds and some small drilling machines. The process remains entirely manual. The choice of the machines was again made by the Swiss parent company. The general lack of modernisation and expansion of the facility, at a time when imports were being liberalised and markets growing, may have reflected partly the lack of interest by the parent and partly the quality of local management. In either case, few investment capabilities were developed or exercised by the local firm.

Small Firms. Of the five small-metal working firms, two make machines, two make structural products of different types and one makes foundry products. They are taken in this order. The two machinery firms, MW5 (Accra) and MW7 (Kumasi), manufacture simple equipment for agriculture, food processing and wood working. They are both well-established (35 years and 20 years respectively), but apart from this they are very different from each other. MW5 was started by a traditional village blacksmith who moved to Accra, started a micro enterprise in a temporary shed and moved to larger size and a more permanent site: another of the few sample firms that 'graduated'. The initial investment was in two used British machines purchased locally from other firms; there was no pre-investment planning or study. Over time other used machines were bought and reconditioned, and some were constructed, by the entrepreneur himself – this was the only case in the sample where some in-house manufacture of equipment took place. Though the ability to recondition old machines and build some in-house shows considerable ingenuity, all the equipment remained fairly simple and of old design. The degree of precision and finish that could be obtained was limited. The technology did not advance over the years.

MW7 was started by a university lecturer at the University of Science and Technology in Kumasi, who had studied and worked in the UK. He started to make teaching aids in the UST workshop and in his garage, then switched to wood-working equipment and set up as a full time manufacturer in a wood magazine in 1972. In three to four years he had added agricultural machinery to his products, and currently concentrates on food-processing machinery, all for the local market. He makes about 30 different items.[8] This firm also 'graduated' in terms of size, but its origins do not lie in traditional metal-working technologies, and it is not included in the 'graduating' firms in the sample.

MW7's initial investment consisted of used machine tools bought in the UK while the entrepreneur was a student of plant engineering there (with money borrowed from his lecturer and repaid on instalment). The purchase was not based on any formal study of production possibilities or a feasibility study. The initial purchase was supplemented by more used UK machines after his return and financed by a small EEC loan. He searched for the machines by looking at catalogues and visiting suppliers; his selection was based on considerations of price, durability and ease of maintenance. His technical background and ability to search for and analyse the available information enabled him to make efficient investment decisions (the equipment is more advanced than that possessed by MW5). He plans to continue buying used equipment because of its cheapness.

The two structural parts manufacturers, both in Kumasi, MW6 and MW9, have different technological characteristics. MW6 makes the simplest kind of metal products (tanks, gates, doors), largely for domestic users, with minimal welding equipment. MW9 makes heavier structures and equipment, with more sophisticated equipment, for the mining industry. MW6 was started 17 years ago by a trainee welder of farming background with a partner (who later left). It started in a shed, with a few old welding machines bought from other firms in the Suame Magazine (an industrial zone in Kumasi). There was no feasibility study or formal planning for the operation. No search was needed for the equipment, nor were any special skills or information required for setting up and initial training. There has been no subsequent investment, and the firm is still without permanent accommodation. Its output fluctuates widely with housing spending: 1990 was a good year while 1991 was poor (the increase in employment registered in 1988–91 does not signify a sustained improvement in performance).

MW9 started 29 years ago as a joint venture between a resident Lebanese and a Ghanaian, with the former managing the firm. It went through a variety of activities. From 1963 to 1972 it reconditioned car and truck engines. From 1973 to 1988 it made articulated and other trailers for carrying timber, a technology involving welding and machining of heavy steel sheets (far more complex than the welding done by MW6). The onset of import competition (with much cheaper trailers coming from Nigeria) knocked out its trailer market, and the firm closed down for a while. After this it started again with fabricated metal parts (like chutes) for the mining industry, which use much the same technology as trailers, and is surviving at very low capacity utilisation in this activity at present.

MW9's initial equipment was bought by the Lebanese partner, who was a qualified engineer with some knowledge of equipment suppliers from his industrial contacts in Ghana. He visited several suppliers in Germany and purchased used equipment. There was no formal feasibility study or plant layout design, but the Lebanese partner himself did the layout and other engineering services for the initial investment. The equipment suppliers trained him in Germany and he trained Ghanaian workers on his return. In 1978 several new machines were purchased (for rolling, cutting and bending), while smaller investments in welding machines were made at different times. All the buying was done by the Lebanese partner. Investment capabilities were thus adequate to the needs of the operation.

Finally, there is the state–private joint venture MW8. This had started life as a private car servicing facility, and was taken over by the government in 1985 to set up a foundry operation (with the government-owned Social Security Bank holding 40 per cent of the equity and the Ghana Association of Garages and Automotive Technical Services 60 per cent). However, the machinery that the firm was to use was already in the country: it had been ordered some two years earlier by the Ministry of Rural Development and Cooperatives to distribute to individual artisans in the Suame Magazine to help raise their productivity (three much smaller foundries already existed in Kumasi). In 1985 it was decided that the foundry equipment would not be distributed but that a new venture would be set up to use it. The Social Security Bank was to provide working capital and take a share in ownership. None of the shareholders had any expertise in foundry technology.

The equipment had been purchased from Hindustan Machine Tools International of India (the trading arm of the country's leading manufacturer of machine tools).[9] The choice had presumably been made because of the line of credit extended by the Industrial Development Bank of India (later the EXIM Bank of India) rather than any evaluation of the specifications and performance of the equipment. HMT itself is a well-reputed public-sector firm, but does not make foundry equipment; it is likely that it acted as an agent for another manufacturer in India.[10]

MW8 thus started with equipment ordered, for a different purpose, with little initial technical study or search, and without management or technical staff qualified in foundry operations. HMT engineers helped in the installation of the foundry, but the furnace could not be made to work from the start. Apparently it needed some relining to make it work with scrap iron, and the formula for inputs had to be carefully controlled. On the first attempt by the HMT installation engineer, the scrap–pig iron mixture did not melt fully and a power cut led to the solidification of the molten mass in the furnace. Despite several attempts (by local staff and German technical assistants, see next section), the furnace remains inoperative till today. The machine shop with HMT tools that went with the foundry has improved its functioning, and accounts for the current 5 per cent capacity utilisation.

It is difficult to decipher the real causes of the disastrous investment in MW8. The evidence suggests a mixture of poor investment and operational capabilities on the part of the firm, incompetence by the supplier and bad luck. The whole may have been compounded by the failure of the owners to take effective action to repair the furnace till now.

To summarise, the metal-working sample has a wide dispersion of investment capabilities, reflecting the interaction of the inherent complexity of the technology with the information and skills of the investors. In the more demanding technologies (such as the 'mini' steel mill and the foundry), it was initially difficult to get and evaluate the information needed for the investment. The equipment had to be new and highly specific, with considerable skill transfer in the initial stages, all calling for the recipient to have access to information and considerable technical and organisational capabilities. This was difficult enough to provide, but the presence of the state as entrepreneur probably did not help. Thus MW1 and MW8 started life, and in the former case continued, with the legacy of badly selected and inadequately mastered technologies.

In the 'easier' technologies, as for the other firms, the equipment needs were relatively simple, consisting mainly of general purpose machine tools, and the processing technologies existed already or could be readily transferred. Even here, however, there were differences in investment efficiency depending on the ability of the entrepreneur to search for the right equipment and to improve it over time. Thus, MW2, MW3 and MW7 were able to find and update their equipment to keep pace with changing demands and skills. MW5 was able to use reconditioned machines effectively but not to upgrade its manufacturing technologies. MW6 remained a small welding workshop. MW9 could get the right equipment to start with, but not to cope with the influx of international competition.

PRODUCTION CAPABILITIES

Process engineering. The analysis of production capabilities follows the same order as above. We start with the two large firms, MW1 and MW2. MW1 has an original installed capacity for 45 000 tons of rods for the construction industry. It is one of three such firms in Ghana. The newest and most cost-efficient is a Taiwanese plant with a capacity of 30 000 thousand tons. The remaining plant is a Hong Kong Chinese-owned plant of 10 to 15 000 tons, the least efficient of the three. None of the plants is anywhere near the state-of-the-art capacities for mini steel plants, which are now approaching 1 million tons, but with efficient technical management they can compete with imports.

Before the enterprise was placed under Indian management in 1991, MW1 was running at 10 per cent of capacity. Many major pieces of equipment were unutilized or under-utilized. Among these, one blast furnace (out of two), the continuous-casting machine and the foundry had never been used. The rolling mill suffered frequent breakdowns because of poor maintenance and because the Italian consultants had changed various settings that made it very difficult to operate properly.[11] The local technical staff could not adjust the machinery to make it work at anywhere near its capacity. Most of the plant needed repair and upgrading. In essence, the lack of production capabilities of the level and specialisation needed meant that the technology had not been absorbed or mastered.

All the engineering effort underway at the time of the interview was concerned with putting the plant back on its feet, to undo the mistakes of past neglect and of inappropriate technology transfer. The new owners imported 17 experienced 'steel men' from India to take charge of all the main technological functions in the plant. They started a thorough process of refurbishment and upgrading of the machinery, with only modest investment in new plant. Maintenance was greatly improved, with personal attention by the expatriates. The process capabilities that they brought to bear led capacity utilisation to rise over threefold to 35 per cent in a year (with the rolling mill working two shifts and the furnaces three shifts, for six days a week). The changes and improvements made affected every area of the plant's operations, so are difficult to describe, but some of the main ones are:

- The second furnace was brought into operation after making some technical modifications.
- The first furnace was improved so that it could produce a larger number of heats, and has been able to achieve operations 24 hours a day (which it could not before).
- The continuous-casting machine was put into operation for the first time, by getting certain missing items made (the previous technical staff could not even identify these deficiencies).
- Ingot production was replaced by billets, and moulds and patterns were changed to suit size needs of the market.
- The rolling mill was adjusted so that the modifications made by the Italian consultants could be reversed. The bearings and skid lengths were changed to prevent frequent breakdowns, raise production and cut processing costs.
- Various motors that were not working were refurbished and put back into action.
- The foundry, which had never worked, was being put into operation, initially to be used for internal needs.
- Refractory products were being developed for use by the furnaces.

The in-house workshop was critical to many of the improvements made, since there was little available by way of local suppliers or technical services (this was contrasted by the firm to India, where a good network of subcontractors and suppliers existed). Given the age of the plant, it could not reach the level of productivity of a new plant like the Taiwanese one, but it was expected to have competitive processing costs when it reached full capacity utilisation. However, the higher costs of some local supplies (like furnace oil) and the difficulty of obtaining local supplies meant that it would be barely profitable when it faced the full force of import competition (the products are highly traceable, though transport costs give some advantage). It was not clear that it would be able to generate the resources to modernise fully and expand the plant as it wanted to. The firm thought that a modest degree of protection (15 per cent was mentioned) would allow it to generate reinvestible surpluses.

Quality control was at British standards, and there was no problem in meeting import competition in terms of quality. There was a small laboratory for quality testing, but there were no facilities for tensile testing and the controller was a secondary-school graduate with six months' training in the Kumasi Institute. The firm made both hard bars (that are used in developed countries) and soft bars (that are preferred in Ghana because they are easier to bend).

The case of MW1 is an excellent illustration of the difference that technological capabilities can make to the absorption and deployment of a reasonably complex technology. With basically the same equipment, the injection of technological skills and experience led to an enormous improvement in efficiency. There was no identifiable technological 'catalyst': the team of expatriate engineers had different specializations, and each contributed in his field. It is likely that their background in another developing country helped greatly in coping with the situation in Ghana. Years of operation under the previous owners had not allowed the necessary capabilities to be built up, because the receptive base of skills, information and instruction were lacking.

MW2 faced much lower demands on technological capabilities. The process of making pots and pans from aluminium sheets is relatively simple. In the first year of the firm's operation, it did not have an engineer and managed with three experienced operators who had worked in this activity in Nigeria. This was enough to operate the process and train other workers, but minor problems with the alignment of the motors and bearings could not be dealt with in-house until an engineer was hired.

There was no system of controlling quality during the production process, but at the end of the process each piece was inspected by eye. There were some rejects because of in-process defects, but these were relatively low (1.5 per cent). It was claimed that quality was much better than local competitors, which is borne out by the market share achieved by the company, and its ability to export a small amount to neighbouring countries. An engineer was hired for plant maintenance, and he instituted a maintenance routine of weekly, monthly and annual checks and servicing. There was an in-house maintenance repair shop.

The maintenance engineer was a technological catalyst in that he changed the motors and pulleys to raise operating speeds. He saved costs by doing in-house the repairs and servicing that previously had to be done by external agents. His input was essential in achieving good performance from used machinery. Given the needs of the technology, this level of technological effort, in combination with a sensible choice of equipment, was enough to establish a leading position in the Ghanaian market. This firm thus appears to be technologically competent.

We come now to the two medium-sized firms, MW3 and MW4. MW3 now has a fairly modern capital stock, since the major machines were replaced in the last two to three years. It had a good maintenance system from the start, instituted by the Israeli partner, and the system was kept up. At the time of the interviews there was a full-time maintenance manager (a qualified mechanical engineer) with a supporting team. There was a regular maintenance schedule, and an annual shutdown for a complete overhaul. Interestingly, the firm had started to implement ISO 9000 quality systems, one of the few companies in the country to do so. This was at the insistence of the foreign construction companies that were operating in Ghana and buying products from this firm. Reject rates, at 1–2 per cent per batch, were claimed to be lower than local competitors, and the quality of the final product was claimed to be higher.

MW3 admitted that the layout of the plant was not optimal, and that production could be speeded up with a different arrangement of plant and equipment. Plans were in hand to change the layout. The firm had made no adaptations or improvements to the machines. Inventory control was done manually, but it was planned to computerise this function over a year or two. There was a scheme for monitoring productivity and for rewarding workers by performance. In general, therefore, the firm displayed good mastery of its technology, with a systematic approach to maintenance and quality and an awareness of its process needs. It is not innovative in its processes, but given the nature of the technology this is not surprising.

MW4 used to be the market leader in aluminium structural products in Ghana, but lost market share steadily (from 85 per cent in 1986 to 30 per cent in 1991) as new competitors appeared. Its old equipment is a handicap. Maintenance is minimal, and there is no in-house repair shop. Repair services are called in when needed. The productivity of the plant apparently declined after the late 1970s when the last Swiss technician left, and it is only after 1990, when a new manager (qualified as a technician) took over that some conscious efforts were made to improve capabilities.

When the new manager took over, there was no system for quality control. He instituted a system of random quality checks for materials and finished products. He claimed that reject rates came down from over 10 per cent previously to 3 per cent in 1991. However, it appears that the quality of the product is still inferior to that of MW3; certainly the care given to this function is far less. The layout of the plant, based on the Nigerian affiliate of MW4, has never been changed. The machinery has not been improved. There is no incentive system for rewarding worker productivity (apparently the parent company does not allow any changes in the salary structure). Thus, despite some improvement in the past two years, this firm remains technologically stagnant.

Coming now to the small firms, we start with the two machinery makers, MW5 and MW7. MW5 is a firm that has grown out of a traditional blacksmith's skills and entrepreneurship. As noted earlier, the entrepreneur showed considerable ingenuity in using old reconditioned equipment, and building some simple machines of his own. However, most of the equipment was very old and apparently in poor condition. There was no maintenance schedule or personnel in charge of this function. The owner himself did all the repairs as the need arose. There was no formal system of quality control; again, the owner inspected all the products himself. Capacity utilisation was low.

The quality of the products was crude, and did not seem to have improved over time. As a result, the firm was rapidly losing market share to imported food processing equipment from India, which was better designed and finished, and offered better performance. However, the owner, who dominated all the functions of the plant, was resistant to any changes in procedures.

MW7 also had old equipment, but the machines were in much better condition. There was a regular maintenance schedule, with a diploma holder and two assistants in charge of this function. The owner only intervened for the more complex maintenance and repair tasks. Many of the old machines had been renovated with in-house manufacture of spares; some of these spares were complicated, like clutches and gears. The level of workmanship was high, with thorough training of workers.[12] The firm was operating at full capacity.

There was no formal quality control system, and, as with the previous case, the owner did all the inspection himself. However, the results seemed much better than with MW5. The careful monitoring of the production process gave the firm a reputation for reliability and quality, leading to a sustained increase in sales despite growing import competition. The firm claimed to match imports in quality, and to be better than the several local competitors making food-processing machines.

Thus, the two firms present contrasting pictures of process capabilities. One is very much a traditional shop, where the master craftsman, in charge of all technical functions, is rooted in old technologies and procedures. The other is a more 'modern' operation with a more systematic approach and greater use of newer production methods. The owner also undertakes all the complex technical functions, but he pays more attention to the quality and training of his staff. On this evidence, the first is technologically stagnant, while the latter is dynamic.

The two structural-parts manufacturers, MW6 and MW9, are at different technological levels. MW6 is a simple welding workshop, one of several in Kumasi, and losing market share to its competitors (all local). It operates in temporary accommodation. Its equipment is old and in poor condition, without proper maintenance. Quality control is primitive (welding is tested by filling tanks with water). The processes are very simple, and have not improved over time. Even given the nature of the technology, the firm is stagnant.

MW9 has more complex equipment and higher production capabilities to fabricate structural metal products. Its equipment is in reasonable condition, but there are no maintenance or quality control procedures. The owner checks the finished products himself. There has been no improvements to the machines or processing techniques, but the technology seems adequate to make the kinds of products required. However, the level of efficiency is not enough to meet import competition, and the firm is barely surviving by switching to simpler products. Thus, production capabilities are adequate but not dynamic.

Finally, MW8 has a mixture of experiences as far as process capabilities are concerned. The foundry, the main part of the plant, has never worked, and there seem to be no capabilities to restore it to working order. The firm is waiting for foreign technical assistance to sort out the problems, but what was provided has been of the wrong kind. In 1990 the German aid agency GTZ undertook to send two engineers, one mechanical and one metallurgical, to complete the project execution, set the foundry working and train the local staff. Instead, the Germans sent one technician and one exchange student, both in mechanical engineering and without metallurgical skills. The two were able to rehabilitate the machine shop, set up a maintenance routine and train the workers in machining. Thus, some capabilities were developed in this section, and the firm is able to machine parts. However, on the whole the state of production capabilities in the firm is rudimentary.

Product engineering. As may be expected, there is no product design capability in the sample firms based on independent search and experimentation. However, there is some capability to carry out minor adaptations. In the intermediate product firms like MW1 there is no need for design; the firm has to implement quality and other standards that are demanded by the market. The only adaptation that it has made has been to make some rods 'softer' because of the local preference for rods that are easier to bend. It also plans to move into the production of flat products, and cast iron products from its foundry. The technology for this will be provided by the Indian technicians running the plant.

MW2's initial designs for aluminium utensils were copied from those being sold in the market, and later some minor changes were made (to the size, shape, handles and so on) based on feedback from customers. There was no separate design department or any systematic effort to explore new designs; all the designing was done by the maintenance engineer.

The two aluminium structural product firms got their product designs by copying foreign products or building to specifications provided by customers. MW3 had to follow stricter standards because many of its customers were foreign contractors, and was working with local architects to develop new products like ceilings and partitions to compete with wood products. It had cut costs by eliminating thermal insulation from doors and windows (this feature, useful in cold climates, was not needed in Ghana). MW4 had introduced one new product based on foreign license (the venetian blinds noted above), and had developed a sun breaker that was being made by another firm. It also bought a technology from the US for door and window frames that were better insulated from rain. This did not require any change to the equipment or the production process.

Product design is more important to the two machinery makers, MW5 and MW7. Both based most of their designs on imported equipment, and both made adaptations and designed products for specific local needs. The owners in both cases undertook all the design work themselves. However, the product engineering capabilities manifested were different. MW5's designs were relatively crude, but those of MW7 were more imaginative, better executed and more appealing to the customers.

The MW7 entrepreneur geared his product adaptations and designs to adding new functions and raising the reliability and quality of the products. For instance, food-processing machines were traditionally made with bronze bearings and were exposed to dirt. This reduced the life of the bearings and meant a lot of 'downtime' on the machines. The entrepreneur substituted imported stainless steel bearings enclosed in a self-lubricating case (made locally from scrap metal), improving greatly the quality and life of the product.[13] In collaboration with the Technology Tansfer Centre of the University of Science and Technology, he developed a shea-butter kneading machine and other simple pieces of equipment (this was a service he sold to the TTC for a fee). He improved the servicing of his products, offering staff and spares to solve any operational problems that his customers encountered. The level of product design capability was not high by the standards of the industry, but even this capability was unusual in the Ghanaian context.

MW6 copies designs for tanks, gates and doors from other local producers. There is no attempt even to adapt them. MW9 copies imported designs, and was able to switch from trailers to structures for the mining industry. The Lebanese partner is the source of these designs. Finally, MW8 copied products that its customers brought into its machining shop, with no attempt at design.

LINKAGE CAPABILITIES

The engineering industry is normally the most linkage-intensive of all manufacturing activities, because its production processes consist of several separate stages that have different technological requirements and can be in separate locations. This lends itself to very fine degrees of specialisation, with accompanying gains in productivity and efficiency, and with active diffusion of technical knowledge and skills. However, the development of such a network requires firms of various sizes with the technological capabilities needed to undertake the specialised forms of production and the technical interchange that linkages involve.

There are few signs of the Ghanaian metal-working industry developing linkages of this type. As in most developing countries in the early stages of industrialisation, there is practically no subcontracting between large modern firms and SMEs in the engineering industry. Traditional small firms in similar activities do exchange information and employees with each other. At the low levels of technology that these firms operate, however, this serves to preserve existing methods of production rather than to increase specialisation and efficiency. To quote Moore on linkages in Ghana,

> Unfortunately there is no interdependent network of firms in Ghana with specialisation in production through subcontracting. The extent of subcontracting is minimal, sporadic and primitive; consequently, the base for growth in the engineering industries is weak, production is limited to a few products, there is no interface between the larger and smaller firms, and the benefits from some integration of activities cannot be achieved with the present structure, organisation, and operations of the industry.[16]

The sample firms illustrate this clearly. The two intermediate product makers, the steel firm and the foundry, have no linkages with other producers. While this is not surprising, the Indian technicians in MW1 noted that the lack of a local supply and servicing network was a handicap relative to India, where a large network had developed over time.

The three aluminium firms also had no production linkages. Though their raw material was local, it was procured in sheet form from the local rolling mill, with no need for special technological exchange. All the components, where subcontracting may have been feasible, were imported since there were no local suppliers with the capabilities to meet the needs of the aluminium firms.

The two machinery manufacturers, the most likely candidates for linkages with other metal-working firms, had no subcontracting with component suppliers, and did not themselves subcontract for larger firms. The same applies to the two structural product firms.

As far as technology institutes are concerned, there are again very few linkages with the sample firms. The Standards Board checks the products of the three aluminium firms and MW7, but offers no technical advice on improvement and is uninformed about international standards for their products.[15] MW3 has informal consultations with the faculty of architecture in UST about the new products it wants to develop. MW6 has taken the advice of the Technical Institute on equipment purchases and machining services. And MW7 has collaborated with the Technology Transfer Centre of the UST to develop the shea-butter kneading machine and other machines. However, this was a service sold by MW7 to the institute rather than a transfer of technology from the institute to the firm. MW8 has purchased some technical assistance from the UST, but no details are available on this.

As with the other industries in the sample, therefore, the engineering industry has minimal linkages within the industry and with the technology infrastructure. This is of particular concern because of the inherent nature of the industry, which is especially reliant for its efficiency and growth on the development of specialisation and subcontracting.

CONCLUSIONS

The sample firms have to be assessed in the context of the industry as a whole. The Ghanaian engineering industry is at a low level of technology. It produces a limited range of products, mostly fairly simple, and mostly at relatively low levels of quality. There is little backward integration or subcontracting. In this context, the sample shows a mixture of strengths and weaknesses. There is evidence of technological competence in some sample firms relative to the rest of the engineering industry. This competence consists mainly in the ability to absorb and use relatively simple technologies rather than to enter into sophisticated engineering activities or to develop new products and processes. Nor does it signify, so far, the emergence of export potential on the part of the Ghanaian metal-working industry.

Notes

Chapter 1 Introduction and Analytical Approach

1. See World Bank (1989), Fransman (1982), Lall (1992d), Stein (1992), Riddell (1990).
2. See Lall (1992a).
3. World Bank (1989), pp. 108–9. Emphasis added. This line of reasoning is also pursued in Lall (1992a), Navaretti (1992) and Wangwe (1992).
4. Ibid., pp. 118–19.
5. See recent work on technological capabilities in developing countries by Dahlman et al. (1987), Enos (1992), Katz (1984, 1987), Lall (1987, 1990,1991, 1992), Pack and Westphal (1986), Teitel (1981, 1984, 1993).
6. As seen below, mastery requires systematic training, searching for technical information, in-house engineering and experimentation. For a detailed analysis of the constituent elements of the 'learning curve' see Adler and Clark (1991).
7. Teitel (1993).
8. Mody (1989) analyses the strategy that firms can adopt to undertake learning and the determinants of rates of learning, focusing on inputs of skilled engineering manpower.
9. See Mody (1989). On the different skill needs of different technologies see Teitel (1982), and on a study of the skill needs in the context of technical change in the US see Howell and Wolff (1992).
10. On the significance of organisational factors in absorbing and innovating technologies, especially in the engineering industry, see Hoffman (1989). Enos (1992) has a perceptive analysis of the institutional needs of capability development.
11. Rosenberg (1976). See also Arrow's classic work (1962b) on the significance of learning by doing.
12. On the significance of networks to TC development see Hakansson (1987).
13. It has been found, for instance, that the best Korean firms have needed from 10 to 20 years to absorb complex capital goods technologies to the level of becoming internationally competitive. See Jacobsson (1993).
14. Lall (1993a).
15. See Lall (1987).
16. On Korea, for instance, see Enos and Park (1987).
17. On the absorptive functions of R&D, see Cohen and Levinthal (1989).
18. See Katz (1984) and Teitel (1982).
19. For an analysis of the economic significance and determinants of extra-market linkages between firms in developing countries, see Lall (1980).
20. The best exposition of the evolutionary theory is by Nelson and Winter (1982). This theory forms the analytical basis of much of the recent work on technology development in developing countries.
21. On the need to develop organizational capabilities, see Chandler (1992).

22. In some activities, the import of equipment combined with some local design and absorption effort may suffice, while in others considerable licensing and local R & D may be necessary. Similarly, in some industries, low wages and the use of somewhat older technologies may allow the country to preserve its competitiveness; in others, the utilisation of state-of-the-art technologies may be essential.
23. See Lall (1991, 1992), Pack and Westphal (1986), OED (1992), and Teitel (1993).
24. See Arrow (1962), Pack and Westphal (1986), Stiglitz (1987, 1989).
25. See Bell et al. (1984).
26. On the risk of government failure, see Biggs and Levy (1990), Shapiro and Taylor (1990) and Lall (1992.b). For a discussion of the requirements for a trade policy geared to industrial development in Africa, see Lall (1993).
27. See Amsden (1989), Lall (1992c), OED (1991), Pack and Westphal (1986), Wade (1990) and Westphal (1990).
28. See Westphal (1990).
29. See Mowery and Rosenberg (1989).
30. See Teitel (1982).
31. Lall (1990, 1992).
32. This set of problems is discussed for Africa by Stein (1992).
33. On the role of foreign investors in transferring technological skills to local partners in the Cote d'Ivoire, see Navaretti (1992).
34. The developed countries now impose the ISO 9000 series of quality standards on most products they import. This has an extremely demanding set of requirements for the process as well as product quality, which is expensive to implement even in the developed countries. The next chapter explains the significance of this series for Ghana.
35. See the Office of Technology Assessment (1990) for an analysis of technology support systems in the US and Japan.
36. Stiglitz (1989).
37. Hoffman (1989), p. 78.

Chapter 2   Background to Technology Development in Ghana

1. See Lall (1992d).
2. Ministry of Industries, Science and Technology (1992), page 1.
3. Ghana used to meet all its bauxite needs locally, but now imports a substantial amount of alumina from Jamaica. It is economical to do this because of the low cost of electricity in Ghana since the refining of alumina to aluminium is highly energy intensive.
4. Technical inefficiency in this class of Ghanaian firms in the wood working industries was investigated for the early 1970s by Page (1980). An earlier paper on Ghanaian industrial efficiency is by Steel (1972).
5. For a comparative analysis see the World Bank (1989), p. 110.
6. These data are from the World Bank, *Ghana: Progress on Adjustment*, Report no. 9475-GH, 16 April 1991.
7. Note that the definition of 'manufactured exports' here is somewhat different from that used by the GEPC. In particular, re-exports and products

like common salt and handicrafts are excluded from the sums shown here.

8. On the concepts of selective and economic interventions in trade regimes and their application in the newly industrialising countries, see Operations Evaluation Department (1992).

9. World Bank, 1985, p. 50.

10. Ibid., p. 58.

11. Under the present rules, the only remaining requirements placed on foreign investors are that they cannot own 100 per cent of an enterprise unless the venture is a net foreign exchange earner (there are no fixed per centages of ownership otherwise). Some investment incentives are dependent on the use of local raw materials. All ventures located in export processing zones are prohibited from selling on the domestic market. According to the Ghana Investments Centre, these requirements are also due to be relaxed in the near future.

12. The skill gaps at the firm level between Ghana and more advanced industrialising countries (India, Korea, Malaysia and Sri Lanka) are highlighted in Chapter 7.

13. Data from the *World Development Report, 1991*. See Lall's (1992) article on African industry for a longer analysis.

14. Data collected from the University in Kumasi.

15. Council for Scientific and Industrial Research, *Draft Science and Technology Plan Options*, Accra, 1990.

16. On R&D figures in Africa see Lall (1992.a), and on other countries Lall (1990).

17. For a detailed analysis of these institutions see Enos (1993).

18. The science and technology infrastructure in Ghana is described in *Institutions Supporting Scientific and Industrial Development*, the Technology Transfer Centre, Accra, 1989.

19. Practically all the total funding for the three institutions came from the government budget; only 1.1 per cent came from the sale of consultancy services. All these data were provided by the CSIR.

20. In contrast to Ghana, where productive enterprises do no significant R&D, in Korea some 1.8 per cent of GDP is accounted for by enterprise financed R&D. This is followed by Taiwan Province, with 0.5 per cent, Singapore 0.2 per cent, and India and Brazil 0.1 per cent each. See Lall (1990).

21. See Enos (1993) for references.

22. Many of these points are made in a memorandum of the Ministry of Industries, Science and Technology, *Memorandum on Reordering of S & T for Maximum Impact on National Development*, Accra, January 1992.

23. This standard has three modules: ISO 9001 covers the areas of design and development, production, installation and servicing; ISO 9002 covers quality management in production and installation; and ISO 9003 covers quality assurance obligations of the suppliers in the areas of final inspection and testing.

Chapter 3 Methodology and Sample Characteristics

1. The Census also has a category for 'micro' enterprises, with 1–4 employees. There are no firms of this size in the case study sample.
2. In the absence of data on sales, FP1 and MW1 are classified as growing firms because of their exceptional increase in capacity utilisation rates in the past two or so years and because interviews suggested that their sales are increasing. Interviews also suggest that TG1's sales grew strongly between 1988 and 1991 (the decline over 1985–91 indicates a decline in early years, which was followed by healthy growth. Two firms, MW8 and TG2, are not regarded as growing even though they recorded some sales growth. In MW8, the growth was from a very low base, and was achieved by providing machining services rather than by manufacturing (its capacity utilisation stayed very low). In TG2, capacity utilisation rates fell in 1991 compared to 1985, and the sales figures provided are slightly suspect. In addition, two firms had misleading data on sales growth. TG3 had closed down in 1986–7, and its capacity utilisation figures in 1992 remain low; this suggests that it resumed some operations but is not a growing firm. The sales data for TG7 are suspect, and interviews suggest that it is stagnant.
3. A full analysis of the panel data is not undertaken here because another team, from the Oxford Centre for the Study of African Economies and the University of Ghana, is doing this. However, the technological characteristics of the panel firms are analysed in the following chapter.
4. See Table 3.2.
5. Using employment growth rates to measure performance, produces a higher proportion of growing firms in both samples than sales performance. The information suggests that 63.0 per cent of the 24 case studies on which information is available registered increasing employment. In the case of the panel 64.4 per cent of the firms had positive employment growth during 1988–91.
6. See Table 3.4.
7. Most of the new producers were concentrated in simple metal products (water coolers, drums, knives) or those with a strong local input base (briquettes from sawdust).

Chapter 4 Technological Characteristics of the Panel Sample

1. Atkinson and Stiglitz (1985).
2. Formally, a principal component is a linear combinations of the 10 original variables (X_1, X_2....X_{10}), the coefficients of which are obtained by maximising the variance explained by the component itself. For each set of n variables n components can be derived, under the constraint that components are not correlated between each other. In other words, principal components are orthogonal, in that they do not provide 'overlapping information': each component explains a specific amount of the sample variability. Components can be ranked in decreasing order, according to the amount of the sample variance they explain. The selection of the number of components one wants to use is obviously arbitrary.

The larger the number of components selected, the larger the amount of variance explained but the less synthetic is the information given by the analysis.

3. There are four reasons for using the principal component instead of one of the size variables directly. First, the principal component embodies the information of all the size variables and not of only one. Second, the variance explained by the component is larger than the variance explained by any of the other variables. Third, the principal component also takes into account the relationship between the size variables and all the other variables considered. Fourth, any principal component is orthogonal to all the other principal components, i.e. there is zero correlation between the principal components.

4. A more standard way of showing the relationship between observations and variables in principal components is a so called 'bi-plot'. In the bi-plot, both variables and observations (firms in this case) are plotted. The coordinates of the variables are given by the correlation coefficients between variable j and component i. As the cosine of the angle between two variables is the correlation coefficient between them, two variables which are close to each other in the plot are also highly correlated. Note that a plot between two principal components is a much more powerful tool than a standard plot between them. The principal components contain most of the information contained in the 10 original variables and the two components are not correlated. If two variables have some degree of correlation, as in the case of our original variables, some of the information is duplicated. Finally, this plot explains a much larger share of variability than any other standard plot (never less than 55 per cent in the case of the 'structural' clusters).

5. Note that the industries are defined rather broadly, and there is the risk that differences in capital intensity in fact reflect differences in products. It is not possible with the information at hand to correct for this, but an examination of the firms involved does not suggest that the problem is a major one. Firms producing 'capital intensive' products are spread across the clusters in each of the four industries. For example, in the case of the textile industry, clothing firms may be expected to be in the lower cluster and textile firms in the upper one - this is not the case.

6. It should be noted that this sample does not include the big affiliates of multinationals that are covered in the case studies below. These affiliates do have high levels of physical and human capital.

7. This is seen clearly when individual firms are considered in the case studies below.

8. This conclusion is strongly supported in the detailed case studies.

9. A multinomial linear logit analysis with the cluster as the dependent variable and the market segments as independent variables was also carried out. The number of observations in each of the clusters was not sufficient to provide interesting and significant results.

10. In addition, the other studies in the larger project, on labour markets, finance and regulations, address in detail issues of market imperfections and their remedies.

11. See Lebart et al. (1984) and Lessler and Kalsbeek (1992).

Chapter 5 Technological Capabilities: a Summary Evaluation

1. As shown in the previous chapter, there is also a clear correlation between the size of the enterprise and capital intensity (the value of capital per employee) in the larger panel sample. Thus, micro firms (employment of 1–9) have average capital per employee of $1195, small firms (10–29) of $4827, medium sized (30–99) of $7920–$8644, and large firms of $8008.
2. The average hourly wage in Ghana in the garment industry was 30 US cents in 1992. This may be compared with $3.22 in Korea, $3.05 in Hong Kong, 92 cents in Thailand and 40 cents in Sri Lanka in 1990; the rates are likely to be higher today. See Lall and Wignaraja (1992).
3. The firm claims that defective equipment was sent and is still involved in litigation with the equipment suppliers.
4. This cannot be blamed on the lack of imported inputs and spares, since import liberalisation had taken place some years earlier.
5. See Appendix B for details.
6. See Chapter 2.
7. This does not mean, however, that these firms will continue to be completely insulated from import competition. Some transactions costs could come down with time, and there may be substitution of low income products with more sophisticated imported ones as buyers become better informed or richer.
8. These are TG5 (the knitwear firm), FP5 (the flour mill), and MW1 (the steel mill). Of these, the flour mill was receiving protection at the time of the study, and MW1 felt that some protection was needed to have reinvestible profits.

Chapter 7 Human Capital and Technology Development

1. Data on the larger panel sample suggest that the average education level of entrepreneurs rises with the size of firm, from middle school for micro and small firm to university level for large firms with over 100 employees. These average levels do, however, conceal a number of interesting variations within the size groups.
2. This is also true of small and medium enterprises in other developing countries. For evidence in the metal working industry of several Asian and Latin American countries, see Maldonando and Sethuraman (1992). The study of Bangalore, India, in the above volume finds that 71 per cent of the heads of 80 sample SSEs, with a median employment size of 14 workers, had university level (Bachelor or Masters) education. A similar analysis of 53 small metal-working enterprises in Rwanda found, in contrast, that 54 per cent of the sample had only reached primary school level, and the remaining 46 per cent had general or technical schooling. There were no university graduates in the Rwanda sample. In Mali, the picture is similar: 50 per cent of the enterpreneurs in a sample of 64 enterprises were illiterate, while another 22 per cent were primary school leavers, and the rest had not gone beyond secondary school. This suggests that many African small-scale enterprises are operating at a different level of sophistication from their counterparts in more industrialised developing

countries. The panel data for the Ghanaian sample shows, as noted above, that the median level of education for enterprises with below 30 employees was middle school, which is better than for Rwanda and Mali, but far below levels in Bangalore.

3. The entrepreneur who took over from his father and revitalised the business (MW3) is a particular indication of the contribution of education to changing attitudes to technology and management.
4. The firms are WW4, WW6 and MW5.
5. The panel sample had a question on the 'average education' of management, which presumably included the production manager. This showed that managers are on average better educated than entrepreneurs at all size levels and in all industries, and that firms in all size classes from 30 employees upwards (medium and large firms) have management with professional education, while smaller firms have management with middle or secondary level education. It is difficult to interpret the average level of education of the entire management, and the present study's focus on the production manager is more geared to the technological aspects of operations.
6. The high percentage figure of 7.7 per cent for one firm, TG7, is misleading because there is only one technician out of a total employment of 13.
7. See Lall and Wignaraja (1992).
8. Figures for India from Lall (1987), Korea from Enos (1992), Malaysia from Lall (forthcoming) and Sri Lanka from Wignaraja (thesis in progress).
9. These firms are locally owned.
10. These firms are locally owned.
11. All the Malaysian firms except for Eng are foreign owned.
12. Brown and Company and Metalux are locally owned.
13. In this context, it may be useful to mention figures of larger samples of Indian and Korean machine tool and electrical firms collected by Chudnovsky, Nagao and Jacobsson (1983). In machine tools, the Indian sample employed engineers as 16.6 per cent of its staff and Korea 8.2 per cent; in electrical equipment, the figures are 21.9 per cent and 13.1 per cent respectively (Table 3.9).
14. For an analysis of the apprenticeship system in Africa, see Bas (1989).
15. From Wignaraja (thesis in progress)
16. An exception is 2 workers from the WW4 company who were sent on an aid-funded scholarship to Italy and Sweden. However, the firm claimed that the courses were not very practical and there was no gain in productivity in the trainees.
17. The Kumasi Technical Institute trains young people in wood working, but does not seem to provide more advanced employee training.
18. See Lall and Wignaraja (1992).
19. An interesting case is TG7, which hires retired and disabled workers at very low wages, and so gains a competitive edge in the Kumasi school uniforms market. This may, however, have disadvantages in terms of worker skills relative to other firms.
20. These certificates are from the former British school certificate system. O levels were taken at 16 and A levels at 18.
21. Moore (1989) comments on the effectiveness of this training by MW7 in raising the quality of its products.
22. Bas (1989).

Chapter 8 Technical Effort

1. This included a contract by MW8 for the foundry which has never worked.
2. These data are from Wignaraja (thesis in progress)

Chapter 9 Incentives and Other Influences on TC Development

1. Foreign buyers come to potential suppliers on the basis of their domestic track record and demonstrated capabilities to improve technology to international levels. See Egan and Mody (1992).
2. This also suggests that simply providing easy access to credit to small enterprises is unlikely to resolve their technological problems. The experience of Kenya, where a lot of money was 'thrown at' small-scale African enterprises but had a very low success rate in terms of enterprises that could reach competitive levels, is instructive.

Chapter 10 Lessons of the Case Studies

1. This was the mechanism used by Korea to counter the risks of granting protection. See Amsden (1989) and Westphal (1990).
2. The World Bank (1990) describes some remaining hinderances to inflows, such as activities reserved for Ghanaians, minimum investment requirements for joint-venture partners, limited access to local capital markets.
3. These priority areas are: food and agro-based industries; forest based industries; earth-based industries; engineering industries; energy-related industries; and chemical industries.
4. For a review see Lall (1992a) on the structural problems of African industry.
5. This is also the finding of World Bank reports on the skill base of vocational and apprenticeship training.
6. Despite the low overall supply of technical manpower, however, there is some unemployment among technically qualified Ghanaians.
7. See also Steel and Webster (1992).
8. See Pack (1987) for a discussion of this in the context of the textile industry in Kenya.
9. 'The GIC guidelines contain elaborate provisions dealing with issues such as duration of agreements, payments, restrictive business practices, criteria for the approval of technology transfer agreements, form and procedure for the approval and monitoring of technology transfer agreements and the training of local manpower.' (Technology Transfer Centre, *Technology Policy and Legal Issues Report*, CSIR, Accra, 1989, p. 3).
10. Para. 3.66, World Bank (1990).
11. This is noted, for instance, for US firms in OTA, 1990.
12. These criticisms are also made in the CSIR's *Draft S&T Plan Options*, 1990.
13. On a recent visit to Malaysia, one of the present authors found that there was a very active public campaign to introduce ISO 9000, and companies that achieved it (several hundred by mid-1993) advertised this in the media. The Standards Board there had taken the lead in promoting

this, with special funding from the government.
14. This approach has been adopted with success in a number of countries like Spain and Portugal, as well as in NIEs like Korea.

Appendix A   Textiles and Garments

1. Statistical Service, Republic of Ghana, *Quarterly Digest of Statistics*, December 1991, Table 10A.
2. Ibid., Table 5.
3. Lall and Wignaraja (1992).
4. See Gherzi Textil Organisation (1985), Vol. I, p. 3.
5. Ibid., p. 4.
6. Ibid.
7. Plan Consult (1991), Table 5.
8. As UNIDO (1986) puts it, "productivity within the industry is low particularly in comparison with international competitors ... The quality of products is therefore very low. In the woven fabrics subsector, 20 defects per 100 meters is considered normal. This compares with a defect rate of 5 per cent in "first quality" export markets' (p. 41). These deficiencies are also noted by the GEPC (1991).
9. Gherzi Textil Organisation (1985), Vol. II, p. 4.
10. This may be contrasted with the experience of Sri Lanka, which also has a relatively underdeveloped industrial structure, but which moved into garment exports after liberalisation in 1977 and, from a very low base, was exporting about half a billion dollars within 10 years. See Wiganaraja (forthcoming).
11. Plan Consult (1991), Table 5.
12. This estimate comes from GEPC (1991), p. 82.

Appendix B   Food Processing

1. For background on the Ghanaian food-processing industry, see the Technology Transfer Centre, 1990.
2. Plan Consult (1991), Table 5.
3. See Teece (1976). On the experience of some African countries with local participation in technology transfer and the costs involved, see Wangwe (1992).
4. This involved doing without glucose or egg powder, using less malt, and offering less expensive packaging.

Appendix C   Wood Working

1. GEPC (1991), pp. 21–22.
2. Plan Consult (1991), Table 5.
3. One of the major requirements for exporting Ghanaian furniture to Western markets is strict control of moisture content levels in the wood which can only be attained by using kiln dryers. Very few firms in Ghana have this equipment, and the GEPC's export development plan highlights this as a major constraint to export activity (p. 76).

4. UNIDO (1988), p. 6.
5. 'Good machinery and equipment maintenance practice is in most cases non-existent. Tools are also not properly handled and these work against an extended life span of expensive machine parts and tools.' UNIDO, p. 76.
6. However, in the early 1980s it bought some new machines for lumbering, and tried unsuccessfully to have a gangsaw rehabilitated with the help of a German consultant.
7. As the UNIDO report says, 'The management's understanding of quality is very high' (p. 11).
8. UNIDO (1987) comments on this, and also on the poor motivation of the staff, the lack of production planning and erratic quality control.

Appendix D   Metal Working

1. For general reviews of the Ghanaian metal working industry, see Baark (1991), Moore (1989), UNIDO (1986).
2. Baark (1991), p. 51.
3. Moore (1989), pp. 23–24.
4. TTC (1990a) p. 40. A survey of small firms in Kumasi found that 95 per cent of the training of entrepreneurs in metal working was apprenticeship (overwhelmingly in other small firms), and only 3.6 per cent in training institutes.
5. Ibid., p. 37.
6. Ibid., p. 38.
7. The details of the search and negotiation are not known because the operators interviewed only took over the plant a year ago.
8. The main ones are cornmeal grinding machines, cassava graters, palm nut crackers, palm fruit digesters, sugar cane crushers, rice and corn hullers, poultry feed mills, gari plants, and shea-nut butter kneaders. See Moore (1989) for an analysis of MW7's capabilities. Moore regards MW7 as a model for small workshops to survive and progress in the new economic environment.
9. For a study of HMT's technological development see Lall (1987).
10. Probably the Heavy Engineering Corporation, the leading makes of metallurgical equipment in India. This is another state-owned enterprise making heavy losses and with a poor reputation for quality and management.
11. The rolling mill was designed to make 16" rods, but had been adjusted to 21" by the Italian consultants. This made alignment very difficult. The Indian engineers subsequently put it at 18.5".
12. This is stressed by Moore (1989) p. 16.
13. See Moore (1989) pp. 15–16.
14. Moore (1989) pp. 4–5.
15. Moore (1989) notes that 'All in all GSB plays little or no active role in the improvement of standards and technology transfer and cannot so much without the reconstruction of the facilities and equipment' (p. 70). New facilities have now been built, but the contribution of GSB remains much the same.

References

Aboyange, A. A. (undated) 'Technology and Employment in the Capital Goods Industry in Ghana', International Labour Office, Geneva, World Employment Programme Research, Working Papers.

Adler, P. S. and K. B. Clark (1991) 'Behind the Learning Curve: A Sketch of the Learning Process', *Management Science*, 37:3, pp. 267–81.

Afriyie, K. (1988) 'Factor Choice Characteristics and Industrial Impact of Joint Ventures: Lessons from a Developing Economy', *Columbia Journal of World Business,* Fall, pp. 51–62.

Amsden, A. (1989) *Asia's Next Giant: South Korea and Late Industrialization*, New York: Oxford University Press.

Arrow, K. (1962a) 'Economic Welfare and the Allocation on Resources for Innovation', in National Bureau of Economic Research, *The Rate and Direction of Innovative Activity*, Princeton: Princeton University Press.

Arrow, K. (1962b) 'The Economic Implications of Learning by Doing', *Review of Economic Studies*, 29(1), pp. 155–73.

Atkinson, A. B. and J. Stiglitz (1985) 'A New View of Technological Change', *Economic Journal*, September.

Baark, E. (1991) 'The Capital Goods Sector in Ghana: Options for Economic and Technological Development', *Industry and Development*, 29, pp. 37–61.

Bas, D. (1989) 'On the Job Training in Africa', *International Labour Review*, 128:4, pp. 485–96.

Bell, M., B. Ross-Larson and L. E. Westphal (1984) 'Assessing the Performance of Infant Industries', *Journal of Development Economics*, 16:1, pp. 101–28.

Berger Louis (1989) *The Metalworking Subsector,* for the Government of Ghana, Paris.

Biggs, T. and B. Levy (1990) 'Strategic Interventions and the Political Economy of Industrial Policy in Developing Countries', in D. Perkins and M. Roemer (eds), *Economic Systems Reform in Developing Countries*, Cambridge (Mass.): Harvard University Press.

Chandler, A. D. (1992) 'Organizational Capabilities and the Economic History of the Industrial Enterprise', *Journal of Economic Perspectives*, 6:3, pp. 79–100.

Chenery, H. B., S. Robinson and M. Syrquin (1986) *Industrialization and Growth: A Comparative Study*, New York: Oxford University Press.

Chudnovsky, D., M. Nagao and S. Jacobsson (1983) *Capital Goods Production in the Third World*, London: Frances Pinter.

Cohen, W. M. and D. A. Levinthal (1989) 'Innovation and Learning: The Two Faces of R&D', *Economic Journal*, 99:4, pp. 569–96.

Council for Scientific and Industrial Research (1990) *Draft Science and Technology Plan Options*, Accra.

Dahlman, C. J., B. Ross-Larson and L. E. Westphal (1987) 'Managing Technological Development: Lessons from Newly Industrializing Countries', *World Development*, pp. 759–75.

250

Dasgupta, P. and J. E. Stiglitz (1988) 'Learning by Doing, Market Structure and Industrial and Trade Policies', *Oxford Economic Papers*, 40, pp. 246–68.

Egan, Mary Lou and A. Mody (1992) 'Buyer–Seller Links in Export Development', *World Development*, 20:3, pp. 321–34.

Enos, J. (1992) *The Creation of Technological Capabilities in Developing Countries*, London: Pinter.

Enos, J. (1993) 'The Effects of Structural Adjustment on the Pursuit of Science and Technology in Sub-Saharan Africa', Draft prepared for UNU INTECH, Oxford.

Enos, J. and W. H. Park (1987) *The Adaptation and Diffusion of Imported Technologies in the Case of Korea*, London: Croom Helm.

Fransman, M. (ed.) (1982) *Industry and Accumulation in Africa*, London: Heinemann.

GEPC (1991) *Export Development Plan*, Accra: Ghana Export Promotion Council.

Gherzi Textil Organisation (1985) *Ghana Textile Study*, Zurich, for the World Bank.

Häkannson, H., (ed.) (1987) *Industrial Technology Development: A Network Approach*, London: Croom Helm.

Hoffman, K. (1989) 'Technological Advance and Organizational Innovation in the Engineering Industry', World Bank, Industry and Energy Department, Industry Series Paper No. 4.

Howel, D. R. and E. N. Wolff (1992) 'Technical Change and the Demand for Skills by US Industries', *Cambridge Journal of Economics*, 16, pp. 127–46.

Jacobsson, S. (1993) 'The Length of the Learning Period: Evidence from the Korean Engineering Industry', *World Development*, 21:3, pp. 407–20.

Katz, J. (ed.) (1987) *Technology Generation in Latin American Manufacturing*, London: Macmillan.

Katz, J. (1984) 'Domestic Technological Innovation and Dynamic Comparative Advantage: Further Reflections on a Comparative Case Study Programme', *Journal of Development Economics*, 16:1, pp. 13–38.

Lall, S. (forthcoming) 'Malaysia: Export Performance and Sustainability', Report for the Asian Development Bank, Manila.

Lall, S. (1993a) 'Understanding Technology Development', *Development and Change*, 24(4).

Lall, S. (1993b) 'Trade Policies for Development: A Policy Prescription for Africa', *Development Policy Review*, 11(1), pp. 47–65.

Lall, S. (1992a) 'Structural Problems of African Industry', in F. Stewart, S. Lall and S. Wangwe (eds), *Alternative Development Strategies in Sub-Saharan Africa*, London: Macmillan.

Lall, S. (1992b) 'Technological Capabilities and the Role of Government in Developing Countries,' *Greek Economic Review*, 14:1.

Lall, S. (1992c) 'Industrial Technology Development and Policy' World Bank, mimeo.

Lall, S. (1992d) 'Technological Capabilities and Industrialization', *World Development*, pp. 165–86.

Lall, S. (1991) 'Explaining Industrial Success in the Developing World', in V. N. Balasubramanyam and S. Lall (eds), *Current Issues in Development Economics*, London: Macmillan.

Lall, S. (1990) *Building Industrial Competitiveness in Developing Countries*, Paris: OECD Development Centre.

Lall, S. (1987) *Learning to Industrialize*, London: Macmillan.

Lall, S. (1980) 'Vertical Inter-Firm Linkages in LDCs: An Empirical Study', *Oxford Bulletin of Economics and Statistics*, 42:3, pp. 203–27.

Lall, S. and Wignaraja, G. (1992), 'Foreign Involvement by European Firms and Garment Exports by Developing Countries', Centro Studi Luca d'Agliano/ Queen Elizabeth House, Development Studies Working Papers, No. 54.

Lebart L., A. Morineau and K. Warwick (1984) *Multivariate Descriptive Statistical Analysis*, Chichester: J. Wiley.

Lessler J. and W. Kalsbeek (1992) *Nonsampling Errors in Surveys*, Chichester: J. Wiley.

Levy, B. (1993) 'Obstacles to Developing Indigenous Small and Medium Enterprises: An Empirical Assessment', *World Bank Economic Review*, 7:1, pp. 65–83.

Maldonando, C. and S. V. Sethuraman (1992) *Technological Capability in the Informal Sector: Metal Manufacturing in Developing Countries*, Geneva: International Labour Office.

Ministry of Industries, Science and Technology (1992a) *Industrial Policy Statement: A Strategy for Industrial Regeneration*, Government of Ghana, Accra.

Ministry of Industries, Science and Technology (1992b) *Memorandum on Reordering of S & T for Maximum Impact on National Development*, Government of Ghana, Accra.

Mody, A. (1989) 'Firm Strategies for Costly Engineering Learning', *Management Science*, 33:4, pp. 496–512.

Moore, F. T. (1989) 'Industrial Development in Ghana', Draft Report for the Industry and Energy Department, West Africa Department, World Bank.

Mowery, D. C. and Rosenberg, N. (1989) *Technology and the Pursuit of Economic Growth*, Cambridge: Cambridge University Press.

Navaretti, G. B. (1992) 'Joint Ventures and Autonomous Industrial Development: The Case of the Cote d'Ivoire', in F. Stewart, S. Lall and S. Wangwe (eds), *Alternative Development Strategies in sub-Saharan Africa*, London: Macmillan.

Navaretti, G. B. (1991) 'Joint Ventures in Developing Countries: an Essay on the Feasibility and the Cost of Autonomy', Oxford University, D.Phil. dissertation.

Nelson, R. (1992) 'The Role of Firms in Technical Advance: A Perspective from Evolutionary Theory', in Dosi, G. et al. (eds), *Technology and Enterprise in a Historical Perspective*, Oxford: Clarendon Press.

Nelson, R. R. and S. J. Winter (1982) *An Evolutionary Theory of Economic Change*, Cambridge, MA: Harvard University Press.

Office of Technology Assessment (1990), *Making Things Better: Competing in Manufacturing*, Washington, DC: US Senate.

Operations Evaluation Department (1992), *World Bank Support for Industrialization in Korea, India and Indonesia*, World Bank.

Pack, H. and L. E. Westphal (1986) 'Industrial Strategy and Technological Change: Theory versus Reality', *Journal of Development Economics*, pp. 87–128.

Page, J. M. Jr. (1980) 'Technical Efficiency and Economic Performance: Some

Evidence from Ghana', *Oxford Economic Papers*, 32, pp. 319–39.

Pietrobelli, C. (1993) 'Technological Capability and Export Diversification in a Developing County: The Case of Chile Since 1974', Oxford University, D.Phil. thesis.

Rhee, Y., B. Ross-Larson and G. Pursell (1984) *Korea's Competitive Edge*, Baltimore: Johns Hopkins.

Riddell, R. and Associates (1990) *Manufacturing Africa*, London: Curry.

Rodrik, D. (1988) 'Industrial Organization and Product Quality: Evidence from South Korean and Taiwanese Exports', National Bureau for Economic Research Working Paper, Series No. 2722, Cambridge, Ma.

Rosenberg, N. (1986) *Perspectives on Technology*, Cambridge: Cambridge University Press.

RPED (1992), 'Economic Reform and the Manufacturing Sector in Ghana', Prepared for the Regional Programme on Enterprise Development, World Bank, by the Department of Economics, University of Ghana, and Centre for the Study of African Economies, Oxford.

Rugman, A. (1981) *Inside the Multinationals*, London: Croom Helm.

Shaked, A. and J. Sutton (1984) 'Natural Oligopolies and International Trade', in H. Kierzkowski (ed.) *Monopolistic Competition and International Trade*, Oxford: Clarendon Press.

Shaked, A. and J. Sutton (1983) 'Natural Oligopolies', *Econometrica*, 51, pp. 1469–84.

Shapiro, H. and L. Taylor (1990) 'The State and Industrial Strategy', *World Development*, 18:6, pp. 861–78.

Steel, W. F. (1972) 'Import Substitution and Excess Capacity in Ghana', *Oxford Economic Papers*, 24, pp. 212–40.

Steel, W. F. and Webster, L. A.(1992), 'How Small Enterprises in Ghana Have Responded to Adjustment', *World Bank Economic Review*, 6:3, pp. 423–38.

Stein, H. (1992) 'Deindustrialization, Adjustment, the World Bank and the IMF in Africa', *World Development*, 20:1, pp. 83–95.

Stewart, F. (1984) 'Facilitating Indigenous Technological Change in Third World Countries', in M. Fransman and K. King (eds), *Indigenous Technological Capability in the Third World*, London: Macmillan.

Stiglitz, J. E.(1989) 'Markets, Market Failures and Development', *American Economic Review Papers and Proceedings*, 79:2, pp. 197–202.

Stiglitz, J. E. (1987) 'Learning to Learn, Localized Learning and Technological Progress', in P. Dasgupta and P Stoneman (eds), *Economic Policy and Technological Development*, Cambridge: Cambridge University Press.

Technology Transfer Centre (1990a) *Report on Capital Goods Sector Study*, Accra.

Technology Transfer Centre (1990b) *Report on Food Processing Sector*, Accra.

Technology Transfer Centre (1989) *Institutions Supporting Scientific and Industrial Development*, Accra, TTC Document No. 1.

Teece, D. (1976) *The Multinational Enterprise and the Resource Costs of Technology Transfer*, Cambridge (Mass): Ballinger.

Teitel, S. (1993) *Industrial and Technological Development*, Washington, DC, Inter-American Development Bank-Johns Hopkins Press.

Teitel, S. (1987) 'Science and Technology Indicators, Country Size and

Economic Development: An International Comparison', *World Development*, 15:9, pp. 1225–35.

Teitel, S. (1984) 'Technology Creation in Semi-Industrial Economies', *Journal of Development Economics*, 16:1, pp. 39–61.

Teitel, S. (1982) 'The Skill and Information Requirements of Industrial Technologies: On the Use of Engineers as a Proxy', in M. Syrquin and S. Teitel (eds), *Trade, Stability, Technology and Equity in Latin America*, New York: Academic Press.

Teitel, S. (1981) 'Towards an Understanding of Technical Change in Semi-Industrialized Countries', *Research Policy*, 10, pp. 127–47.

UNIDO (1992) *Industry and Development Global Report 1991/1992*, Vienna.

UNIDO (1988) *Technical Report: Improving Productivity in Ghana's Furniture Industry*, report by S. Cinar, Vienna, No. DP/ID/ SER.A/991.

UNIDO (1986) *Industry Development Review Series: Ghana*, Vienna, PPD.18.

Wade, R. (1991) *Governing the Market*, Princeton: Princeton University Press.

Wangwe, S. (1992) 'Building Indigenous Technological Capacity in African Industry: An Overview', in F. Stewart, S. Lall and S. Wangwe (eds), *Alternative Development Strategies in Sub-Saharan Africa*, London: Macmillan.

Westphal, L. E. (1990) 'Industrial Policy in an Export Propelled Economy: Lessons from South Korea's Experience', *Journal of Economic Perspectives*, 4:3, pp. 41–59.

Wignaraja, G. (forthcoming) 'Trade and Industrial Policies and Experience in Sri Lanka', in G. K. Helleiner (ed.), *Trade Policy and Industrialization in Turbulent Times*, London: Routledge.

Wignaraja, G., 'Manufactured Exports, Outward Orientation and the Acquisition of Technological Capabilities in Sri Lanka', Doctoral thesis in progress, Oxford University.

World Bank (1991a) *Ghana: Progress on Adjustment*, Report No. 9475-GH.

World Bank (1991b) *World Development Report 1991*, Washington, DC.

World Bank (1990) *Ghana: Towards a Dynamic Investment Response*, draft, West Africa Department.

World Bank (1989) *Sub-Saharan Africa: From Crisis to Sustainable Growth, A Long Term Perspective Study*, Washington, DC.

World Bank (1985) *Ghana: Industrial Policy, Performance and Recovery*, Report No. 5716-GH.

Index

Notes: References to figures and tables are given only when they appear separately from relevant text and are indicated by page numbers in *italics*.
Abbreviations: ITD industrial technology development; R&D research and development; SMEs small- and medium-sized enterprises; TC technological capabilities.